INDUSTRY AND POLITICS IN THE THIRD REICH

Ruhr coal, Hitler and Europe

JOHN GILLINGHAM

COLUMBIA UNIVERSITY PRESS
NEW YORK 1985

Printed in Great Britain

Library of Congress Cataloging in Publication Data

Gillingham, John.
Industry and politics in the Third Reich.

Bibliography: p.
Includes index.
1. Industrial mobilization—Germany—History—20th century. 2. Coal trade—Germany—Ruhr (Region)—Military aspects—History—20th century. I. Title.
UA18.G4G55 1985 355.2'6'0943 85-11307
ISBN 0-231-06260-5

CONTENTS

LIST OF TABLES

LIST OF FIGURES

ACKNOWLEDGEMENTS

The production of a book such as this requires time, money and sacrifice. The University of Missouri/St Louis, and especially Professors Edwin Fedder (Director of the Center for International Studies) and Neal Primm (Chairman of the History Department) have assured the provision of sufficient release time to allow me to complete this project. They deserve to be thanked first. Professor Baron Karl Otmar von Aretin (Director of the Institute for European History, Mainz) has given constant moral as well as frequent material support over many years. A mere acknowledgement is a poor expression of the depth of my gratitude. I am also very fortunate to have benefited from the generosity of several distinguished institutions. Research on this book began during a year spent as a fellow of the Alexander von Humboldt Foundation and continued over summers in which my archival visits were supported by the Foundation, by the Berlin Historical Commissions and by the University of Missouri/St Louis. A six-month research grant provided by the Volkswagen Foundation in collaboration with a project conducted by the Institute for European History enabled me to write the first four chapters.

The *sacrifice* involved was shared in ample measure by all concerned with the project. The notes give some indication of my great indebtedness to those who administer and, in at least two cases, who have actually created, the several archives consulted in the course of this research: above all, Herr Bodo Herzog of Gutehoffnungshütte Aktienverein; Dr Ottfried Dascher of the Westfälisches Wirtschaftsarchiv in Dortmund; Agnes Peterson of the Hoover Institution, Stanford; as well as the staffs of the US National Archives, the Rijksinstituut voor Oorlogsdocumentatie in Amsterdam, the Wiener Library in London, the Bergbau Museum in Bochum, the Bergbau Bibliothek in Essen, the Politisches Archiv des Auswärtigen Amtes in Bonn, the Rheinish-Westfälisches Wirtschaftsarchiv in Köln and, of course, the Bundesarchiv in Koblenz. Dr Hugo Lacher, director of the library at the Institute for European History, has aided me (and every other past or present scholar at that institution) with words of kindness and good counsel as well as with books. My thanks go also to those who offered their comments on the manuscript –

Professors Werner Abelhauser, Volker Berghahn, Howard Miller, Alan Milward, Neal Primm and Mr Claus Scharf. They are responsible for numerous significant improvements in the text, although none, of course, of the remaining shortcomings. I would like to thank Kathy Pottebaum-Bauer and Mary Hines who, as well as those who worked under their direction, typed the manuscript under very strenuous conditions. The patience of Stephanie Horner, at Methuen, was no less unfailing than that of the typists. All of them now qualify as experts in reading foreign language notes written in my illegible scrawl. But I have asked the greatest sacrifices of my wife, Barbara, and daughters, Anne and Nicole. I can only hope that they will eventually agree that it has all been worthwhile. My son John was born within a week of the manuscript's completion and could have been only dimly aware of its existence.

John Gillingham, 1985

INTRODUCTION

The history of German business during the Third Reich is a subject of extraordinary sensitivity. It belongs to what is called 'the unconquered past' *(die unbewältigte Vergangenheit)*. Countless tens of thousands of men and women throughout Europe must live with memories of months and years spent as slave labourers in Nazi factories, and figures still prominent in the economic life of the Federal Republic can recall when, because of alleged complicity in Hitler's crimes, German private enterprise stood under Allied sentence of death. They would still rather not talk about what happened between 1933 and 1945. As a result, their critics have seldom been answered.

Marxist authors have so far written the history of German business during the Third Reich. Within months of Hitler's takeover the first of a stream of books appeared, blaming Germany's producers for having brought the Führer to power and purporting to disclose how they controlled the political machinery of national socialism. This line remains unchanged. There is much to recommend it. Over the past thirty years the historians of the German Democratic Republic have scoured the archives in search of evidence, published periodically, linking German business to Hitler's crimes. Their work, impressive in its sheer bulk, leaves no doubt that German industry supported Hitler: helped fund his rise to power, encouraged and profited from rearmament, exploited slave labour and ransacked much of occupied Europe.

Yet the Marxist approach is not satisfactory. To equate German business with Hitler's policies requires a special aptitude for overlooking the obvious. Is one really to believe that the man had no will or ideas of his own? The Marxist approach also leaves a number of basic questions unanswered. One would like to know how closely the regime controlled business, how much autonomy business preserved and whether business restrained Hitler's power or extended it. One would like to know how business used its autonomy: to Nazify itself, merely defend its interests, or pursue independent strategies of development? And one would like to discover the range of possible business reactions to the regime and how they varied from industry to industry.

Non-Marxist historiography provides few answers. The disillusioned Ruhr steel industrialist Fritz Thyssen launched the first defence of industry in *I Paid*

Hitler (New York, 1941). In his view the Führer's economic plans amounted to a form of socialism which, whether employers recognized it or not, could only be realized at their expense. Few have followed Thyssen's lead. One can only cite as noteworthy the book by public relations man Louis Lochner, *Tycoons and Tyrant: German Industry from Hitler to Adenauer* (Chicago, 1954), based on accounts provided by prominent industrialists. It describes them as at worst unwilling accomplices and at best secret opponents of Hitler but in any case victims. Although these ideas may have some merit, they have not yet been explored. Because German business has preferred to sweep the entire episode of the Third Reich under the carpet, no major figure from industry or finance has yet published his memoirs. With precious few exceptions, private archives remain closed.

Nor have non-Marxist scholars done much to modify the Marxist view. While there have been some noteworthy attempts to build 'models' identifying business as one of several main influences on Hitlerian policy, none of them has been supported by extensive empirical research.[1] To the historian, they are useful mainly as hypotheses. Technical studies of the national socialist political economy, such as Petzina's study of the Four Year Plan and Milward's of war production, contain the best descriptions of business practices in the Third Reich.[2] Exposés such as Joseph Borkin's *The Crime and Punishment of IG Farben* (New York, 1978) recross ground covered more thoroughly by the historical profession in the German Democratic Republic. No single branch of industry, not to mention industry as a whole, has yet been seriously studied. The lack of such research makes it impossible to generalize confidently about business in the Third Reich. Historical discussion of the serious issues raised by Marxist writers has really just begun. The main issue at hand – the subject of a fierce debate by 'traditionalists' led by Henry Turner of Yale and 'Neo-Marxists' defended by David Abraham of Princeton – is the responsibility of big business for Hitler's rise to power. This increasingly bitter controversy has not yet touched, however, on the more important issue of producer behaviour in the Third Reich itself.[3]

This book deals with a single branch of industry, but the intention is that it will be a step towards more comprehensive studies. Its approach is that of business history. It examines an industry's competitive position and management strategy, demonstrates how these considerations governed its responses to the political and economic challenges of the period, and evaluates the results.

My subject is the collieries of the Ruhr. I chose this industrial sector for two main reasons, one of which is the unique abundance of source material. In addition, the mines provide a suitable vehicle for discussion of more general problems than those merely of the industry itself. Coal and the related steel and manufacturing industries, which, in customary English usage, are conveniently lumped together as 'The Ruhr', have traditionally provided much of the leadership – often contested to be sure – for German business as a whole. This remained true for the years after 1933. Another thought must also be borne in mind. Because of its size, structure, strategic importance and partially competitive position, Ruhr coal offers many worthwhile points of comparison with the one enterprise which, due to its intimate involvement with the regime, has been studied in detail. This is IG Farben, the model Nazi corporation.[4] It provides a good standard with which to judge Ruhr coal.

The example of Ruhr coal also sheds light on some of the main questions raised by the history of the Third Reich, one of which concerns Hitler's strategy. Was there any substance to either *Autarkiepolitik* (economic self-sufficiency) or the attempt to build a European Economic New Order? Or was Germany doomed to defeat? As the primary source of German and west European energy the mines were critical to economic mobilization, the utilization of the industrial potential of France, Belgium and the Netherlands, and the attempt to match allied armaments production. Another question concerns Hitler's boast that he would overcome class conflict. As the largest employer of German blue-collar labour, and a traditional arena of social conflict, the mines presented Hitler with an imposing challenge. His success in dealing with it provides an 'acid test' for the now famous but still largely undocumented 'Neo-Marxist' thesis that the working class resisted the regime.[5] The question as to whether the years from 1933 to 1945 represent a case of break or continuity with the German past presents a third problem. The Ruhr industry was old, had strong corporate traditions and was as important economically to the lands west of Germany as to the Reich itself. How much of this non-Nazi tradition survived?

The study of Ruhr coal can also lead to new approaches. The historical literature tends to equate the Germany of the 1930s with the Hitler regime.[6] (The myth of the all-powerful dictatorship dies hard!) It has proved difficult to discover the workings of long-term secular social and economic trends during the Third Reich common to all industrial societies. Certain of them come to light through an examination of Ruhr coal in a European rather than a purely German context. The responses of German mining directors and foundrymen to the problems of depression and war were basically similar to those of their counterparts in the rest of Western Europe. Indeed, during these years a common outlook developed within the management of heavy industry in Germany, France and the Low Countries. Out of it grew a tradition of trans-national co-operation which provided the substructure for the economic integration of the Continent as realized through the formation of the European Coal and Steel Community in 1951.

Notes

1 See Franz Neumann, *Behemoth* (New York, 1943) and Arthur Schweitzer, *Big Business in the Third Reich* (Bloomington, 1964).

2 Alan S. Milward, *The German Economy at War* (London, 1965); Dietmar Petzina, *Autarkiepolitik im Dritten Reich: Der nationalsozialistische Vierjahresplan* (München, 1968).
3 See the Turner and Abraham letters in the October 1983 issue of *American Historical Review* 88 (4), 1143–9.
4 See the promising forthcoming book on this subject by Peter Hayes.
5 This thesis is developed most fully in Tim Mason's *Arbeiterklasse und Volksgemeinschaft* (Opladen, 1975). For alternative points of view see Ludolf Herbst, 'Die Krise des nationalsozialistischen Regimes am Vorabend des Zweiten Weltkrieges und die forcierte Aufrüstung', *Vierteljahrshefte für Zeitgeschichte*, 26 Jg./Nr. 3, 1978, and John Gillingham, 'Ruhr coal miners and Hitler's war', *Journal of Social History* 15 (4), 1982, 637–53.
6 David Schoenbaum's *Hitler's Social Revolution* (Garden City, NY, 1966) is an important exception.

1

AN INDUSTRY IN CRISIS

The importance of coal – and particularly that of the Ruhr region – in the development of Germany is without parallel in the history of any other modern nation. This fact is due not so much to the industry's size, although it is immense, as to its role in economic development and its political power. Much of Germany's industrial economy is built on coal, the huge steel and manufacturing plants in the literal sense, and the vast and successful chemical industry in the more figurative, technological and scientific sense. Whether as fuel or raw material, most German industries rely on coal. Its share in overall energy consumption has traditionally been greater in Germany than in other major industrial nations. The political power of the industry derives not only from its economic importance but the strength of its internal organization and its close association with steel. The Ruhr coal syndicate, the Rheinisch-Westfälisches Kohlensyndikat (RWKS), founded in 1893, is often considered to be the first modern industrial cartel. RWKS enabled the operators not only to market their products as a unit but to speak in political matters with a single voice. The tie-in with the giant steel and manufacturing firms made the Ruhr the political and economic centre of gravity in the Reich. Modern Germany has been built not so much on 'Blood and Iron' as on coal and iron, and more specifically *Ruhr coal* and iron.[1]

Never did the Ruhr coal industry seem so powerful as in 1926. Politically it had long commanded fear and respect. Its potential to inflict economic damage was immense: without coal nothing ran, and when it became too expensive nothing could be sold. In 1904, to suppress the recurring nightmare that the industry would use a national emergency as an occasion for blackmail, Kaiser Wilhelm II took the unusual step of acquiring control of the Hibernia Mine on behalf of the Prussian state. In 1919 the Reichstag enacted a special law, the *Kohlenwirtschaftsgesetz* to regulate the industry. It provided for both a *Reichskohlenverband*, the so-called 'coal parliament', and a *Reichskohlenrat* (coal council), each composed of representatives of the state, labour and consumers as well as the operators. They were to supervise the marketing operations of the coal syndicate. But neither the Wilhelminian nor the Weimar approach represented a serious challenge to the industry. The Ruhr crisis of

1923 provided an awesome demonstration of *die Kohlenmacht* – the coal weapon. By withholding deliveries of fuel the government of the Reich, supported by Ruhr industry, destroyed the value of the franc. This forced France to drop the policy of 'bleeding' Germany and accept its partnership in a programme of European economic recovery. This was the most dramatic change in the European diplomatic climate of the 1920s.[2]

Economically as well, in 1926 Ruhr coal seemed to be advancing towards new peaks of power. Thanks to inflation, it had been able to eliminate nearly all of its long-term debt, and due to the British miners' strikes, it was enjoying success on export markets. The German economy itself was entering a period of expansion which would continue until 1930. Finally, there were the anticipated benefits deriving from 'rationalization'. The idea behind this programme was to make the mines the most modern and efficient in the world. It involved consolidation of working points, mechanization of underground operations, construction of giant cokeries of a new design, the setting up of new installations for by-product refinement, extension of the gas net, promotion of research into new fields such as synthetic petroleum, and elaboration on the complicated maze of power and pipelines known as the *Verbundwirtschaft*, which connected coal and other sectors of Ruhr industry in a common energy grid. The *Verbundwirtschaft* added a technological link to those of politics, organization, ownership and common history which tied the industry to its major industrial customers – steel, chemicals and the utilities.[3]

But in spite of the Ruhr's good short-term prospects, by 1926 an era of crisis and decline had begun for the entire world coal industry which, in its essentials, continues down to the present. For Europe it did not involve the immediate displacement of coal as the main source of energy but rather a steady reduction in its overall share of consumption and the lack of any significant growth (Table 1). The situation was brought about by high

Table 1 Apparent consumption of primary sources of energy in Europe, 1913–1949

	Solid fuels	*Fuelwood*	*Natural gas*	*Hydro-electricity*	*Liquid fuel*
1913	556	(133)	0.05	10	6.4
1925	537	(142)	0.91	32	12.7
1929	636	(138)	1.28	43	19.8
1937	633	(127)	2.95	65	32.4
1949	618	(123)	3.10	93	50.4

Source: Ingvar Svennilson, *Growth and Stagnation in the European Economy* (Geneva, 1954), 103.

Notes:
Solid fuels – millions of tons of coal equivalent
Fuelwood – millions of m^3 (estimated)
Natural gas – 1000 millions of m^3
Hydroelectricity – 1000 millions of kwh
Liquid fuel – millions of tons

production costs, excess capacity, efficiencies in fuel consumption, but, above all, competition from new sources of energy and shifting patterns of demand.[4] The dramatic impact of these changes was first felt outside the Ruhr. American coal output dropped from over 500 million tons in 1913 to about 480 million tons in 1929. By 1930 several British coal districts, most notably South Wales, had become areas of chronic unemployment and economic misery. Even before the Depression mining in the southern basin of Belgium and northern France required public subsidies. To survive, the Ruhr coal industry would have to adjust to increasingly competitive conditions on world energy markets.

The Ruhr coal industry, while relatively ill-equipped by nature, was thought to be well-equipped by history to deal with the impending crisis. Its strengths were organizational in character and extended to all areas of operation. Paternalism, combined with encouragement of technical schooling, had produced a labour force which was relatively conservative and highly productive. Thanks to a tradition of sponsoring research through such institutions as the Bergbau-Verein, Ruhr mining technique was as advanced as any in the world. The industry led the way in such diverse fields as land reclamation, briquette-making, winding methods, cokery design, the physics of thermal energy, and in coal chemistry generally. Ruhr coal enjoyed great advantages in marketing as well. The tie-in with steel assured preferential treatment to about 15 per cent of total output. RWKS served as the sales outlet for the remainder, except for small amounts reserved for sale at the works and payment to miners in kind *(Deputatkohle)*. In addition, a tonnage levy on production, the famous *Umlage*, enabled the syndicate to subsidize sales in some markets with its monopoly profits from others. Associated informally with the coal syndicate and operating on similar principles were so-called specialized cartels for the various by-products. These strengths led the French commentator Maurice Baumont to conclude in his 1928 study, *La grosse industrie allemande et le charbon*, that of the various European coal industries, the Ruhr stood the best chance to weather the impending crisis.[5]

But geography and geology limit the amount of Ruhr coal that can be mined commercially. Total known and probable reserves have been variously estimated at between 121,300 million tons and 213,600 million tons, roughly on a par with those of Great Britain and Silesia but puny by comparison to the 1,975,205 million tons of the USA and the approximately similar amounts of the Soviet Union. The coal beds lie some 400–800 m below the surface, occurring first along a line running in the south from the Ruhr valley eastward to Hamm and westward across the Rhein to the Dutch frontier, then pitching downward as they move to the north as far as Münster. The positioning of the seams can be described as only fair. They vary from 0.4 to 2 m thick, are badly faulted, and dip from 0° to 90°. Roof formation in some areas is weak. But the quality of Ruhr coal is generally good, and over two-thirds of it is suitable for coking.[6]

The district was well served by its transportation system, a critical matter given the low ratio of coal value to bulk. Two main canal systems connected the mines to the Rhein. The Rhein–Herne canal runs along the centre of the district, from the two main coal harbours Ruhrort and Duisburg eastward to Dortmund where, bending north, it extends to Münster and beyond. The second system, Wesel–Datteln–Hamm, connects the increasingly important mines of the northern part of the district to the Rhein port of Walsum. During the interwar period, over one-half of Ruhr coal exports normally left the district by waterway. The district was also served by four important rail connections: east to central Germany over Hannover, north-east over Osnabrück to the coast, south-west to Aachen, and south to Köln and Frankfurt.[7]

The geological situation of the mines provides for no alternative to working at lower and lower depths. In 1892 5 per cent of total Ruhr output was mined at depths of 600–1100 m. By 1926 this had increased to over 52 per cent. Operations therefore became increasingly capital-intensive, requiring longer terms of amortization, and higher degrees of mechanization. Unfortunately the Ruhr seams were not thick enough to be suitable for the most advanced inter-war mining methods, which involved continuous undercutting and scraping. By 1939 mechanical cutter-scrapers *(Schrämmaschine)* were responsible for about 55 per cent of British output and virtually none of the Ruhr's. Its seams were, however, well-suited to the second best technology available, the pneumatic pick *(Abbauhammer)*. It was normally employed in advancing long-wall operations (Table 2). During the inter-war period the industry lacked the resources to make the transition to full mechanization. As a result average pithead costs of Ruhr coal per ton remained above those of Silesian, British and American mines, about on a par with those of the Dutch and Flemish, and, making allowances for differences in grade, below those in either France or southern Belgium.[8]

To operate at a profit, the Ruhr had to find markets for the considerable variety of sizes, shapes and weights which turned up with every ton of coal yield. This was by no means easy since the various grades varied widely according to burning, storage and travelling characteristics, and usages. This is what the industry termed the *Sortenproblem*, the grade problem.[9] The sensitivity of coke sales to the business cycle was another difficult problem. Both this and the grade problem were constant concerns of the marketing and research arms of the industry. Finally, profitability required high levels of operation. The break-even point in the years 1928–38 stood at about 90 per cent of total estimated capacity of 125 million to 130 million tons per year.[10]

The proximity of competitors also affected the marketability of Ruhr coal. Before the First World War, Great Britain had been the chief rival. With total output and exports considerably larger than those of the Ruhr, Britain

Table 2 Percentage of mechanical and manual methods in Ruhr coal-getting, 1913–1938

	Pneumatic pick	*Cutter-scraper*	*Hand or explosives*
1913	—	2.20	97.80
1925	36.50	11.50	52.00
1926	56.50	10.90	32.60
1927	74.36	8.49	17.15
1928	83.93	6.43	9.64
1929	87.37	5.54	7.09
1930	93.80	—	6.20
1931	95.90	—	4.10
1932	88.80	8.10	3.10
1933	88.51	7.52	3.97
1934	89.27	7.68	3.05
1935	87.87	8.31	3.82
1936	90.27	6.34	3.39
1937	89.74	6.80	3.46
1938	89.40	7.23	3.37

Source: Bergbau-Verein, *Statistisches Heft. Produktions-unds wirtschafts-statistische Angaben aus der Montanindustrie* (Essen, 1939), 120.

dominated the European bunker coal market, held the upper hand in Scandinavia and along the Mediterranean basin, was responsible for the bulk of French and Dutch imports and even shared in deliveries to the German North Sea ports. British sales outside of this area were contested only by non-European producers. Belgium was another, albeit less formidable, European competitor whose mines sold heavily to the French railways. The Silesian mines defined the eastern boundary of the Ruhr's market area. They were the sole Reich exporters to Russia, important suppliers to the Danubian area, and dominant in sales to Reich markets east of Berlin and north of Bavaria within a radius of roughly 675 km from Gleiwitz. To the south, the Ruhr faced competition from the Saar. Its mines provided a portion of the coal requirements of the district's steel industries, supplied additional amounts to those of the *Reichsland* Elsass-Lothringen, and occasionally made forays into the area of the Baden-Württemberg region.[11]

A very simplified diagram of Ruhr coal marketing areas would be three concentric circles, each centred on Essen. In the outer circle the industry competed only for exceptional reasons, because sales often required subsidies. The middle circle included stable markets for important export products, especially coke, with western Europe absorbing about a fifth of total outputs. The inner circle represented the so-called protected area falling within a radius of approximately 375 km from Essen. This was the destination of about 11–12 per cent of total coke and coal outputs. Finally, the Ruhr district itself consumed about 28 per cent of total coal and 34 per cent of total coke outputs.

Nearby industrial consumers provided the Ruhr with its greatest marketing advantage.[12]

The First World War and the post-war political settlement created new competitors for the Ruhr mines both at home and abroad and disrupted traditional coal marketing patterns. The catastrophic wartime fall in German coal output – from 190 million tons in 1913 to 147 million tons in 1915 had two severe long-term consequences. First the Netherlands, which before 1914 had been the Ruhr's largest export customer, embarked on a programme of coal self-sufficiency. Dutch outputs increased from 1.8 million tons in 1913 to 4.1 million tons in 1920 to 12.2 million tons by 1930, giving the Ruhr a powerful new competitor in the markets of the Lower Rhein.[13]

More serious in the long run was the new competition from the young brown coal industry, which had been built up by the Reich during the war. There are three important German brown coalfields – the East Elbian, the Middle German and the Rhenish, west of Köln. Brown coal, or lignite, is slow burning, has low volatility and produces an undesirable amount of smoke. Its great bulk and low calorific content make it expensive to transport. It can, however, be mined at the surface in automated operations and at very low cost. It is well-suited for consumption by thermal generating plants and can be formed into a low quality but cheap briquette suitable for use in home heating. (As events would later demonstrate, it was also well-adapted to use as a new material for synthetic petroleum produced by the hydrogenation process.) German lignite output increased from 87.2 million tons in 1913 to 101 million tons by 1918, and 174 million by 1929. Brown coal was the unlikely but highly profitable glamour industry of Weimar.[14]

The post-First World War settlement exacerbated problems of over-capacity in both western and eastern European coal markets. France, which had imported 3.2 million tons of German coal in 1913, stepped up domestic production from 24.3 million tons in 1920 to 53.9 million in 1930. Belgium, whose Southern Basin contained the oldest and least-efficient mines in Europe, put the Campine, or Kempen, district in operation during the 1920s. It added another 10 million tons per year to Belgian capacity. The Aachen mines also presented a problem. They had lost their main market when Luxembourg entered the Belgian customs union after the First World War. Still, the district's output increased from 3.2 million in 1913 to 6 million tons in 1929, creating a flood of coal on the markets of the Lower Rhein.[15]

Changes in eastern Europe were no less disruptive. The Russian market was lost to Germany (representing 2.3 million tons in 1913) when the Soviet Union discontinued coal imports. In 1930 the Soviet Union returned to European coal markets, this time, however, as an exporter. In the meantime output had been raised from the pre-war record of 24 million tons per year to 56 million tons, and it would rise to 126 million tons by 1936. The transfer of Upper Silesia to Polish jurisdiction as a result of the 1922 plebiscite had an even more far-reaching impact on coal markets. The Silesian seams were the best in Europe and could be worked cheaply but were located far away from major industrial markets. Poland's desperate hard currency shortages played a major role in their development. By means of subsidies and numerous export premiums output in the Upper Silesian mines increased some 9 million tons in the first year after the plebiscite, and would increase another 8 million tons per year by 1929. Finding markets for this production was no easy matter. After 1925, the Reich simply boycotted Polish coal. Although the Poles managed to wrest the eastern Baltic from the British, they were unable to create a protected market area elsewhere. Polish coal therefore led a vagabond existence. Prices, sales and destinations fluctuated wildly not only in response to demand but to Poland's foreign exchange position. In the portions of Upper Silesia which remained in the Reich and the somewhat less important fields of Lower Silesia, production also increased by about 6 million tons, partly because of the introduction of a new rail tariff which moved the 'Demarcation Line' between the two main German coal districts some 200 km to the west. It was not until late 1931 that Ruhr lobbying succeeded in having the tariff amended with a view to restoring the pre-First World War status quo.[16]

But as production capacities increased, advances in thermal technology decreased demand for coal. The German steel industry reduced average coke consumption from 1457 kg to 1258 kg per ton between 1913 and 1930. Over the same years, the gas works lowered coal requirements per m^3 by some 46 per cent, and the electricity works their needs per kwh from 1.30 kg to 0.680 kg. The Reichsbahn achieved economies of 20 per cent per work unit during the 1920s. The industry estimated that these savings reduced total German coal requirements by some 25–30 million tons annually.[17]

Competition from oil and electrical power presented Ruhr coal with its greatest challenge over the long run. For most purposes, the new sources of energy were superior: cleaner, better suited to large-scale operations, easier to convey, more reliable in supply and standardized in grade, and generally cheaper. The market relationships between them and coal are quite intricate. Before 1930, coal and *oil* were, at least in Europe, seldom directly competitive. The market for bunker fuel was an important exception. It provides an instructive example of what the future would hold. By 1930, oil had replaced coal in most merchant marine vessels, less because of the superiority of the motor to the steam turbine than because of petroleum's superior handling qualities and lesser bulk. Other than for bunkering, the rise in European petroleum consumption between the wars was due almost entirely to the increase in motor-car ownership. By the late 1920s the coal industry had attained a foothold in this growth market and was actively attempting to strengthen its position.[18]

Relationships between coal and electrical power were complicated by the fact that in the Reich, as elsewhere, utilities were the largest industrial consumers of solid fuels. A case could be made that cheap electric power translated into additional coal sales. But while in 1913 coal was responsible for generating 12 (US) billion kcal, by 1930 brown coal had replaced coal as the largest supplier to the electrical utilities – 63 billion kcal versus 60 billion kcal – and water was responsible for another 24 billion kcal.[19]

The availability of these new energy sources also altered the economic environment, making possible the creation of new industries, such as aluminium, which competed with traditional coal customers, opened up whole new regions to industrial development far removed from sources of coal, and raised environmental standards to levels coal could not meet. They represented a threat not only to the coal industry but to the power of the Ruhr itself.

To explain Ruhr coal's response to these challenges, one must begin with its business traditions. Cartelization had, first of all, virtually eliminated entrepreneurship. According to William Parker's detailed 1951 study of the industry's marketing methods this could take only two forms: the improvement of operational efficiency and the reduction of the purchasing price for labour and raw materials. A firm's 'marketing strategy' was effectively limited to the acquisition of mine properties or larger quotas, both of which added to its power in RWKS councils and increased the degree it could vary by grade the coal supplied to fill its quota.[20]

The steel industry held the upper hand in relations with coal. (This was less a function of size than of differentials in growth rate.) *Konzerne* controlled over half of total output (Table 3). The domination of steel did not imply interference in mining matters; in every *Konzern* the 'coal side' operated autonomously. But from the standpoint of the managing directors of the trusts, the mines' primary *raison d'être* was to provide a reliable supply of coke to the steel industry. They were categorically opposed to the collieries' developing into independent 'profit centres'.

Coal was run by technicians of a rather special type. These were the *Bergassessoren* (mining engineers). They had been schooled in the virtues of technical excellence and an authoritarian approach to management. Believing coal-mining to be a quasi-sacred task, they viewed themselves as custodians of a precious and depletable asset. Their overriding concern was not return on investment but yield per ton of coal output.[21] The mine managers' business strategy was consistent with this priority. It aimed at lowering production costs, tightening control of existing markets, increasing the sale of by-products, and developing new uses for both coal and its by-products through research. A curtailment of mine operations was simply never considered. Nor was the transformation of coal into a diversified energy industry, whether by means of merger, acquisition, the set-up of 'communities of interest' or exchanges of patents and processes. Such a strategy might have worked. The late 1920s was a period of massive business reorganization in all the major industrial nations. In its search for new coal markets, the industry was also entering many key growth areas. With appropriate management, these opportunities might have supported a solid new kind of enterprise. As it was – fundamental conservatism notwithstanding – the industry was on a perilous course. Even though by 1928 the German production index had reached pre-war level Ruhr coal could not make a profit. Thus the viability of the industry, and during the Depression its very survival, came to depend chiefly on political rather than on business decisions.

The effort to lower costs involved, first of all, concentrating production. In 1925 twenty-seven mines producing some 4.3 million tons were shut down. With the exception of 1927, some 1.3–1.5 million tons per year were taken out of operation during the rest of the decade. After 1927 there was a significant reduction in the number of working points, from 16,700 to 12,500 by 1929. The number in operation fell even more drastically during the Depression years. Over the same period output per working point increased impressively. By 1937, it was possible to produce at 1928 levels with only 355 working points.[22]

The pneumatic pick made these efficiencies possible. In 1913 there were only 189 in use underground. By 1925 some 35,600 of them accounted for slightly over a third of total output and by 1929 this share had increased to 89 per cent. The new technology enabled the industry to increase daily coal production from 378,695 tons to 407,101 tons in the years between 1913 and 1929 while reducing employment from 424,627 to 375,711. The pneumatic pick also brought an increase in the percentage of large lumps, that is of useable sizes, in the overall yield. But the instrument also had its disadvantages. Management, recognizing that it destroyed the 'artisanal character' of mine labour, believed that it undermined morale. Certainly the pneumatic pick took a heavy toll on both physical and psychic health. It tore at the muscles, stiffened the joints, ruined the ears, and aggravated the traditional hardships of the mines: extremes of temperature, dampness, dust and darkness. But the pneumatic pick had a favourable influence on other areas of mine operation; it brought improvements in lighting systems and ventilation and a steady modernization in conveyance systems. These facts are reflected in the increase of electrical power consumption per ton of yield from 9.5 kwh in 1913 to 15.4 kwh in 1929. There were proportionate increases in requirements for steam and compressed air. Still, operations remained only semi-mechanized: roof construction involved timbering, and loading and backfilling were done almost entirely by shovel.[23] In short, mining remained the most physically demanding of all jobs.

In addition to lowering production costs, the industry tried to increase tonnage yields by overcoming the grade problem – the fact that a given volume of mined Ruhr coal normally contains pieces of various sizes, with different combustion and storage characteristics, and for which demand varied considerably. Over 70 per cent of the burden was normally 'fat coal'

Table 3 Members and tonnage quotas, 1939

Mine	*Coal quota*	*Coke quota*	*Briquette quota*	*Total use*	*Total quota*
Steel Trust					
Vereinigte Stahlwerke AG	24,376,100	7,779,930	3,565,350	13,250,420	37,626,520
Concordia Bergbau AG	1,850,000	702,400		350,000	2,200,000
					39,826,520
State-owned Mines					
Saargruben AG (Reich)	22,906,000	1,317,000		780,000	15,686,000
Hibernia AG (Prussia, VEBAG)	11,906,700	4,223,400	712,100	2,051,600	13,958,300
Alte Haase (Vereinigte Elektrizitätswerke Westfalen – VEW)	452,900		385,900	257,100	710,000
Gottessegen (VEW)	287,000		244,600	163,000	450,000
Caroline (VEW)	274,300		144,300	155,700	430,000
					31,234,300
Flick Combine					
Harpener Bergbau AG	10,949,200	4,033,800	192,620	727,600	11,676,800
Essener Steinkohlenbergwerke	9,199,000	1,815,570	2,116,100	350,000	9,549,000
Siebenplaneten	865,500	189,500	231,800	349,100	1,215,000
					32,440,900
Krupp					
Friedrich Krupp AG	2,211,100	744,400	418,200	3,116,300	5,327,400
Ver. Constantin der Große	3,682,600	1,300,200	223,350	193,800	3,876,400
Emscher Lippe	2,314,200	1,231,750		121,700	2,435,900
					11,639,700
Other steel companies					
Eschweiler Bergwerks Ver. (Arbed)	8,806,600	4,296,600	949,150	60,000	8,866,600
Hoesch AG	6,810,000	2,384,750		1,900,000	8,710,000
Ewald-König Ludwig (Thyssen)	7,215,500	2,474,500			7,215,500
Klöckner-Werke AG	4,048,000	1,902,800	72,000	1,705,200	5,753,200
Gutehoffnungshütte Oberhausen AG (Haniel)	3,517,600	777,200	1,013,600	1,831,200	5,348,800
Gebrüder Stumm GmbH	4,149,100	1,415,100	128,700	335,000	4,484,100
Mannesmannröhren-Werke	3,958,000	1,625,500	214,900	1,128,300	5,086,300
Friedrich der Grosse (Ilseder)	888,600	240,000		596,700	1,485,300
					46,949,800
Stinnes interests					
Mathias Stinnes/Mülheimer Bergswerks Verein/Diergardt-Mevissen I–III	7,330,500	961,300	2,448,700	160,000	7,470,500

Table 3 Members and tonnage quotas, 1939 *(continued)*

Mine	*Coal quota*	*Coke quota*	*Briquette quota*	*Total use*	*Total quota*
IG Farben					
Rheinische Stahlwerke/Admiral/Hermann V	6,465,600	2,529,000	400,400	1,409,800	7,875,400
Auguste Victoria	950,000	37,300		1,050,000	2,000,000
					9,875,400
Other chemical interests					
Lothringen Bergbau (Wintershall)	5,072,900	1,627,700	577,400	140,000	5,212,900
Dahlbusch (Solvay-Lib. Owens)	1,589,200	619,800			1,589,200
Sachsen (Salzdetfurth)	1,160,000	450,400			1,160,000
Mansfeld AG (Salzdetfurth)	484,620	300,000		300,000	784,620
					8,746,720
Wendel interests (French)					
Friedrich Heinrich/Norddeutschland	1,172,500	225,000		1,077,500	2,250,000
Heinrich Robert AG	1,625,000	291,700		375,000	2,000,000
					4,250,000
Deutsche Erdöl AG					
Victoria Mathias/Friedrich Ernestine/Graf Beust	4,987,800	300,000		50,000	5,037,800
Rheinisch-Westfälische Elektrizitätswerke	1,348,000	739,100		544,775	1,892,775
Westfalen (Dessauer Gas)	1,350,000	312,000		350,000	1,700,000
					3,592,775
Miscellaneous					
Niederrheinische AG (Michel)	1,100,000	359,300			1,100,000
Rheinpreussen/Rheinland	4,466,400	1,566,800		334,700	4,795,100
Neumühl Gewerkschaft	2,069,700	807,200			2,125,700
Carolus Magnus (Palenberg)	1,750,000	640,000			1,750,000
Carl Alexander (Aachen)	1,152,000	38,600		48,000	1,200,000
Sophia Jacoba (Aachen)	2,100,000		330,000		2,100,000
Heinrich Gewerkschaft	973,100		528,900		973,100
Langenbrahm Gewerkschaft	809,300		120,000		809,300
Carolus Magnus (Essen)	617,800	241,300			617,800
					15,415,000

Quota totals 1939	*Coal quota*	*Coke quota*	*Briquette quota*	*Total use*	*Total quota*
Ruhr mines	142,501,820	43,850,500	14,098,220	34,374,995	176,876,815
Saar mines	14,906,000	1,317,000		780,000	15,686,000
Aachen mines	13,808,600	4,975,200	1,279,150	108,000	13,916,600
	171,216,420	50,142,500	15,377,370	35,262,995	206,479,115

Source: OMGUS (Decartelization Branch), 'A Survey of German Cartels', 1946.

(*Fettkohle*), which could not be stored and was usually coked. Coking coal and coke were therefore in surplus except when steel demand was high. In the 1920s the industry spent heavily to develop a cheap storable briquette from fine fat coal which could be both sold for domestic heating purposes when steel demand was weak and consumed at the foundries when it was strong. The coke briquette also used previously wasted grades of fine and ballast coal as a binder. The industry invested considerable sums in the 'swelling' process as well. It provided a method of increasing the volatility of normally hard-to-sell 'thin coals' (*Magerkohle*). When 'swollen' they could substitute for, or be mixed with, a number of different grades in a variety of industrial uses.[24]

Still more important for the long-run, the Ruhr mines sought to increase yields by developing markets for the by-products of the coke-making process. One ton of coal, when coked, normally yields 0.72 tons of coke and, in addition, 11,000 cubic feet of gas, 3.5 lb of sulphur, 9 lb of ammonia (NH_3), 7.0 gallons of crude tar, and 2.6 gallons of benzole. The perceived importance of these by-product markets was both cause and consequence of the cokery construction in the period 1925–9. Between May 1925 and August 1928 some thirty-five new cokeries were built in the Ruhr. These were new regenerating ovens, which produced as much as 27.8 metric tons per 24-hour day as compared to 5.15 metric tons in the older type of oven. Ruhr coking capacity was rated at 40–42 million annual tons.[25]

To make use of the approximately 1 billion m^3 of gas generated by the new cokeries, Ruhr coal entered the business of gas transmission. On 11 October 1926 the A.G. für Kohleverwertung, later called Ruhrgas, was founded by five of the largest mines (Harpen, Hibernia, Köln-Neuessen, Essener Steinkohlen-bergwerke and Konstantin der Grosse). The new company planned to construct five lines radiating out from the Ruhr to connect with city gas nets already in place: to reach Hamburg and Bremen over Kiel; Berlin and Stettin over Hannover, Braunschweig and Magdeburg; Thuringia and Saxony over Kassel; and finally, Hesse, Baden and Württemberg from a feeder along the Rhein. It was also hoped eventually to connect with the grids of Silesia and the Saar. Coke gas, like natural gas, burns clean and therefore competed directly with electricity for household use. It had the additional advantage of costing virtually nothing to produce, since it would otherwise have been wasted.[26]

The transmission business was confronted with serious problems from the outset. First, it put the Ruhr in competition with itself: it had supplied gas cokes to the very gas works it would have to supplant. The transmission plans also aroused almost instantaneous opposition from the representatives of a newly formed association of communes headed by Frankfurt and Köln. They were justifiably wary of becoming totally dependent on the Ruhr as a supplier. Although in the late 1920s the Ruhr disposed of huge surpluses of gas, demand for coke determined gas outputs, and gas outputs depended on the vicissitudes of the steel market. To aggravate the problem, pipe-laying required large outlays of capital. The Ruhr reckoned that delivery contracts would have to run for a minimum of ten years and would require exclusivity. Many large communal gas suppliers such as Hamburg, Düsseldorf and Braunschweig also planned to extend their own gas operations. Finally, it was by no means evident that Ruhrgas could offer a significant cost advantage over electricity, even for heating. By 1928, only some 500 km of pipe had been installed, mainly in the Sauerland. This doubled the pre-war length but was still disappointing.[27]

The most commercially valuable of the chemical by-products whose outputs grew as a result of the new cokery construction were the coal tars or aromatics, whose unique chemical structure resembles a ring. When distilled, these compounds yield a number of derivatives such as pitch (for binding), solvent naphtha, creosote oil (a preservative), tar acids (raw materials for various disinfectants, plastics and drugs) and benzole (see Figure 1). Benzole was both a high-grade motor fuel with properties similar to petrol and a raw material for toluene (for explosives) and xylene (for pharmaceuticals). From 1910 to 1929, German output of distilled tar products increased from 984,000 tons to 1,615,000 tons, and the percentage of raw tar distilled from 83.9 per cent to 90 per cent. The Gesellschaft für Teerverwertung, a mine-industry owned corporation, purchased over one-half of this output. It was marketed through specialized cartels essentially similar in structure to RWKS, but like gas, coal tar production depended in the first instance on coking activity and therefore was not market-responsive.[28]

The production of surplus benzole put Ruhr coal into the petroleum business, at least in a half-hearted way. Liquid fuel matters were handled by the relevant cartel, the Benzol-Verband, formed in 1898. It had been pushed into the market for supplying motor vehicles in 1915–16 when Romania, the Reich's previous supplier, entered the First World War on the side of the Entente. The end of reparations in kind in 1924 opened the way to German distribution of the product. At first benzole was retailed through coal merchants and chemists or sold by the drum. In late 1924, the coal industry set up an independent distribution network. In 1926 the brand name 'BV-Aral' (Benzol-Verband und Aromatische und Aliphatische) was trade-marked, and the Reich thus had its first major non-foreign-owned chain of service stations. It was for all intents and purposes identical to the others except that its product was coal- rather than petroleum-based. The Benzol-Verband also sold the USSR petroleum under contract until 1929. In that year, the Soviets set up their own chain, DEROP. But none of this committed Ruhr coal seriously to the motor fuel business. It did not seek its own independent sources of supply or even enter refining. From first to last, the network of service stations existed primarily to provide markets for coal products.[29]

In the 1920s the industry conducted numerous experiments with coal as a motor fuel. While none of them was commercially successful, they all had

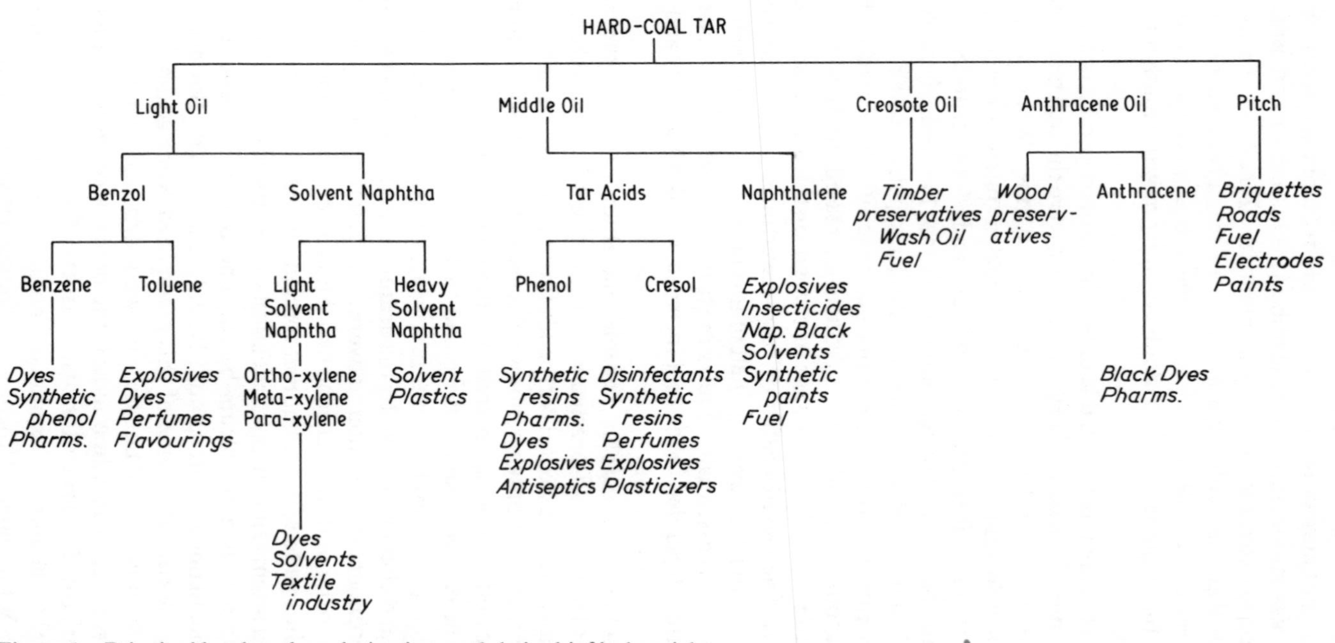

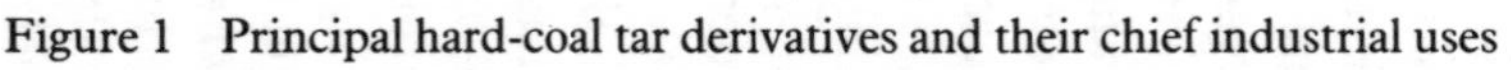
Figure 1 Principal hard-coal tar derivatives and their chief industrial uses

some application to wartime conditions. At Hibernia mine, Wanne-Eickel, a methane 'gas station' was built to supply delivery vans with distilled by-product gas from coke ovens. Lack of steady supplies and the cumbersomeness of the high-pressure tanks and hoses necessary for fuelling operations limited the applicability of the approach. The Koppers Co., an important manufacturer of coal-mining and processing equipment, estimated that its procedure for burning coal in 'gas-sucking generators' *(Sauggasgeneratoren)* would reduce German fuel imports by 350,000 tons annually, assuming that one-half of all trucks and buses were equipped with them. But vehicles using the device could not climb gradients without supplementary petrol carburation.

The Gesellschaft für Teerverwertung actively promoted the use of coal tar oil as a motor fuel. In the First World War it was often burned in diesel engines which, however, required special compressors no longer in production. Because of the low volatility of coal tar, research concentrated on developing an improved ignition system. But downhill or bumpy motion tended to overheat or extinguish the firing points resulting in stalling or fires. Tar oil was therefore considered to be satisfactory for use only in stationary engines. Coke gas appeared to have a much more promising future. German supplies, as measured in energy equivalents, were estimated at twice normal petroleum consumption requirements. The fuel could be burned in a petrol engine merely by replacing the carburettor with a reduction valve. But the smallest removable tank weighed 75 kg, too heavy for passenger car use. The alternative, built-in storage tanks, required high-pressure compressors, which had to be operated on a more or less continuous basis. They were considered suitable only for bus systems running to a tight schedule. Finally, the industry continued to promote the development of a steam-powered truck. In this field it could benefit from improvements in boiler design, firing systems, and safety standards which had resulted from the industry's effort to stave off the introduction of oil-fired steam and diesel locomotives like those already common in the USA. But steam-powered trucks were heavy, smoky, and offered no price advantage over those powered by petroleum fuels. In 1929 only 400 were operating within the Reich.[30]

The principal emphasis in Ruhr coal's research programme was the production of synthetic petroleum. In 1926, Professor Franz Fischer and his assistant Hans Tropsch, working in the industry's Coal Research Institute (Kohlenforschungsinstitut) at Mülheim, successfully produced the new product by the gas synthesis process. Its essential feature is the passage of a gas containing hydrogen and carbon monoxide over a cobalt catalyst to form a series of hydrocarbons. The hydrocarbons are then condensed, distilled, and passed on to a refinery for treatment. In addition to synthetic petroleum, the process yields paraffin and a gas similar in structure to coke gas. But the Fischer–Tropsch process did not monopolize the synthetic petroleum field.

It faced severe competition from the so-called hydrogenation process controlled by IG Farben. This was based on the work of Professor Bergius who, in 1916, produced a high-grade gasoline by combining hydrogen and oxygen at extremely high temperatures and pressures. IG Farben took over developments of the patent after the war and by 1927 commercial production of synthetic fuel had begun at the new Leuna works at Oppau.[31]

There was plenty of opportunity for the two patent holders to pool their processes. Each one had respective advantages and disadvantages. The Fischer–Tropsch process could be built on a smaller scale and was generally cheaper to operate. Hydrogenation was safer and yielded a higher grade of petrol and, unlike the Fischer–Tropsch process, no by-products. The latter process was slightly more flexible: it would work equally well with brown coal or any grade of hard coal. Hydrogenation worked best with brown coal, well with most grades of hard coal, and not at all with either hard-to-sell heating coke or swelled coke. Most experts agreed that neither process was inherently superior: success would depend on the financial strength of each patent holder and on demand levels for their processes' somewhat differing outputs. But the Ruhr coal industry was uninterested in any kind of arrangement to spread financial risks or share markets for synthetic petroleum. It was concerned mainly with creating markets for hard-to-sell coal. The Ruhr coal industry, while it disliked IG's hydrogenation plans, therefore did strangely little to counter them. The mines' only move was increase the budget of the Mülheim researchers in the hope that the 'bugs' could be worked out of the Fischer–Tropsch process.[32]

Another critical concern of the industry after 1926 was to develop new markets for coke and coal. This was the responsibility of the Rheinisch-Westfälisches Kohlensyndikat (RWKS). Often cited as a *Paradebeispiel* of the modern industrial cartel, RWKS has had numerous imitators and spawned a vast literature.[33] Organizationally, it was both an association in public law and a corporation owned by its members with shareholdings based on output quotas. The syndicate normally sold in three ways. In 1928 it delivered 16.81 per cent of saleable production directly to large consumers such as the utilities, the railways and export markets. RWKS marketed another 60.52 per cent through wholly-owned merchanting companies, the *Syndikatshandelsgesellschaften*. They enjoyed a sales monopoly in the uncontested area around the Ruhr. One of them, the Kohlenkontor in Mannheim, also sold in the *contested* area of central and southern Germany. Merchanting companies owned by individual mines marketed another 12.67 per cent in the contested areas, and independents the remaining 0.6 per cent. The mine-owned merchanting companies, while required to purchase all Ruhr coal through RWKS, could also acquire coal from other districts on the open market. In the uncontested areas the syndicate charged fixed prices, exclusive of transportation and handling charges; in the contested areas, it offered rebates as required. Foreign sales were usually conducted by contract. The syndicate paid merchanting companies a fixed commission of 6 per cent on total sales at official prices *(Richtpreise)*. The *Umlage* (levy) was levied initially to cover commissions plus overheads and later, as rebating became more common, developed into a device for subsidizing sales.[34]

The distribution of the levy between 'pure' mines and those owned by Konzerne plagued the cartel from its inception, at times even threatening its existence. But by 1925 this problem had largely been solved because of the merger of 'pure' mines into Konzerne and other trusts. Levels of Umlage assessment became a more troublesome matter than its distribution. In the period from 1904–15, calculated on the basis of 4 to 12 per cent on total output, they amounted to RM 0.50 to RM 1 per ton. These were not levied in the period 1916–23, but set at RM 0.50 per ton when resumed in February 1924, then soon rose to between RM 1.20 and RM 1.50 per ton in 1925. And from there they increased to RM 1.29 in 1927, RM 1.94 in 1928 and RM 2.28 in 1929. While these increases aggravated differences between mines which benefited from sales in export markets and those which sold locally, they did not jeopardize the existence of the syndicate. RWKS had come to be regarded by its members as indispensable. Some of them also foresaw an expanded role for it in the future, namely as a key component in a kind of super-cartel for west European heavy industry.[35]

In the international field events in coal followed those in steel, one of which was of particular importance. This was the formation of the International Steel Cartel (ISC) in 1926. It concluded more than two years of negotiations between French and German foundrymen aimed at ending the disruptions on west European iron and steel markets resulting from the terms of the Versailles peace settlement. The modalities of the Franco-German understanding were highly complicated but the key to it was the Ruhr cession to French producers of a steel import quota. In return the Germans secured an agreement from France not to raise tariffs against the importation of their manufactures. This arrangement was tied to another between German foundrymen and manufacturers, the so-called 'AVI Pact'. It committed the steel industry to providing rebates for exporters of finished products as compensation for increases in domestic prices.[36]

These two agreements forged bonds of great strength between German and French steelmen and preceded broader negotiations with their counterparts in Belgium and Luxembourg to regulate international steel markets. The four west European producers represented a tremendous concentration of power. In 1926 they produced 29.67 million long tons of a total world raw steel output of 91.79 million long tons and 65 per cent of total world raw steel exports. From the first, Ruhr foundrymen conceived of the ISC negotiations as a step toward a single west European *Montanindustrie*. Accordingly, they proposed the adoption of the Stahlwerksverband (Steel Producers' Association), the steel analogue to RWKS, as a model to their counterparts in France, Belgium and Luxembourg. While far too radical a step, given the scars of war, this proposal forced the other steel industries to recognize that regulation of international sales required corresponding control on domestic market. The ISC agreement assigned each producing nation an annual quota which included both domestic and international sales and provided a compensation scheme to penalize those who exceeded it to the benefit of those who did not.[37]

As the largest exporter of coke and coking coal to the steel industries of eastern France, Belgium and Luxembourg, Ruhr coal was a silent partner in the ISC negotiations. Clearly, the agreement stood no chance of working in the absence of a Ruhr coal commitment to act as a reliable and 'loyal' supplier. The parties to the ISC took for granted that RWKS would 'discipline' its members, abandon the 'coal weapon' in matters touching on steel, and make financial sacrifices when necessary. Ruhr coal none the less stood to gain from any increase in western Europe's overall share in world steel exports and from the stabilization of coke and coal markets which would result from the successful cartelization of steel. While there was no coal sequel to the ISC agreement – largely because it would have had to involve different principals – the steel negotiations did lead to coal conferences in 1927 and 1929, sponsored by the League of Nations. The second of these resolved that 'international agreements between producers should be arranged concerning outputs, markets, and prices'.[38]

But might such arrangements as the ISC and those discussed for coal have broader significance? Emile Mayrisch, the managing director of the giant Luxembourg steel complex known as ARBED, believed that they could provide the institutional basis for a lasting Franco-German political reconciliation. He spelled out his ideas in a December 1927 note entitled 'Les ententes économiques et la paix'.[39] Mayrisch's immediate concern was to create stable economic conditions in western Europe. He blamed the governments of the area for having failed in this respect and assigned the task to businessmen. Arguing that commercial stability could only be assured through the creation of a network of international cartels, Mayrisch went on to explain that two conditions were indispensable to the success of such arrangements. One was the improvement of business co-operation through exchanges of capital, the organization of new holding companies, and the setting up of new types of pooling arrangements. Another was public support. This would require successful appeals to the material interests of consumers and the provision of adequate social security measures. This, he explained, would make it possible for producers to circumvent obstructive parliaments.

Mayrisch, who had few illusions, none the less felt strongly enough about his proposal to organize a discussion group composed of industrialists and academic dignitaries called 'Comité franco-allemand d'information et de documentation'. The head of the ISC until his death by motor-car accident in 1928, he influenced the thinking of a number of prominent industrialists. The 1930s and the war would prove unexpectedly propitious for Mayrisch's ideas. They would witness the arrival of authoritarian government, an increase in producer co-operation and a rise in the popularity of paternalism.

As the end of the 1920s approached, Ruhr mine managers could not afford the luxury of thinking about the future. By then it had become evident that their business strategy was failing badly. RWKS enjoyed but little success in creating new markets for coal. Although by the end of the decade domestic sales of 68 million tons exceeded the 65 million tons of 1912, this was due largely to the increase in household consumption of heating coal. The increase barely covered the reduction of deliveries to industry. Nor did it prove possible to influence industrial consumption requirements for coal by *grade*; the same varieties remained hard to sell. Ruhr coal for domestic market sales increased only in one place, the North Sea ports. These gains, which were made at the expense of the British, approximately offset the loss to Silesia in 'contested areas'. These were due to the eastern district's favourable treatment in the matter of freight rates. Prices for the main Ruhr coal grades never recovered to the high levels of 1924, advancing only slightly between 1925 and 1929. Fat coal *(Fettkohle)* which normally comprised over one-half of the total Ruhr output, reached RM 20.60/ton on 21 January 1924, declined to RM 15.00/ton on 1 April 1925, and by 16 December 1928 had recovered only RM 16.97/ton. Prices for large cokes *(Hochofenkoks)* were particularly dismal. They hit RM 36.40/ton on 24 January 1924, but slipped to RM 25.00/ton on 1 April 1925, and fell to RM 23.50/ton by 16 December 1928. The weakness in large coke markets was in part the result of cut-throat competition for exports. Most galling of all was the situation in western Europe, the one large foreign growth market. While exports of coke increased from 5.5 million annual tons in 1913 to 9.8 million annual tons in 1939, average Ruhr coke export prices fell from RM 23.1/ton to RM 17.3/ton. The attempt to hold on to these markets was behind the rising export *Umlage* of the late 1920s.[40] Nor were hopes of raising tonnage yields realized. The increase in the value of total mine output from RM 1,834,471,000 in 1926 to RM 2,195,118,000 in 1929 was due almost entirely to increased sales of coal. By-product sales were distressing, cokeries operated at a growing loss, yield fell on tar and pitch, and only pressed coal (used mainly for domestic heating) showed an impressive gain. Nominal yields per ton decreased steadily from RM 1.27 in 1913 to RM 0.68 in 1926 to RM 0.65 in 1927 and RM 0.38 in 1928 – at a time when an adequate return on capital, figured at 9 per cent, would have required yields of RM 2.95 ton.

But the situation was even worse than this. The published balances did not provide adequately for depreciation. This was the opinion of both the

Schmalenbach Commission, set up by the industry in 1927 to study its financial situation, and the famous Enquête-Ausschuss organized by the Reichstag to investigate the general condition of German business. According to the Schmalenbach Report, adequate depreciation allowances would have shown the industry operating at a loss of RM 0.27/ton in 1928. The Reichstag-appointed committee corroborated this conclusion, citing with special concern the alarming deterioration of the industry's capital structure. Costs for debt servicing – before the war RM 914,491.90 and wiped out during the post-First World War inflation – jumped to RM 9,197,869.10 in 1924 and increased from there to RM 13,841,591.15 by 1927. This approximated one-quarter of the book value of mine machinery. To make matters worse, about 90 per cent of this debt was short-term. The Enquête Ausschuss concluded that 'the results of our findings are cause for grave concern. . . . The figures indicate that . . . often and in many cases for considerable time large portions of the German mining industry have operated with little or no success.'[41]

The mines were in a difficult position. To restore profitability there was no alternative but to reduce the one large variable in production costs, wages. As of June 1926, wages comprised 52 per cent of total yield, salaries another 6.93 per cent, and employer social contributions another 8.06 per cent, totalling 67 per cent of all costs. The 'rationalization' of underground operations brought about some improvement. Between 1927 and 1930 wages per ton decreased from RM 7.54 to RM 7.31. High though these costs were, wages do not appear to have been excessive. They compare favourably with those of other districts. In the years from 1927 to 1929 wage costs per ton of mined coal averaged 69.1 per cent in Great Britain, 56.2 per cent in Belgium, 52 per cent in the Ruhr and at 49 per cent were lower only in the highly mechanized mines of the Netherlands. Ruhr miners were, if anything, paid too little for their work. Their status relative to other occupational groups was also slipping. After 1928 construction replaced mining as the best-paid industrial labour.[42] Further reductions could only damage morale and increase the difficulties of recruitment.

Inadequate pay and increased job stress created an explosive mood underground. Although the leaders of the main miners' union (Alter Verband) and the 'moderate' wing of the Social Democratic Party tried hard to contain it, their efforts went unthanked. The Bergassessoren blamed their labour problems on the political system. Their immediate solution was to eliminate the reforms introduced by Weimar governments to reduce class conflict. Mine management waged a dogged campaign to lengthen the work day, refused to submit to official wage arbitration, and opposed all wage increases. By 1930 frustration over the 'labour problem' had put the operators into the camp opposed to the continuation of the Weimar system.[43]

The mining industry also had a long-term plan for coping with employee problems. It involved a full-scale attempt to change attitudes by means of modern personnel methods. Through them the Bergassessoren hoped to restore the 'Herr in Haus' status they imagined themselves to have enjoyed before the First World War.[44] In this respect the industry could fall back on special traditions.

German mining is distinguished from that of other nations by a military-bureaucratic form of organization on the one hand and a strong sense of corporate identity on the other. Both stemmed from the era of Direktionsprinzip (1776–1851), when Prussian officials supervised the administration of the mines. Legally, their power was absolute: mining rights belonged to the sovereign and could not be alienated. Permission to mine was subcontracted to *Kuxeninhaber*, individuals who did not acquire title to the property in question and who were required to follow official production plans. Within the mines themselves, quasi-military discipline prevailed. At the same time, miners were privileged. They lived in special state-chartered mining communities *(Bergstädte)* normally located at the site of operations and enjoyed tax relief, freedom of movement, and wood-gathering rights, as well as the privilege of organizing special mining associations. These *Knappschaften* were initially little more than fraternal organizations but soon took on a variety of civic and social functions: burials societies, to promoting self-improvement, and to providing sickness, accident and life insurance. In the *Knappschaften* one finds the most characteristic forms of miner culture: uniforms, special music, tool symbolism, and ritual associated with its ceremonies as well as an ethic of 'obedience and discipline, of honour and rank consciousness'.[45]

The paternalism of the operators, who after 1870 exercised effective control of the mines, brought these two traditions together. While not tampering with the structure of authority in the pits, they promoted those traditions which gave miners a sense of belonging to a privileged and distinct group. They took over the financing of the *Knappschaften* (which provided the most comprehensive industrial insurance coverage available to any occupational group prior to the First World War), subsidized residential communities near the pithead *(Bergarbeitersiedlungen)*, provided garden plots for their residents, and in addition, sponsored consumer and savings co-operatives, sports clubs, choral societies, and diverse social activities.[46]

In the 1920s, this paternalism both at the mines and in heavy industry generally was being worked into a purportedly new theoretical approach to labour relations, *betriebliche Sozialpolitik* or BSP (factory-oriented social policy). Its avowed purposes were to eliminate all 'non-factory disturbances' *(ausserbetriebliche Störungen)* from unions, parties, churches, state welfare institutions as well as other 'factory-foreign influences' *(betriebsfremder Gebilde)* and to secure the 'soul-loyalty' of the employee to the factory *(seelische Einstellung der Belegschaft zum Werk)*. BSP used the most modern methods. Through the *Werkspflege* (factory social service) the influence of the mine extended even into the home. Company social workers looked after family health, ran crèches and kindergartens, and took over responsibility for the education and training of wives. As one admirer put it,

> The training of capable housewives is important for several reasons. The wife is responsible for the life of the miner outside of the factory [but also] for rearing the next generation of miners [*Pflege des Nachwuchses*]. Clearly, raising the cultural level of miners' wives means an improvement in the profession itself. The worker must be rooted through his family.

The overall mission of the factory social service, in effect, was 'to combat the proletarian sense of desperation that is the death of initiative, self-sufficiency, and happiness'.[47]

Labour training was the most important part of BSP. Before the First World War, miners were trained on the job as necessary for production. Instruction was purely technical in character. The impetus to change stemmed from the new industrial pedagogy movement of Dr Carl Arnhold. Arnhold argued for the establishment at the works of a new kind of technical training programme based on the apprenticeship system familiar to *Handwerk* (artisanal labour) and designed to serve the requirements of manpower development and, at the same time, provide a 'school for citizenship'. Arnhold sought to inoculate workers against Marxism by inculcating an attachment to the firm, a sense of pride based on one's role in the production process, and a belief in the supreme importance of work as a measure of moral value and status and a source of human creativity. This new sense of professional pride – this *Berufsethos* – would, he promised, transform mass man *(Massenmensch)* into achievers *(Leistungsmenschen)*.[48]

In 1925, Arnhold found a prominent sponsor in the person of Albert Vögler, director of Vereinigte Stahlwerke (VS), which controlled some 40 per cent of total German raw steel capacity. The result of their collaboration was DINTA (Deutsches Institut für technische Arbeitsschulung), headed by Arnhold, promoted by Vögler, funded by business and set up to spread the new gospel of *Arbeitspädagogik* throughout industry. In 1925, Arnhold established training programmes at VS. The following year, as director of instruction for the VS-controlled coal company, Gelsenkirchen Bergwerk AG (GBAG), he organized the first new training programmes for the mines. By 1930, three-quarters of the coal firms in the district were following the GBAG example. The new schools provided above-ground training for 15- to 17-year-olds (who by law were barred from labour in the pits), followed by regulated apprenticeships under the supervision of certified miners *(Hauer)*, and for *Hauer*, eventual promotion to work party supervisor *(Steiger)* and ultimate advancement to section supervisor *(Fahrsteiger)*. In 1930, an estimated 53 per cent of underground workers had received training in the new technical schooling programmes.[49]

The new employer labour policy was but one manifestation of a widespread belief within Ruhr industry that it could not do business under Weimar. Far-reaching changes of an authoritarian character were believed to be in order. But precisely which ones? Numerous plans were sounded: the declaration of emergency rule under Article 48 of the constitution; the establishment, by amendment, of a kind of presidential dictatorship under Field Marshall von Hindenburg; and the restoration of the monarchy. Occasional sympathy was even expressed for the Nazis. But it would be wrong to identify the sentiments of the coal and steel producers with any of these particular ideas. They were opportunistic rather than doctrinaire, their loyalties determined by a process of accommodation with whichever group was best-positioned to protect their interests. This approach allowed for movement across a broad band of right-wing politics, neither foreclosing nor predetermining alliance with any of its factions. Two considerations were ultimately decisive in determining the political loyalties of the Ruhr in the years between 1930 and 1933; the economic impact of the Depression and the collapse of the political system.

In coal even more than in other sectors, the Depression created a *Subventionswirtschaft* – an economy of subsidies – and without it the mines would have foundered. This economy of subsidies included a gamut of measures: railway tariff reductions, tax relief, import quotas and protective tariffs, bilateral trade and payments agreements, and direct capital participation by the Reich. The bank crisis which began on 11 May 1931 with the collapse of the Austrian Kreditanstalt was a hard blow to the German economy. It necessitated government intervention into the field of international payments (the imposition of foreign exchange control and the principle of bilaterality in foreign trade) and a reorganization of the banking structure. In the process the Reichsbank acquired one-third of the capital of the Deutsche Bank, two-thirds of the capital of the Commerzbank, and the entire capital of the Dresdner Bank.[50]

The next massive Reich reorganization occurred a year later and involved VS. The threatened collapse of the economic empire of Friedrich Flick precipitated this intervention. Through a series of deals during the 1920s, Flick had acquired a controlling interest in GBAG and, through it, the largest holding in VS. When, thanks to a deliberate press indiscretion, it appeared as if French interests were about to acquire controlling interest in the Konzern by buying up shares on the open market at low prices, the Minister of Finance offered Flick RM 100 million for his interest – a sum equal to nine-tenths the nominal value of the entire company and three times their market value. The Reich thereby became the largest shareholder in VS, even adding to its position so that by January 1933 it controlled some 50 per cent of the company.[51]

The perilous situation of Ruhr coal in the Depression was due above all to the collapse of export markets. World coal output declined from approximately 1.3 (US) billion tons in 1929 to 965 million between 1929 and 1933 and the west European market for coking coal shrank by one-half due to a fall in demand for steel products. The beggar-thy-neighbour policies adopted by each coal exporting nation intensified competition in these markets. For the Ruhr, the worst of them was the British devaluation of the pound by 30 per cent in September 1931, a measure followed five months later by the imposition of a 33⅓ per cent *ad valorem* duty on steel imports. They caused coal export prices to plummet. While Ruhr export tonnages declined from 37,762,354 to 21,552,298 between 1929 and 1932, the value of these sales fell from RM 749,473 million to RM 279,477 million. To maintain the Ruhr export position the *Umlage* had to be increased steadily from RM 2.37 per ton in 1929 to RM 4.08 in 1933, or about 40 per cent of total value of exports at frontier. Sales in domestic markets also slipped. The result was a decrease of output from 123,590 million tons in 1929 to 73,277 in 1932, and a fall in the average value of coal mined (including by-products) from RM 17.66 per ton to RM 12.45 per ton. By 1933 the industry was on the verge of bankruptcy.[52]

For Ruhr coal, survival depended on politics. Its difficulties had begun in the mid-1920s, when the Bergassessoren launched it on a technically ambitious and in many ways commendable 'rationalization programme', whose benefits could, however, only be realized over a long period of strong demand and from which there was no turning back. By 1929 the strategy had failed so utterly that the operators had come to regard a reduction in wage and social costs as their only way to earn a profit. Then came the Depression, which hit coal markets with exceptional severity. The industry required a government that would respect its autonomy, impose a wage reduction, provide secure markets and offer the necessary subventions. There was no shortage of Chancellor candidates committed to such policies. Heinrich Brüning was reputed to be 'the best Chancellor that business ever had', and Franz von Papen featured as 'the man of the hour'. Finally, there was Hitler, who, from the standpoint of the Ruhr, was distinguished from the other two less in respect of his attitudes towards business or political ideas than in his ability to govern.[53]

Notes

1 Office of Military Government, (OMGUS) (Decartelization Branch), 'Report on German Cartels and Combines 1946: Vol. II survey of Germany's major industries', 1 March 1946, 12–34; Friedrich Schunder, 'Die wirtschaftliche Entwicklung des Ruhrbergbaus seit der Mitte des 19. Jahrhunderts', in K.E. Born (ed.), *Moderne deutsche Wirtschaftsgeschichte* (Köln/Berlin, 1960); OMGUS (Decartelization Branch) 'The major German cartels' (1945), i–xi, 1–26.

2 Elaine Glovka Spencer, 'Business bureaucrats and social control in the Ruhr, 1896 to 1914', in H.U. Wehler (ed.), *Sozialgeschichte Heute: Festschrift für Hans Rosenberg zum 70. Geburtstag* (Göttingen, 1974), 452–66.

3 Robert A. Brady, *The Rationalization Movement in German Industry: a study in the evolution of economic planning* (Berkeley, 1933), 84 f.; Erich Wedekind, 'Die Rationalisierung im Bergbau und ihre ökonomischen und sozialen Auswirkungen' (diss., Köln, 1930).
4 Ingvar Svennilson, *Growth and Stagnation in the European Economy* (Geneva, 1954), 102 f.; International Labour Office, *The World Coal Mining Industry*: vol. 1 *Economic Conditions* (Geneva, 1938), 9 f.
5 See Volkmar Muthesius, *Ruhrkohle: 1893–1943* (Essen, 1943); Schunder, op cit. 229 f.; Maurice Baumont, *La grosse industrie allemande et le charbon* (Paris, 1928); Gerhard Gebhardt, *Ruhrbergbau. Geschichte, Aufbau, Verflechtung seiner gesellschaftlichen Organisationen* (Essen, 1957); Bergbau Verein, *Der Ruhrbergbau im Wechsel der Zeiten* (Essen, 1933).
6 Norman J.G. Pounds, *The Ruhr: a study in historical and economic geography* (New York, 1965), 135 f.; Bergbau Verein (BV); *Statistisches Heft. Produktions- und wirtschaftsstatistische Angaben aus der Montanindustrie* (Essen, 1934).
7 Ministry of Economic Warfare, *Economic Survey of Germany* (ESG), *The minerals industries* (London, 1944), 42.
8 Institut für Konjunkturforschung (ed.), *Vierteljahrshefte zur Konjunkturforschung* (Sonderheft 34) 'Die Wettbewerbslage der Steinkohle' (Berlin, 1933), 22 f.; ILO, op. cit., 163 f.; Neil K. Buxton, 'Coal mining', in Neil K. Buxton and Derek H. Aldcroft (eds), *British Industry Between the Wars* (London, 1979); Norman J.G. Pounds and William N. Parker, *Coal and Steel in Western Europe: The Influence of Resources and Techniques on Production* (London, 1957), 264 f.
9 William N. Parker, 'Fuel supply and industrial strength: a study of the conditions governing the output and distribution of Ruhr coal in the late 1920s' (diss., Harvard, 1950).
10 G. Schmalenbach *et al.*, 'Gutachten über die gegenwärtige Lage des Rheinischen-westfälischen Steinkohlenbergbaus', (Berlin, 1928), 5 f.; Ausschuss zur Untersuchung der Erzeugung- und Absatzbedingungen der deutschen Wirtschaft [Enquête-Ausschuss], *Die deutsche Kohlenwirtschaft* (Berlin, 1929), 160 f.
11 ILO, op. cit., 128 f.
12 Parker, op. cit., 85.
13 Institut für Konjunkturforschung, op. cit., 7.
14 ILO, op. cit., 105 f; E.G. Lange, *Steinkohle. Wandlungen in der internationalen Kohlenwirtschaft* (Leipzig, 1936), 65 f.
15 ibid, 53 f.
16 Gabrielle Unverferth, 'Die verbandspolitische und ökonomische Entwicklung des Ruhrbergbaues von der Machtergreifung bis zum Vierjahresplan' (MA thesis, Ruhruniversität Bochum, 1975), 134 f.
17 Svennilson, op. cit., 105 f.; Lange, op. cit., 92 f.
18 Rudolf Regul, *Energiequellen der Welt* (Schriften des Instituts für Konjunkturforschung. Sonderheft 44) (Berlin, 1937), 32.
19 ibid., 29.
20 Parker, op. cit., 129.
21 Klaus Tenfelde, 'Mining festivals in the nineteenth century', *Journal of Contemporary History*, 13 (2), April 1978, 377–412.
22 BV, op. cit., 16–17, 177.
23 H. Bahnhoff, 'Stand und Entwicklungsmöglichkeiten in der Zechenkraftwirtschaft des Ruhrbergbaus', *Glückauf*, 29 December 1933; Horst-Günter Buck, 'Die Entwicklung des Ruhrbergbaus seit der Weltwirtschaftskrise' (diss., Köln, 1950), 55.

24 Ministry of Economic Warfare (ESG), *The Minerals Industries*, op. cit., 55.
25 ibid., 59 f.; Archives of Gutehoffnungshütte (GHH), 400101301/3 'Fortschritte in der Nebenproduktengewinnung der Kokereien', *Rheinisch-Westfälische Zeitung*, 31 December 1937; W. Scheer and W. Grobner, *Die Entwicklung der Steinkohlenveredlung in der letzten 20 Jahren* (Essen, 1941), 5 f.
26 Ministry of Economic Warfare (Section D) (ESG), *Fuel, power, and public utility services*, 63 f.; United States Strategic Bombing Survey, *The Coking Industry in Germany* (January 1945) n.p.
27 Erich Wedekind, 'Die Rationalisierung im Bergbau und ihre ökonomischen und sozialen Auswirkungen' (diss., Köln, 1930).
28 Ministry of Economic Warfare (ESG), *Fuel, power, and public utility services*, 73 f.
29 Willy Becker, 'Die deutsche Mineralölwirtschaft' (diss., Berlin, 1936), 32 f.
30 Erich Wiester, *Ausbau der deutschen Treibwirtschaft*, (Dortmund, 1935), 9 f.
31 Wolfgang Birkenfeld, *Der synthetische Treibstoff 1933–1945. Ein Beitrag zur nationalsozialistischen Wirtschafts- und Rüstungspolitik* (Göttingen, 1964), 13 f.; BIOS, 'Report on the petroleum and synthetic oil industry of Germany' (London, 1947), 5; Unverferth, op. cit., 113 f.
32 BIOS, 'Technical report on the Ruhr coal field', vol. I (London, 1947).
33 Most recently Lon L. Peters, 'Coal and bureaucrats: preliminary remarks on some recent research' (unpublished manuscript, August 1978).
34 Muthesius, op. cit., 228 f.; Parker, op. cit., 113 f.; ILO op. cit., 236 f.
35 Bergbau Museum (BM) B13/1833: Edward Loerbroks, 'Wie hat sich die Wirtschaftskrise auf die Verkaufs – und Verbrauchsbeteiligung der Zechen beim Rheinisch-Westfälischen Kohlensyndikat ausgewirkt?' (n.d.); Ministry of Economic Warfare (ESG), *The Minerals Industries*, 35 f.
36 Ervin Hexner, *The International Steel Cartel* (Chapel Hill, 1943); Ulrich Nocken, 'Interindustrial conflicts and alliances in the Weimar Republic: experiments in social corporatism' (diss., U.C. Berkeley, 1974).
37 Bundesarchiv Koblenz (BA) R13I/613: J.W. Reichert, 'Ein Rückblick auf das zehnjährige Bestehen der internationalen Stahlverbände', in *Stahl und Eisen*, Heft 48, 1936; US Federal Trade Commission, *Report on International Steel Cartels* (Washington, 1948).
38 ILO, op. cit., 11.
39 Centre de Recherches européenne, *Emile Mayrisch, Précurseur de l'Europe* (Lausanne, 1967), 47–51.
40 Parker, op. cit., 88; BV, *Statistiche Angaben* 54.
41 Wedekind, op. cit., 40; Enquête-Ausschuss, 169.
42 Berndt Weisbrod, *Schwerindustrie in der Weimarer Republik: Interessenpolitik zwischen Stabilisierung und Krise* (Wuppertal, 1978), 65; ILO, op. cit., 216, 218.
43 See Hans Mommsen, 'Der Ruhrbergbau im Spannungsfeld von Politik und Wirtschaft in der Zeit der Weimarer Republik', in *Blätter für deutsche landesgeschichte*, 108 Jg/1972, 160–75 and 'Die Bergarbeiterbewegung an der Ruhr 1919–1933', in Jürgen Reulecke (ed.), *Arbeiterbewegung am Rhein und Ruhr* (Wuppertal, 1974).
44 Weisbrod, op. cit., *passim*; Rudolf Tschirbs, 'Der Ruhrbergmann zwischen Privilegierung und Statusverlust: Lohnpolitik von der Inflation bis zur Rationalisierung (1919 bis 1927)' in Gerald Feldman (ed.), *Die deutsche Inflation. Eine Zwischenbilanz* (Berlin and New York, 1982), 309–46.
45 Klaus Tenfelde, 'Bergarbeiterkultur in Deutschland', *Geschichte und Gesellschaft*, 5.Jg./Heft 1, 1979, 19 f.; Hans Mommsen, 'Sozialpolitik im Ruhrbergbau', in D. Petzina *et al.* (eds) *Industrielles System und politische Entwicklung in der Weimarer*

Republik (Düsseldorf, 1974), 306 f; and id. (ed.), 'Die Bergarbeiter und der Ruhr, 1918–1933', *Arbeiterbewegung und Nationale Frage* (Göttingen, 1979), 318–45.

46 Tenfelde, op. cit.; Gebhardt, op. cit. 114.

47 Rudolf Schwenger, *Die betriebliche Sozialpolitik im Bergbau* (Schriften des Vereins für Sozialpolitik 186/1) (München and Leipzig, 1932), 179.

48 Rolf Seubert, *Berufserziehung und Nationalsozialismus. Das Berufspädagogische Erbe und seine Betreuer* (Weinheim, 1977), 70 f.; Theo Wolsing, *Untersuchungen zur Berufsausbildung im Dritten Reich* (Schriftenreihe zur Geschichte und Politischen Bildung, Bd. 24) (Kastellaun, 1977), 81 f.

49 Schwenger, op. cit., 68 f.

50 Arthur Schweitzer, *Big Business in the Third Reich* (Bloomington, 1964), 420 f.; Maxine Y. Sweezy, *The Structure of the Nazi Economy*, (Cambridge, Mass., 1941), 26 f.

51 US National Archives (USNA) RG 260/OMGUS German Industrial Complexes – Flick, Box 27-2/11, 'The Flick Complex'; 'Report on German Cartels and Combines,' 16.

52 BV, *Statistisches Heft*, 63, 66; Buck, op. cit., 196.

53 Heinrich A. Winkler, 'Unternehmerverbände zwischen Ständeideologie und Nationalsozialismus', *Vierteljahrshefte für Zeitgeschichte*, 17 Jg. 1969, 4 Heft/ Oktober, 369; Henry A. Turner, 'The *Ruhrlade*, secret cabinet of heavy industry in the Weimar Republic', *Central European History* III, 1970, 195–228.

2

RUHR COAL ENTERS THE THIRD REICH

In the Third Reich business was both powerful and privileged. It ran the economy for Hitler. The relationship between producers and the regime was not perfect; loyalties on both sides were always conditional. But it was mutually satisfactory, and it grew in strength over time. Hitler gave business the political conditions necessary for survival, growth and for domination of the European economy. Business generated full employment, produced enough 'guns and butter' during the period of lightning war *(Blitzkrieg)* to sustain standards of living while provisioning the armies in the field, and finally stepped up output sufficiently to support total war. The ultimate collapse of Hitler's work is no proof of the fragility of the arrangement between German business and the national socialist regime; on the contrary, the expansion of the Third Reich in the face of overwhelming odds and its refusal to accept defeat attests to their strength.

Upon closer examination, weaknesses in this relationship do appear, of which perhaps the most important was in the energy sector. When Hitler mobilized the economy, shortages of coal provided the main limitation on industrial outputs. During the war they were a bottleneck to production in both western Europe and the Reich. The origins of this situation were not political. Neither employers nor employees 'resisted'. Nor were there any shortages of coal in the ground which could not have been overcome with proper planning. Inadequate production was the result of management failure, stemming from the unsatisfactory adjustment of the collieries to the economic-political environment created after the seizure of power.

This difficulty is not easy to explain. The coal operators were initially well-disposed towards the Hitler government. Moreover, many of the policies enacted by his regime were the very ones advocated earlier by business, finance and officialdom. These also brought about the desired results, namely they staved off economic collapse and set the stage for a return to prosperity. If these facts were not appreciated, it was because the Ruhr coal industry viewed change itself with fear and suspicion. This profound conservatism was responsible for having made Ruhr coal's entrance into the Third Reich unpleasant and uncomfortable for both industry and regime. The *Gleichschaltung* of the mines was far from perfect.

The term *Gleichschaltung*, which has now lost most of its original meaning, refers to the process of administrative co-ordination which Hitler set in motion in an effort to seize command control over all spheres of German life. It involved the elimination of some institutions (supposed proponents of 'class warfare'), the creation of others, and the militarization of all remaining ones including those of business. But the changes in *economic* institutions resulting from this process of administrative reorganization were less the work of the regime than of finance and industry. This was true, first of all, in the field of foreign trade and payments. Although administered exchanges are often loosely associated with *Gleichschaltung*, Chancellor Heinrich Brüning had originally set them up as an emergency measure. The commercial section of the Foreign Office was responsible for managing the operations of the system. Likewise, producers themselves organized the new, stronger industrial associations Hitler ordered to be founded. With regard to labour, while the regime abolished the unions and created its own substitute, the new Deutsche Arbeitsfront (DAF) was modelled partly on the ideas of DINTA. In sum, *Gleichschaltung* reinforced rather than weakened the power of business. This was no less true for Ruhr coal than for other branches of industry.[1]

The reaction of the Bergassessoren to *Gleichschaltung* was peculiar. For example, they gave the government no credit for adopting foreign trade policies which prevented the collapse of the industry. Without them, the exportation of coal would have ceased. These policies were not adopted with the specific requirements of the mines in mind, but because of a more general problem. The collapse of international commerce which occurred in 1931 had a devastating impact on the Reich, which needed a trade surplus to offset payments to numerous foreign creditors. After the pound fell in September 1931, Chancellor Brüning restricted imports rather than risk the political consequences of devaluation. Thereafter bilateral trade and payments conventions, along with subsidies, regulated German foreign trade. Hitler's government merely systematized these emergency measures.[2]

As they evolved, the workings of the Reich's system of import and export regulation were extremely complicated. In 1932, the first bilateral trade and commercial commissions were set up with France and Switzerland. They provided for the conduct of trade on a quota basis, payment being made internally. Both agreements allowed the Reich a small but critical foreign exchange surplus *(Devisenspitze)* with which to service, at least partially, its foreign creditors. Germany arrived at similar arrangements with its other main trading partners. For nations outside of these, the Reichsbank issued so-called ASKI marks at discount to foreign importers. To complicate matters still further, a so-called 'scrips procedure' applied in both areas. The instrument used in it here was a RM-denominated certificate issued as partial repayment to foreign creditors, traded at a discount outside the Reich, and honoured at par by the Reichsbank when used to finance exports. In June 1934 Dr Hjalmar Schacht, Reichsbank director and Minister of Economics, introduced a measure of consistency into these practices: Germany, he announced, would import no more from any trading partner than it was able to export to it. At the same time, he gave a new impetus to exports by introducing the so-called ZAV-procedure *(Zusatzausführvergütung)*. It consisted of a self-assessed industry-wide tax levied to defray losses on foreign sales.[3]

The coal industry had little reason to complain about the new system of foreign trade regulation, at least until full employment was attained in 1937. Export tonnage (unadjusted) rose from 20,353,910 in 1932 to 39,023,273 in 1937 while the *Umlage* declined from RM 3.78/ton in 1934–5 to RM 2.12/ton in 1938–9. ZAV deserves a good deal of credit for this result. It covered two-thirds of the total export subsidy, and was paid almost entirely by other industries.[4]

As for the reorganization of industrial associations and cartels – the real core of business *Gleichschaltung* – the Ruhr operators protested vehemently that the process was unfair. They objected less to the relatively infrequent interventions of the regime than to its supposed lack of support in conflicts with other producer and dealer interests. The mining directors, acting in the narrow spirit of *Interessenpolitik* for which they blamed others, overlooked the great gains attained through *Gleichschaltung* not to mention the still greater ones they might have made if they had been more co-operative. They gave the regime little credit.

The *Gleichschaltung* of industrial associations and cartels was an important step towards 'organized capitalism'.[5] It greatly strengthened the networks of producer and employer associations, regional organizations and lobbies known collectively as *Verbandswesen*. 'Administrative co-ordination' had both public and private dimensions. First, it changed the legal status of trade associations. Membership for firms became compulsory in branch industry organizations with broad powers. These were the Wirtschaftsgruppen (business groups), and they became the basic building blocks of the national socialist system of industrial organization. In addition, all enterprises were required to join local chambers of commerce. At the national level, the Wirtschaftsgruppen reported to Reichsgruppe Industrie (RGI), which succeeded the Reichsverband der deutschen Industrie as the national industry association. The less important chambers of commerce reported to the Reichshandelskammer, which succeeded the Deutsche Industrie-und Handelstag.[6]

These mandated changes were of far less immediate significance than those occurring in the private sphere. The *Gleichschaltung* process also included a number of directives aimed at strengthening existing cartels and setting up new ones in industries not so organized. The impact of such edicts naturally varied considerably from industry to industry. It was not necessary to create cartels in chemicals or other industries dominated by a single producer. In industries such as cement, where intense competition had been the rule, the regime itself organized cartels. By the end of 1935 the entire industry of the Reich was declared to have been cartelized.

The *Gleichschaltung* of coal was supposed to take place in three successive stages: the formation of a new Wirtschaftsgruppe, followed by the organization of a national cartel for producing districts and including dealers, concluded by an unspecified substitute for the regulatory mechanisms of the 1919 coal statute *(Kohlenwirtschaftsgesetz)*.[7] Results at the first stage prefigured the others. In keeping with the general policy of recognizing existing cartels, the regime did not require individual collieries to join Wirtschaftsgruppe Bergbau but allowed RWKS to represent them as a whole. Thus the Ruhr utterly dominated the new official organization, which incidentally also included producers of other minerals. In practice it had little more than a shadow existence. Power within it gravitated to its regional affiliates. Bezirksgruppe Ruhr (der Wirtschaftsgruppe Bergbau) served as the chief intermediary between the district and Berlin. Its officers were appointed by RWKS.

RWKS also conducted the discussions intended to lead to a merger with the Aachen and Saar districts, the brown coal producers and the independent dealers. It did this under protest. A history of conflict stood between the Ruhr and each of these interests. *Gleichschaltung* ameliorated some of them: Aachen and the Saar joined RWKS, putting it for the first time in a position to represent the interests of all West German coal producers. For the rest, results were unsatisfactory. No agreement was reached with lignite, assuring that the product would continue to make inroads into steam coal markets. Nor was there a deal with the coal trade, and this left a legacy of resentment which could be exploited almost at will by ambitious spokesmen for the *Mittelstand* (lower middle class) element in the National Socialist Party. The existence of such unresolved issues made it impossible to arrive at an alternative to the coal statute of 1919.

The RWKS negotiations with the Aachen district were conducted with exceptional bitterness on both sides, a legacy of previous conflict. The Aachen district was in a very special situation: although it contained four mining companies, Eschweiler Bergwerk AG produced two-thirds of its output. This mine belonged to the Luxembourg steel firm, ARBED and, along with the Köln-based electro-manufacturing firm Felten Guilleaume, it was a component of this binational Luxembourg-German Konzern. The Depression-induced collapse in international trade, which hit ARBED particularly hard, left Eschweiler with far more coal than it could sell. It therefore cut prices drastically. As a result, Aachen output increased from 5.5 million to 7.5 million tons in the years between 1928 and 1932. While the Ruhr's 1933 production was a mere 68 per cent of 1913 levels, Aachen's was 231 per cent.[8]

The RWKS tried repeatedly after 1929 to dam up Aachen output by means of a coke convention. The most recent attempt, in August 1932, had left RWKS chairman Erich Fickler 'embittered' at the 'improper' behaviour of the Eschweiler delegates who demanded a 9.5 per cent quota of Reich coal production, and later raised this figure to 11.5 per cent even though its share had averaged only 7.5 per cent during the three previous years.[9] To get around the impasse, the business manager of the Reichskohlenverband, a supervisory agency set up by the 1919 statute, recommended that Aachen merge with RWKS rather than enter a convention with the Ruhr. Rejected at the time by the RWKS as 'government dictation' *(Zwangswirtschaft)* this idea was revived after the national socialist seizure of power.

In July 1933 negotiations were resumed at the behest of Berghauptmann Winnacker of the Mines Section of the Ministry of Economics, this time with a greater sense of urgency. ARBED was, after all, a foreign firm with an uncertain German future. Its director, the Luxembourger Aloyse Meyer, thus proposed that RWKS acquire Eschweiler, while offering a long-term supply contract to ARBED. When this deal broke down over financial considerations, Winnacker dictated the terms of settlement. Eschweiler was to join RWKS, its quota to be based on 1932 levels of output. Price-cutting was to be ended. Finally, Aachen was to sell through RWKS and bear a portion of the costs for the *Umlage*. These were the most important provisions of the Berlin Agreement concluded on 28 December 1933.[10]

This agreement was advantageous for both sides. Eschweiler secured treatment as a 'German firm', a privilege later extended to the Luxembourg components of ARBED. The higher RWKS price levels at which the mine was required to sell enabled it to operate at a profit. The reactions of the Ruhr to the Berlin Agreement do not do it justice. In a stream of complaints to the Ministry of Economics, RWKS protested against it on the petty grounds that the agreement did not order the dissolution of independent coal firms in the Aachen district. The syndicate failed to recognize that it both eliminated an unwelcome competitor and set the stage for a further westward extension of its influence.[11]

The extension of influence would occur with the shift of the Saar from the French to the German customs zone. For the Ruhr pits, this transfer presented two special problems. The French state had nationalized the Saar mines, which meant that it was politically and administratively simplest to turn them over to a new Reich *Regie* and the Saar's supposed significance as an outpost of Germandom foreshadowed a large party role in the further conduct of its affairs. For these reasons, it was impossible for the RWKS to negotiate with its Saar counterparts. Instead, the Ruhr had to accept sacrifices imposed upon it and seek compensation elsewhere. Even so, it proved better to have the Saar 'inside looking out' than 'outside looking in'.

Franco-German negotiations for the restoration of the Saar to the Reich began in early July 1934. Coal and steel were the main issues on the agenda. Through the ISC, arrangements first were made for the Ruhr to find German markets for the bulk of the Saar output previously sold in France in return for which it received a larger export quota. Arrangements in *coal* were handled by the Quai d'Orsay and an inter-ministerial trade committee headed by the Foreign Office (Handelspolitischer Ausschuss). The December 1934 Rome Agreement 'Regulating the Status of the Saar', which concluded their negotiations, contained two coal-related points. First, the Reich was to purchase the mines from the French state using 9 million francs removed from circulation during the switch over to the RM as circulating medium as well as 2 million tons of annual output as payment in kind. The new enterprise was named Saargruben AG. A second provision allowed the French to lease from the Reich the mines of the Warndt district immediately adjacent to the border.[12]

The Ministry of Economics laid down the terms of the Franco–German transfer settlement for Saar coal. These were tough. The Ruhr found itself saddled with the *Saaropfer* ('Saar-sacrifice') obliging it to market without benefit of *Umlage* the 4.4 million tons of annual output the Saar could no longer sell in France. It was also powerless to block the ambitious development programme undertaken by Saargruben AG for reasons of political prestige. Still, it forced the *Regie*'s director Waechter to drop a demand, supported by *Gauleiter* Bürckel, that the party be represented on the boards of all syndicate dealers in Saar-Pfalz. In February 1938 RWKS instigated the 'sacking' of *Oberberghauptmann* Schlattmann of the Saar as head of the Mining Section of the Ministry of Economics. Deprived of the support of his office the Saar had little influence in RWKS councils.[13]

Perhaps understandably RWKS used somewhat questionable methods with the lignite industry in an attempt to wrest from it compensation for the shoddy treatment received at the hands of the Saar. The basis for an understanding between Ruhr coal and Rhein lignite was clear. The two sold to the same large consumers of steam coal, above all the Rheinischwestfälisches Elektrizitätsgesellschaft (RWE), a giant holding company, supplied most of the Ruhr with power. RWE was closely interwoven with the two main Rhenish lignite producers. There were also strong financial ties between Rhein lignite/RWE interests and the heavy industry group in the Ruhr, represented by the VS managing director, Albert Vögler. For these reasons the lignite industrialist Paul Silverberg had proposed exploring merger possibilities several times in the late 1920s. After 1933 Ruhr coal continued to act too hesitantly, found itself outmanoeuvred by Minister of Economics Schacht, and ended with nothing.[14]

The brown coal industry was politically vulnerable. It was capital-intensive at a time of high unemployment; it had increased both output and profits during 1931 and 1932 when virtually every other branch of German industry sustained huge losses; and it was owned mainly by Jews. For those reasons it was the target of frequent press attacks. An article in the *Völkischer Beobachter* (12 May 1934) demanded the 'reorganization' *(Neuordnung)* of the Mitteldeutsche Braunkohlensyndikat on the grounds that it was in reality 'a cartel of company dealers using more or less tricky methods'. With regard to the Ostelbischen Braunkohlensyndikat the same commentator insisted upon 'restructuring the sales organization on the basis of the achievement principle *(Leistungsprinzip)* and reducing the interests of the "non-Aryan" Petschek interests'.[15]

Ruhr coal circles were quick to exploit such sentiment in order to achieve their long-term goal of restraining brown coal output. Bergassessor Georg Lübsen, the senior official in charge of Gutehoffnungshütte's mining operations, endorsed the regime's *Neuordnung* plans as a means to this end. Others shared his sentiments. Professor E. Storm argued in the *Kohle und Erz* issue of 1 October 1933 that recovery policy should favour coal over lignite on the grounds of job creation. Within days, the hard-pressed operators of the minor Saxon district had organized a leaflet campaign imploring the public to buy coal rather than lignite briquettes because, 'For every man who loses his job in lignite, sixteen lose theirs in coal.' Several months later, the general director of the Concordia Mine, Gustav Dechamps, proposed in the semi-official coal industry newspaper that markets be allocated between the two industries to reflect the greater socio-economic importance of the hard combustible. It employed 4.7 times as much human energy per unit of output.[16]

But before such ideas could be considered, Minister of Economics Schacht got to the 'milk-cow'. To their utter dismay, he 'invited' the directors of the main lignite firms to subscribe a portion of their capital to a new company founded to construct a hydrogenation plant for the manufacture of synthetic petroleum. It was to be named 'Braunkohle-Benzin AG', abbreviated to BRABAG. To finance construction, the industry was also required to provide some RM 250–300 million annually, which corresponded to a RM 2/ton levy on output. BRABAG was to produce 500,000 tons of petrol annually from 7.5 million tons of brown coal.[17]

This intervention effectively undercut the Ruhr effort to impede brown coal's development: thereafter lignite production had to be promoted for national-patriotic reasons. Still, negotiations for a soft coal–hard coal agreement dragged on through the year 1936. The 'stumbling block' was area demarcation versus tonnage quotas. The former approach to 'market sharing' would have permitted lignite to take over local markets completely, forcing minor Saxon and Silesian mines to the wall. The latter and equally disingenuous approach, while restricting brown coal output, would have enabled Ruhr mines to benefit from the sale of more profitable grades of coal.

Thus the two sides continued to talk past each other – a missed opportunity for the Ruhr. Brown coal sales by value increased from RM 304.6 million in 1932 to RM 396.8 million in 1936.[18]

Ruhr coal's failure to arrive at a new agreement with the independent coal dealers had serious political consequences. Some 58 per cent of Germany's 65,000–70,000 coal retailers were located in towns and villages of less than 10,000 inhabitants and some 36 per cent of those in cities had an annual turnover of less than RM 10,000. The dealers belonged to the *Mittelstand* element in the national socialist movement, comprised of those who fully expected the seizure of power to result in radical economic change, and, although this failed to be the case, they persisted in the erroneous belief that Hitler would eventually somehow 'set things right'. *Gleichschaltung* did, however, strengthen the power of dealers to act as an interest group. Reichsgruppe Handel (RGH) emerged as the trade counterpart of RGI and the dealers enjoyed their first effective representation at the national level, thanks to the reorganization of the Centralverband der Kohlenhandler Deutschlands.[19]

It is not surprising that the Ruhr operators rejected the numerous Centralverband reform proposals made between 1933 and 1937. They were both radical and politically unrealistic. The dealers wanted the Fuhrer to appoint a 'Leader of the Coal Economy', whose responsibilities would include both production and supply. His office would head two organizations of equal power, one composed of producers as well as importers (and which would therefore have diluted the influence of the Ruhr), and the other composed of dealers. The dealers also wanted to strip the syndicates of the right to sell at the retail level. Finally, they wanted to reorganize existing wholesale companies *(Syndikatsgesellschaften)* to allow a 50 per cent representation to dealers. These bodies would set wholesale and retail prices. The coal leader was to have the final word in cases of disagreement between production and trade. Such schemes lost ground steadily in the years after the seizure of power. Indeed in 1938 the dealers received a crushing blow when the new Labour Front (Deutsche Arbeitsfront–DAF) was assigned the coal retailing operations of the officially dissolved 'red' and 'black' co-operatives. This only increased the dealers' bitterness and extremism.[20]

In spite of its complaints, RWKS was not altogether dissatisfied with the outcome of the organizational *Gleichschaltung*. The 1935 report of Concordia mine noted that 'the desirable consequences of the union with Aachen, namely the reduction of competition . . . and in the *Umlage* assessment . . . have become increasingly apparent over the year'.[21] The Ruhr had also blocked the Economics Ministry's half-hearted attempts to impose central control over production by creating new regulatory machinery. At issue was the revision of the Kohlenwirtschaftsgesetz of 1919. This effort passed through a series of distinct phases – Bennhold (Autumn 1933), Schlattmann I (1934–6), Schacht–

Kirdorf (1936), Schlattmann II (1937–8) and Gabel (1939) – all but one of which (1936) began with an initiative on the part of a new chief of the Mines Section at the Ministry of Economics. Each such campaign began with quick-step urgency but soon bogged down in RWKS foot-dragging. Syndicate spokesmen consistently maintained, doubtless sometimes tongue-in-cheek, that since the new regime had eliminated the abuses of the 1919 coal law there was no need to revise the statute. In fact, it had long since ceased to have any meaning. When the business manager of the *Reichskohlenrat* retired in April 1939, its statutory apparatus was quietly dismantled. Thus ended both the effort to draft a new coal law and the attempt at the 'administrative co-ordination' of the Ruhr coal industry.[22]

The operators' reaction to the 'administrative co-ordination' of the mine labour force fits a depressingly familiar pattern. The regime froze wages, strengthened the business-run official machinery to regulate the supply and training of labour, abolished the unions, and set up new institutions patterned on the DINTA model. Although these moves put a stop to open 'class warfare' at the pits and lowered wage costs as a percentage of yield, the mine managers failed to rally to regime policy. This reaction was due partly to the obtrusive bumbling of the new pseudo-union, DAF, and the political ambitiousness of its leader, Robert Ley. The Bergassessoren none the less should have been grateful for the suppression of the Nationalsozialistische Betriebszellen Organisation (NSBO) from which an opposition led by Nazi workers might have emerged.[23]

Beyond this, the regime provided precisely those labour conditions which the operators felt essential to the resumption of profitable operation. The law of 20 January 1934 for the Regulation of National Work (Gesetz zur Ordnung der nationalen Arbeit), usually referred to as the AOG, served as a kind of Nazi labour charter. It presupposed the absence of all 'factory-foreign influences', labour unions above all. According to one commentator,

> Every rational man who reads it should be happy. For the AOG gives him a free hand in all matters relating to the factory. Even more, [it] requires employees *(Gefolgschaft)* to be expressly loyal and not to disturb the peace of the factory unless they want to appear before a social honour court. For it is their obligation to preserve the honour of the boss *(Betriebsführer)*.[24]

Employers monopolized the conduct of labour relations outside as well as inside the factory. A May 1934 ordinance established as appanages of the Reich the office of *Treuhänder der Arbeit*. These 'labour trustees' were responsible for setting wages, hearing grievances, making appointments to factory councils *(Vertrauensräte)* and supervising working conditions. With a single exception, the labour trustees were former legal experts of employer organizations. Business influence was also paramount at the Labour Ministry (Reichsarbeitsministerium), as well as the regional Labour Offices (Arbeitsämter). These offices, along with the chambers of commerce, were responsible for administering the industrial apprenticeship programmes launched in 1933.[25]

Despite this, employers were not able to monopolize the field of labour relations during the Third Reich, for they had to contend with that vast and amorphous entity, DAF. DAF is difficult to describe in a single breath. It owed its existence to two facts – the regime's need to provide some sort of employee representation and the empire-building mania of Reichsarbeitsführer Dr Robert Ley. It owed its peculiar structure to a third one, a statutory inability to perform the functions of a union. DAF specifically could not bargain for wages or benefits, administer pensions or social insurance funds, order improvements in working conditions, or run apprenticeship programmes. Its indirect influence over such matters was also very limited. DAF was primarily an agent of labour propaganda and its major theme was self-realization through work. This was the *Leistungsideologie* (gospel of achievement). It was glorified in factory psychodramas *(Werkspiele)*, inculcated in annual national skills competitions *(Reichsberufswettkämpfe)*, and commemorated in innumerable odes to *die Schönheit der Arbeit* – the Beauty of Work. DAF was also a bureaucratic octopus; it appropriated and created as many responsibilities as could be linked, if only tenuously, to the work process. Thus Ley absorbed Arnhold's organization. DINTA entered DAF as the Amt Für Betriebsführung und Berufserziehung (Office for Factory Leadership and Technical Training), where it operated autonomously. Ley also organized the vast *Kraft durch Freude* (Strength through Joy) programme for mass tourism and entertainment, authored the Volkswagen project, became chief houser and feeder of foreign slave labour and even tried through a surrogate to take over the coal mines. While DAF was never of great importance at the factory level, it was an unsettling influence. Ley, himself a brash drunkard, and his organization, were profoundly distrusted.[26]

Yet DAF was a valuable adjunct to business power. Its task in Hitler's scheme of things was to tame the working class and transform it from an oppositional force to a serviceable instrument of policy. This process began with the restoration of order within the factory during the *Gleichschaltung*, an undertaking of immense magnitude. Hitler took power in spite of the working class, as demonstrated by the results of the nation-wide factory council elections held in March and April of 1933. Although technically 'free' these elections took place against a background of official intimidation. Yet the Nazis won only a quarter of the votes despite the inclusion of white-collar employees *(Angestellten)* as well as workers.[27]

Preferring to divide and weaken the opposition rather than 'smash' it, Hitler at first promoted the NSBO as a 'radical' alternative to the Marxist parties. It was composed of worker members of the party and dominated by the influence of the Strasser brothers. To it flocked malcontents from a variety of political backgrounds, including many former 'reds'. Apart from hunger for power, a vague commitment to syndicalism held it together. NSBO planned to take over control of the economy through domination of factory councils.[28]

After failure in the March and April elections, Hitler tried other ways to build up the power of NSBO. In June NSBO-Kommissare took over the assets and staffs of the former Free Unions. Unfortunately they 'proved themselves incompetent, regarding the objects of their administration merely as booty, as suitable rewards for their long years of party service'.[29] NSBO soon came to stand for 'Noch Sitzen Bonzen Oben!' ('The Party Hacks Still Rule!') and Hitler found himself in need of an alternative labour organization.

At this point DAF entered the scene. On 10 May 1933 Ley had managed to gain a kind of legitimacy for DAF, then a shadow organization, by signing a 'co-operation agreement' with Reichsverband der deutschen Industrie. Soon Hitler ordered him to bring the factory councils *(Betriebsräte)* under control. This difficult process was essentially completed by the end of 1935.

Factory councils were of great importance in the production process. Although in the 1920s they exercised a number of statutory responsibilities, their real function was to serve as forums for employee grievances. At the same time, factory councils were valuable management tools, enabling employers to obtain insights into worker morale, serving as 'sounding boards' for new proposals, and providing 'transmission belts' for orders and directives. The factory council had a special role at the mines. Wages were based on piecework *(Gedinge)*. A miner normally belonged to a work gang for which a production quota would be set. Premiums were paid for exceeding it, penalties for shortfalls. The bounties or niggardliness of nature, however, often determined the size of the wage packet. Confidence in the equitability of rate-setting was therefore a constant concern. To maintain it, a working factory council was essential.[30]

It took DAF three years to transform the factory council *(Betriebsrat)* into the council of trust *(Vertrauensrat)* – that is, to Nazify the institution. This was by all odds more difficult in coal than in other branches of production because of traditional morale problems and high unemployment. In 1929 the mines had employed 375,711; in 1935 only 235,329. As late as August 1935 the industry failed to provide even twenty-one work days per month – not enough in the view of Gauleiter Fritz Terboven of Essen for a living wage. In summer 1935 he therefore launched a 'large-scale emergency relief action' *(groszzügige Hilfsaktion)* on behalf of the miners. Ley, in an ostentatious demonstration of public sympathy for the plight of the miners likened them on May Day 1935 to the 'heroes who sail the seas', promising to introduce a commemorative festival in their honour. The press organ of *Gau* Essen, *Der Ruhr Arbeiter*, contained as a regular feature a column supposedly addressed specifically to miners' needs, 'Hier Spricht der Bergmann!' ('The Miner Speaks!'). The political reports *(Stimmungsberichte)* of *Gau* Essen in the years 1934 and 1935 none the less depict miner morale as being singularly low.[31]

In the mines as elsewhere the transformation of the *Betriebsrat* into the *Vertrauensrat* required a change in election procedures, the elimination of NSBO influence, and a process of political 'confidence building'. Factory council elections were again held in spring 1934 and 1935, but this time no political opposition was tolerated. Employees were merely summoned to endorse a list of candidates compiled jointly by management and representatives of DAF. Only 50 per cent of those eligible voted.

But a bitter struggle had taken place. After the failure of the March/April 1933 elections, members of NSBO had simply taken over those places on the councils to which communists and social democrats were elected. Thereafter they demanded, usually in a harsh and threatening manner, exclusive rights to make appointments to the bodies.[32] Thanks to repeated interventions by DAF at the behest of management, 'oppositional elements' were gradually driven out of the plant. Thus at Concordia mine when in spring 1933 the leader of the NSBO faction made the customary demand to dominate the factory council, the production chief, Meuthen, solicited the intervention of party member Staubach of *Fachamt Bergbau* (Mines Section) of DAF. After a certain amount of dithering, Staubach denounced the Nazi miners as 'mutinous' and expelled them from a list of conservatives and obedient Nazis. None the less, the annual report of the mine blames NSBO agitation for causing a substantial decline in productivity during the first half of the year. In 1934 the situation was somewhat better. Bergassessor Knepper of GBAG reported on 6 June to the board of managers *(Vorstand)* that 'a perceptible fall in productivity can be traced back to the elections for the councils of trust which have created a distinct sense of unrest among employees', adding that, 'This observation is valid not only for our own company but for the mines as a whole.' But by 1935 there was a marked improvement, and Concordia could state in its annual report that while 'certain members of the *Vertrauensrat* have attempted to serve as mouthpieces for all kinds of extreme demands, such difficulties have been eliminated by general firmness. Co-operation with the Labour Front has on the whole been good.'[33]

Although the council of trust demonstrated its value mainly after the shift to rearmament in 1936, the confidence-building necessary for its effectiveness had been initiated in 1933 and continued to the end of 1935. By that date the New Order in factory and mine had secured, if not enthusiastic support, then at least grudging acquiescence from those who toiled. This was due in part to the effectiveness of the Gestapo. By the end of 1935 it had thoroughly combed out the pitiful remnants of would-be social democratic and communist resistance movements in the Ruhr.[34] Their importance in the district remained negligible until the final phase of the war. But attitudes in the pits also changed due to the improvement in business conditions and the decline of miner unemployment from 114,000 in January 1933 to 66,000 in October 1936. The council of trust also made a contribution to improving the climate of labour relations. In an otherwise highly critical book about national socialist labour policy, Hans-Georg Schumann describes the council as having 'contributed over the space of time to positive cooperation between labour and capital, . . . [which] had an encouraging measure of success in influencing social policy, . . . and brought real gains for the employees'.[35] Although its exact causes are not fully understood, virtually all accounts attest to a gradual improvement in miner morale. The 1936 annual report of Concordia is typical:

> The employees *(Gefolgschaft)* were absolutely quiescent. The few disputes that did occur in the factory were easily cleared up. During the first quarter of the year employees still suffered from numerous lay-offs, even though the nearby mines of Gutehoffnungshütte operated full-time. All the more remarkable, then, that even the more ambitious among them remained loyal to the mine in spite of the lay-offs, and that there was no general resentment.[36]

Throughout industry, employers were generally satisfied with the New Order in labour relations. The American trade commissioner in Berlin, George Conty, reported in January 1935 that

> Conversation with heads of American subsidiaries here all reveal that the present system [of *Vertrauensräte*] is infinitely preferable to that which was in force prior to the Hitler regime. As one [confidant] stated, 'Under the previous regulations, our employees . . . were working for the socialist movement; today they appreciate their jobs while endeavouring to maintain their respect as German Party members. I personally do not find this disadvantageous to my company's interests in Germany.'

Conty's informant added that in each case when the German shop steward had 'proved obnoxious' to the American manager, DAF settled the dispute without permanent damage to employer interests. Conty's confidant also reported that DAF officials had helped discipline party workers who abused time off given for the conduct of official business, noting that in one case it even supported the refusal of a US firm to grant paid leave to an *Obmann* (foreman) who had spent an unauthorized vacation training for the Brown Shirts.[37]

But admissions from the Bergassessoren that DAF was in any respect a useful instrument of labour policy were few and far between, and always grudging. In their view the mines had long provided a model for social policy and attempts from 'outside' to improve it were by definition meddlesome. The operators steadfastly opposed all DAF efforts to establish an organizational presence at the pits. The attitude of RWKS chairman, Bergassessor Kellermann was characteristic. Kellermann refused to join the DAF committee on the grounds of professional ethics *(Berufsmoral)*, to place a ban on the hiring of non-DAF members and to require the payment of dues or to allow their collection on company time. He denied the council of trust both office and telephone facilities as well as objecting to any participation in factory formations, May Day parades, social drinking with employees, factory competitions, skills battles, and factory psychodramas. He declined to have any dealings whatsoever with DAF in his capacity as chairman of RWKS, delegating responsibility for such matters to an operator with good party connections, Ernst Tengelmann of Hibernia mine. The latter deserves the credit for having managed to keep DAF generally at arm's length. In spite of its cancerous growth into new fields, DAF never developed into an effective representative of employees interests, at the mines or elsewhere.[38]

A system of 'industrial self-administration' emerged from *Gleichschaltung*. While this institutional arrangement committed producers to following Hitler, it also strengthened their hold over production and increased their power to regulate the economy. Hitler did not have 'industrial self-administration' in mind when he launched the *Gleichschaltung* process. It none the less worked better than any type of political economy that he or his movement might have devised. It combined power and know-how with responsibility, limited the growth of stifling bureaucracies and gave producers a huge stake in the political system. The success of 'industrial self-administration' would depend on business initiative – the ability of managements to seize profit-making opportunities created by Hitler's policies. Ruhr coal's behaviour during *Gleichschaltung* was not promising. The industry overlooked some opportunities, missed others because of a reluctance to compromise and refused to recognize benefits forced upon it by the regime. The persistent conflict between the mines and other economic interests, the Berlin ministries and party operatives created further complications. It not only made the Ruhr new enemies but prevented the effective mobilization of the Reich's energy resources, without which Hitler's strategy was bound to fail.

Notes

1 K.D. Bracher, W. Sauer and G. Schulz, *Die nationalsozialistische Machtergreifung* (Zweite Auflage, Köln/Opladen, 1962), 186 f.; Henry Laufenberger and Pierre Pflimlin, *La nouvelle structure économique du Reich. Groupes, cartels et politique des Prix* (Paris, 1938), 126; Ingeborg Esenwein-Rothe, *Die Wirtschaftsverbände von 1933 bis 1945* (Berlin, 1965), 141 f.; Arthur Schweitzer, *Big Business in the Third Reich* (Bloomington, 1964), 420 f.; Robert A. Brady, *The Spirit and Structure of German Fascism* (London, 1937), 288; Wolfram Fischer, *Die Wirtschaftspolitik Deutschlands 1918–1945* (Lüneburg, n.d.), 55; Dietmar Petzina, 'Germany and the Great Depression', *Journal of Contemporary History*, 4 (4), October 1969, 65.

2 Allen T. Bonnell, *German Control over International Economic Relations* (Urbana, 1940); Claude W. Guillebaud, *The Economic Recovery of Germany. From 1933 to the Incorporation of Austria in March 1938* (London, 1939), 62 f.
3 US National Archives (USNA) RG151/1631 (US Commercial Attaché, Berlin) 'Annual economic review, Berlin, 1937'; RG151/1481 'Weekly reports, financial', 1934–5.
4 Gutehoffnungshütte (GHH) 400101320/10 'Entwicklung der Grundumlage nach Beitritt der Aachener Zechen'; Bergbau Verein (BV), *Statistisches Heft. Produktions- und wirtschaftsstatistische Angaben aus der Montanindustrie* (Essen, 1934), 63 f.; 400101307/14 'Entwicklung der von dem verschiedenen Wirtschaftsgruppen aufgebrachten . . . Beiträge' (n.d.); 400101320/137 '. . . Besprechung in RWM, 22 September 1937. (Aktenwermerk Janus)'.
5 Esenwein-Rothe, op. cit., 141.
6 Otto Bühring, *Wesen und Aufgaben der industriellen Wirtschaftsgruppen als fachliche Spitzengliederung der Industrie im Rahmen der Organisation der gewerblichen Wirtschaft* (Berlin, 1940); J. Herle, 'Die Unternehmerverbände im neuen Deutschland', *Der deutsche Volkswirt*, 1 September 1933, 1377.
7 NI 1154 'Entwicklung der Organisation im Bergbau', by W. Hoelling; Unverferth, op. cit., 23 f.
8 GHH 400101320/8 'Mitgliederversammlung', 11 December 1933; 400101320/12 'Sitzung des Vorsitzenden den Syndikatsausschüsse', 10 April 1933; 400101320/12 'Besprechung des Vorsitzenden . . .', 10 August 1932; 'Sitzung der Vorsitzenden', 8 July 1932; 400101320/10 'Förderung des Ruhrreviers/Förderung des Aachenerreviers'.
9 GHH 400101320/12 'Besprechung der Vorsitzenden . . .', 10 August 1932.
10 GHH 400101320/12 'Sitzungen', 8 July 1933, 11 October 1933, 11 December 1933, 17 May 1934; Westfälisches Wirtschaftsarchiv, Dortmund (WWA), F26/464 'Richtlinien über die Neuordnung der Aachener Handel'.
11 GHH 400101320/12 Lübsen to Reusch, 21 March 1934; 400101320/8 'Mitgliederversammlung', 31 October 1933.
12 *Documents on German Foreign Policy, 1918–1945* (Series D, 1933–45) III, London, 1949, (DGFP) doc. 372, 'Director of Department II to the embassies of Great Britain, France *et al.*', 4 December 1934; No. 412, Circular of the Ministers of Economics, II 100/35, 5 January 1935; USNA, RG 151/1503 'Monthly economic review, January 1935'.
13 GHH 400101320/115 'Besprechung von Syndikatsvertretern mit dem RWM', 12 July 1934; Bergbau Museum (BM), B13/1832 'Verhandlungen des Geschäftausschusses', 17 April 1936.
14 USNA OMGUS (Legal Division), RG 260 German Industrial Complexes, Box 27–3/11 'The RWE Complex'.
15 Bundesarchiv R13/145 'Fragen der Braunkohlenwirtschaft', *Völkischer Beobachter*, 12 May 1934.
16 GHH 400101320/115 Lübsen to Reusch, 5 August 1933; 400101320/12 'Aktenvermerk, 12.6.34'; BA R13/145 'Arbeitsbeschaffung durch Steinkohle, Braunkohle und Wasserkraft'. *Deutsche Bergwerks-Zeitung*, 24 April 1934.
17 Wolfgang Birkenfeld, *Der synthetische Treibstoff 1933–1945. Ein Beitrag zur nationalsozialistischen Wirtschafts- und Rüstungspolitik* (Göttingen, 1964), 37 f.
18 GHH 400101320/15 Rheinisches Braunkohlen-Syndikat to Reichskohlenverband, 22 April 1936; WWA, F26/503 Bierhaus to Beckemeyer, 20 July 1936; 400101320/115 Niederschliesisches Steinkohlen-Syndikat to Reichskohlenverband, 22 April

1936; GHH 400101320/115 Ostelbisches Braunkohlensyndikat 1928 to Reichskohlenverband, 23 April 1936; BA R7/anh.59 'Die zukünftige deutsche Kohlenwirtschaft' by K.H. Otto, 31 August 1945.

19 BA R7/2017 'Erweiterte Beiratssitzung der RGH', 7 April 1949; 'Beiratssitzung der Wirtschaftsgruppe Vermittlergewerbe', 20 December 1940.

20 GHH 400101320/15 'Wünsche zum neuen Kohlenwirtschafts-Gesetz', *Deutsche Bergwerkszeitung*, 1 September 1936; 400101320/15 'Gespräch mit Herrn Gewerbeassessor Dr Loth', 26 August 1937; 400101320/115 'Beitrag des Kohlenhandels zur beabsichtigten Neuordnung der deutschen Kohlenwirtschaft' (n.d.); 400101320/115 'Fachgruppe Handelsvertreter und Handelsmakler in der Wirtschaftsgruppe Vermittlergewerbe. Rundschreiben 1937 Nr. 1/5', 20 January 1937.

21 Westfälisches Wirtschaftsarchiv (WWA) F26/24–1 'Jahresbericht der Concordia Bergbau AG für das Geschaftsjahr 1935'.

22 GHH 400101320/115 'Im Brennpunkt', *Rheinisch-Westfälische Zeitung*, 30 September 1936; 400101320/115 'Reformgedanken zum Kohlenwirtschaftsgesetz, *Frankfurter Zeitung*, 13 May 1937; 400101320/115 'Besprechung mit Schlattmann, 26 August 1936; 400101320/115 'Sitzung des engeren Ausschüsses zur Neufassung des Kohlenwirtschaftsgesetzes', 1 July 1936; NI–4364 'Besprechung in RWM', 25 November 1933; GHH 400101320/115 Lübsen to Reusch, 11 August 1933; WWA Dechamps to Board of Managers, 5 October 1936; BM 55/12400 Nr. 12 (GBAG) 'Absatz und Marktlage des Geschäftsjahres 1934/5'.

23 John Gillingham, 'Ruhr coal miners and Hitler's war', *Journal of Social History*, 15 (4), 1982, 640.

24 Cited in Heinz Hartmann, *Der deutsche Unternehmer: Autorität und Organisationen* (Frankfurt, 1968), 98.

25 Hans-Gerd Schumann, *Nationalsozialismus und Arbeiterbewegung*. (Hannover/Frankfurt, 1958), 82.

26 Karl Teppe, 'Zur Sozialpolitik des Dritten Reiches am Beispiel der Sozialversicherung', *Archiv für Sozialgeschichte* 17, 1977; id, 'Gesetzentwurf zur Ausschaltung der Deutschen Arbeitsfront im Jahre 1938', *Archiv für Sozialgeschichte*, 17, 1977, 297 f.

27 WWA F26/350 'Aktennotiz', 3 April 1933.

28 WWA F26/390 'Sitzungen des Vertrauensrates', 7 May 1934, 2 August 1935, 14 December 1935, 30 December 1935.

29 Schumann, op. cit., 65 f., 118.

30 Fritz Heina, 'Buchführung und Bilanz im Ruhrbergbau', in Ernst Herbig and Ernst Jungst (eds) *Bergwirtschaftliches Handbuch* (Berlin, 1931), 625.

31 'Leistungsbericht der Deutschen Arbeitsfront, März 1935', *Der Ruhr-Arbeiter*, Jg. 4, Nr. 11; 'Die Sorge um den Kumpel', *Die deutsche Volkswirtschaft*, Nr. 12, April 1934; 'Der Tag des Bergarbeiters', *Der Ruhr-Arbeiter*, Jg. 4, Nr. 22; 'Der Führer hilft dem Bergmann!', *Der Ruhr-Arbeiter*, Jg. 4, Nr. 23.

32 Schumann, op. cit., 128.

33 BM 55/12400 Nr. 12 (GBAG) 'Sitzung des Vorstands', 6 June 1934; WWA F26/24 'Jahresberichte der Concordia Bergbau, 1933, 1934'; F26/24–1 'Jahresbericht der Concordia Bergbau 1935'; F26/390 'Sitzungen des Vertrauensrats', 7 May 1934, 2 August 1935, 14 December 1935, 30 December 1935.

34 Günter Plum, 'Die Arbeiterbewegung während der nationalsozialistischer Herrschaft', in Jürgen Reulecke (ed.) *Arbeiterbewegung an Rhein und Ruhr* (Wuppertal, 1974), 355–383.

35 Schumann, op. cit., 130; *Statistisches Heft* op. cit., 112.

36 WWA 26/24–1 'Jahresbericht der Concordia Bergbau 1936'.

37 USNA RG151/1503 Special report No. 39, 'American branch factories in Germany', 7 January 1935.

38 GHH 400101330/1 Letter from Padberg, Amtsleiter des Fachamites Bergbau, DAF', 30 June 1937; 4001026/98 'Kellermann durch Hilbert, Betr. DAF', 25 March 1938; 4001012003/15 Krecke to Kellermann, 27 January 1934; 4001012003/15 'Entwurf für eine Neufassung der Betriebsordnung.

3

RUHR COAL AND THE COMING OF THE WAR

It is difficult to exaggerate the importance of coal to Germany in the two world wars. In peacetime, this combustible normally supplied directly or indirectly no less than nine-tenths of the Reich's total fuel consumption requirements. In war the nation's dependence on coal was even greater. This was a lesson that should have been learnt in August 1914 when Ruhr daily output fell to 51 per cent of January–June levels because of disruptions caused by the call to the colours. From that point on, the battle for coal production was hard and futile. The winters of 1914 and 1915 brought severe supply bottlenecks which imperilled manufacturing. Thanks to the forced employment of nearly 100,000 foreigners and PoWs output rose for a brief period in 1916 to near peacetime levels, but in spite of the declaration of the Hindenburg programme and the release from military service of 15,000 miners, it soon fell again because of raw materials shortages, equipment breakdowns and human fatigue. The severe winter of 1916–17 froze canals and caused worse railway hold-ups than before. The release of another 38,000 miners in early 1917, together with the virtual abandonment of maintenance work *(Aus- und Verrichtungsarbeiten)*, made it possible to stave off a production collapse for the rest of the year, but this was clearly borrowed time. By mid-1918 the end had come for the mines as well as for the Reich. The failure to maintain coal output was second only to the economic blockade in causing the economic strangulation that brought imperial Germany to its knees.[1]

Hitler's strategy implied an even greater role for coal than in the First World War. The Führer never tired of reminding his associates of the Kaiser's stupidity for entering the fray dependent on overseas sources of food and raw material or of declaiming to audiences the need for a policy of autarchy as a preparation for war. Hitler and his strategists none the less failed to take the essential steps towards energy planning during the mobilization process; once again, Germany would go into battle unprepared.

Germany's economic preparations for war began with the announcement on 10 September 1936 of the Four Year Plan. In the thirty-six months of full employment which followed, and during the war itself, the Reich's appetite for coal would increase by millions of tons per year, reaching consumption levels far above any known previously. However, planning for this contingency was completely inadequate. Not until 1939 did the technocrats of the Four Year Plan begin to forecast future coal consumption requirements, but by then it was too late to increase capacity. Coal shortages were the rule from 1937 to 1945.

The effort to step up output concentrated on labour. It involved increasing mine employment but also lengthening the work day and intensifying the production process. There was almost no chance that such a policy could have worked. Recruitment was difficult not only because of the unpopularity of mining as a career but because better job opportunities were readily available. There was also little incentive to work harder: wage increases were blocked and consumer goods rationed. Yet despite this outputs were maintained, a remarkable result. Even before the war both plant and labour had begun to wear out and so inevitably productivity suffered.

It is incorrect to interpret the fall in average daily miner output as an indication of worker 'resistance'. Productivity normally declines after prolonged operation at full capacity. Beyond this, there is no documentary evidence to suggest that miner opposition reduced coal outputs.[2] The belief that this happened can be attributed to a misunderstanding of the mood at the mines. It is true that morale was poor but this had little to do with politics. Experienced face workers considered it both dangerous and degrading to work with the untrained labour hired after 1937; above all, they were tired of being overworked – of more hours spent underground each week, less leisure, falling standards of living, fatigue and illness. It is hardly surprising that they were fed up.

The Ruhr coal industry was at least partly responsible for the inadequacies of coal policy; it kept its distance from the Four Year Plan, which was responsible for formulating it. This characteristic national socialist economic institution was apparently intended by Hitler to serve as an economic directorate. Its two chief responsibilities were to oversee the armaments build-up and sponsor the creation of synthetics industries that would pave the way to autarchy. Through a process of functional and personal interpenetration of byzantine intricacy, the Four Year Plan exercised a kind of hegemony over other Reich ministries and agencies. It also housed the new offices set up to steer production and investment, allocate raw materials, distribute foreign exchange, direct labour placement and enforce rationing. Finally, the plan launched the vast new industrial investment programmes which stimulated the economic growth of the immediate pre-war years.[3]

Yet neither Hitler nor Hermann Göring, the Plenipotentiary-in-charge, actually ran the Four Year Plan. This job was done by businessmen acting on the basis of powers delegated to them by the regime. Most of these businessmen worked for a single enterprise, IG Farben. Karl Krauch is largely responsible for the fact that the Four Year Plan became, in effect, the IG Farben plan. The protégé of the 'politically progressive' Carl Bosch who designed the Leuna works, Krauch had gained recognition early in the 1930s as Germany's leading expert in the field of hydrogenation. Through the 'petroleum agreement' *(Benzin-Vertrag)* of December 1933 Krauch got the regime to pay subsidies for up to 300,000–350,000 annual tons of synthetic aviation fuel. In the period from 1934 to mid-1936 Krauch acquired virtual domination over the synthetic fuels field. In mid-1939 he added to his mandate planning responsibilities in the fields of artificial rubber, aluminium, powder and chemical warfare. To the extent that any single individual directed the Reich's mobilization for war, Krauch did.[4]

By dint of its size and strategic importance the Ruhr coal industry should have exercised an influence in the Four Year Plan equal to IG Farben's, but this was never the case. The collieries refused to abandon the business strategies developed in the late 1920s in favour of the new opportunities dangled before their eyes by the regime. Ruhr coal did not take over its originally assigned role in the synthetic fuels programme. Nor would the industry consider the expansion of mine operations, both from fear of creating still more excess capacity and incurring still more debt. It was also reluctant to increase labour inputs for cost reasons. This conservative outlook prevented the Ruhr coal industry from occupying a prominent position within the Four Year Plan. There was no coal version of Krauch. An obscure staff officer, Major Czimatis, headed the Energy Section of the plan's Office of German Raw Materials, which was nominally responsible for coal matters. His bureau served as a transmission belt for conveying demands made on the industry. As a lobby for the interests of Ruhr coal, its influence was negligible. The Four Year Plan also had to share authority in coal policy with competing agencies.

The Ruhr mines never received the priority necessary to improve the coal supply. Its representatives therefore complained chronically of inadequacies in allocations of labour, raw materials, transport and capital. Such disputes over production and supply policy eventually broadened into a struggle that threatened the existence of private enterprise in the Third Reich. The Ruhr mines not only became the scapegoat for the fuel shortages, but would be the first branch of German production to be placed under the administration of a party-appointed commissar.

The lack of Ruhr coal influence in the Four Year Plan was due to its having failed to take an active hand in the development of the synthetic fuels programme. This, the plan's most important project, was actually launched by military staff planners in the 1920s. They agreed with Hitler's diagnosis of defeat in the First World War, shared his belief in the need to increase and develop domestic energy outputs, and would support his decision to conclude the 'Benzin-Vertrag'. They also stood behind Schacht's decision to organize BRABAG. The next step was for Hitler to set up the Dienststelle Sonderaufgabe deutsche Roh- und Werkstoff (Office for Special Materials Tasks) under the party-connected businessman, Wilhelm Keppler. This task force, which Krauch belonged to, drafted the first fuels programme of the Four Year Plan in October 1936. It would be the last fuels programme to involve substantial Ruhr coal participation.[5]

This was not inevitable. Ruhr coal might have participated more actively either by promoting its own Fischer–Tropsch process, or by taking over the rights to the IG hydrogenation method. The latter would have been more promising. After years of efforts the chemical Konzern got Ruhr industry to agree in 1933 to set up a study commission for the hydrogenation of hard coal. The armed forces promoted this effort because they needed the high-octane compound yielded from coal for aviation fuel. Still, only one colliery would consider building a Bergius facility, the state-owned Hibernia mine, which disposed of excess low-grade coal. Construction of the Scholven works began there in July 1935. Aided by a generous subsidy on the Leuna model, plant operations commenced in October 1936.[6]

In the same month the Four Year Plan's first synthetic fuels programme was announced. It called for the production of 5.3 million tons of various grades of petroleum within twenty-four months. Part of this amount was to be produced at the two operating lignite-based hydrogenation installations of Leuna and BRABAG, another 180,000 tons from Scholven. The rest was to be produced at new installations, one-half operating with the Bergius process, one-half with Fischer–Tropsch. The Fischer–Tropsch plants were to be built in the Ruhr. In a conference of 6–7 October 1936 Schacht declared that he would not bully the coal-mines as he had the lignite industry but rather would 'work through existing firms in order to secure their co-operation in the execution of the programme'.[7] The district's relative importance in the fuel programme declined abruptly thereafter. Only one additional hydrogenation plant was built in the Ruhr, by GBAG. It yielded 150,000 annual tons and, along with Scholven, supplied some 12 per cent of the Reich's total artificial fuel output. The Fischer–Tropsch process, whose patents the mines controlled, was never really tested. It supplied less than one-tenth of the Reich's total synthetic fuel output. These results are difficult to understand.

While Fischer–Tropsch did not yield aviation fuel but rather a wide range of products from heating oil to lubricants, and the plants proved less reliable than expected, there was no flaw in the process that could not have been overcome at relatively low cost, no shortage of the low-grade coal it consumed, and certainly a paucity of its diverse products.[8] With greater political pressure on the part of the industry more Fischer–Tropsch installations could have been built. The Ruhr might then have gained a greater degree of influence over the critical Four Year Plan decisions with regard to coal policy.

But responsibilities over solid fuel remained entangled in competing jurisdictions, for

> working in . . . coal planning and concerned with the same questions were the Keppler Bureau, the Mining Section of the Ministry of Economics, the Geological Terrain Agencies, the supervisory offices for Iron and Steel as well as those for non-precious metals, numerous Wirtschaftsgruppen with their sub-groups, DAF with its Reich factory Community Mining Groups, the research centres of German science, the military planning agencies and the Office for Raw- and Production Material, not to mention numerous local authorities which [felt] themselves called upon now and then to intervene such as the Four Year Plan, the Gauleiter, the Office for Technology of the National Socialist Party, and local scientific agencies.[9]

The distinguished Dr Pott, inventor of an improved version of the Fischer–Tropsch process, complained that the coal industry was 'not in any way informed as to the scope of the Four Year Plan . . . or as to what particular demands will be made upon us'.[10] This situation did not improve. As noted in the 10 August 1937 minutes of the informal directorate of RWKS,

> As feared, the numerous individual estimates of increased requirements for Four Year Plan projects do not coincide with the figures provided by the Plenipotentiary of the Four Year Plan. The mistakes caused by the discrepancies are so huge as to discourage any optimism.[11]

The industry did not fill the breach in planning. From first to last, fear of creating surplus capacities dominated its thinking. The industry's representatives in the Bezirksgruppe proved highly inventive in finding reasons for not expanding underground operations. They were normally variations on two themes: either it was denied that shortages were permanent or asserted that the industry lacked the financial strength to invest on the necessary scale. Industry spokesmen maintained until late 1936 that output increases could be attained by hiring the 20,000 miners still unemployed, argued in 1937 that the armaments boom would be followed by sharp setbacks, insisted in 1938 that increases in demand had levelled off, and offered assurances in early 1939 (following the sharp decline in world trade in the second half of 1938) that savings for the domestic economy had been gained from a fall in exports. The operators also complained of the high tonnage costs of further tunnelling, pleading that export subsidies and new above-ground investment had perilously weakened balance sheets. They did not, however, seek alternative financing from the Reich.[12]

The planning exercises of 1935 take on critical significance in retrospect. Since seven years were normally required to put a new mineshaft into production, a decision to expand underground operations would have had to be taken before 1937 to have affected the outcome of the war. In November 1935, Wirtschaftsgruppe Bergbau circulated the results of an industry-wide survey, which, while admitting the impossibility of predicting when or how war would break out, concluded that enough Ruhr coal could be dug without major new investment in underground operations to provide for any realistic contingency. Maximum potential output was set at 142.8 million annual tons, some 19 million tons above the record year of 1929. This wildly optimistic estimate presupposed the availability of necessary labour, a 300-day work-year with overtime, and optimum conditions of supply. The survey added that any further requirements could be met by reducing exports. The industry operated on these assumptions until 1939.[13]

But reliance on *Arbeitseinsatzpolitik* (manpower policy) was badly misplaced. The industry was unwilling either to break with traditional labour management methods or improve compensation out of a fear of raising production costs. This was a critical point given full employment after 1936. The first shortages of skilled labour appeared in early 1937. By June 1939 over 23,000 Ruhr mine jobs remained unfilled. Moreover, the opportunities for advancement opened by such vast construction projects as the Reichswerke Hermann Göring in Salzgitter, the synthetics plants of IG Farben, and the Autobahn and Westwall of Dr Todt acted like a magnet on skilled Ruhr metal and electro-workers and supervisory personnel. It was well-known that work in the pits was hard, dirty and hazardous, also that advancement was slow and discipline severe. The general lack of co-operation between industry and regime complicated the effort to solve the personnel problem.[14]

One modest success involved increasing slightly the number of miners employed underground from 290,000 to 310,000 through intense recruitment campaigns. This was accomplished by sacrificing 'quality'. Reports on the calibre of mine recruits are appalling. To cite a characteristic example, one consultant noted that

> most youths directed to the mines [are sent] in the face of express opposition from parents, as well as over their own protests. They are predominantly young persons whose inferior capabilities make them otherwise unemployable. Subsequent entries of young people from other professions have become unusually rare and are normally due to failure.[15]

The increase in the total number of miners employed underground masked a loss of those from the most productive age groups. Younger categories were underrepresented, older ones overrepresented. As of June 1939, those 14–21 years of age were but 53 per cent of the theoretical normal size, those 22–25, 29 per cent and those 26–30, 27 per cent. This stands in sharp contrast to the senior age categories; 31–5, 141 per cent, 36–40, 158 per cent, 41–5, 114 per cent.

Finally, miner health deteriorated as the number of average days and hours worked increased. This was obvious as early as summer 1938. According to one Dr Steckelberg, whose medical opinion is echoed in a plethora of reports,

> The excessive demands being made upon the physical strength of the miners cannot continue for any length of time without running the danger that not only the health of the individual but the productive process itself will soon be disturbed.[16]

The mine operators shared this concern. At a meeting of October 1938 summoned to deal with the problem of miner health,

> Herr Kocker [of Harpen mine] mentioned that many hard-working people had come to him to plead that they were too exhausted to work any more. He could not believe that these people were 'faking it' . . . and expected that the heavy strains being made on miners would further exhaust them.[17]

It is anything but surprising that productivity, as measured by daily man-shift output per underground worker, declined slightly from 2054 kg in 1937 to 1970 kg in 1938 even though it did rise slightly to 2058 in the second half of 1939.[18]

The regime's most serious effort to step up miner output – by lengthening the work day forty-five minutes and providing a bonus – proved to be a failure. This was the so-called Göring directive (Verordnung des Beauftragten für den Vierjahresplan zur Erhöhung der Förderleistung und des Leistungslohnes im Bergbau), which was published in spite of vehement objections from management that it would be a costly failure. The factory directors insisted that it would provide windfalls for the few and demoralize the rest, adding that the planned 15–16 per cent nominal earning increases were of doubtful value because of price controls. Miners complained acidly that although they could buy refrigerators it was impossible to obtain food to put in them. Further, the longer working week ordered in the Göring directive reduced the time they normally spent raising vegetables and domestic animals for personal consumption. The catastrophic fall in miner pig-raising evident by mid-1939 more than offset the nominal gains in purchasing power resulting from the Göring directive.[19]

It did, however, prove possible for the regime to halt the deterioration of miner morale. The operators fully expected to encounter difficulties as a consequence of the transition to full employment. Concordia Mine's annual report for 1937 noted that over the year

> the employee structure has been fundamentally altered. Instead of dealing with people who have been schooled and trained to work together, we must make do with [those] who have been unemployed for six or seven years and have grown unaccustomed to labour. Many of them are embittered and have no comprehension whatsoever of the idea, incorporated into the Labour Regulation Law, of co-operation between leadership and followership. It is evident that only one thing can help, a painful process of education. But the fast pace of work leaves no time for it![20]

So-called *Bummelei* (malingering) was the main symptom of the morale problem. The term was a catch-phrase for a wide range of misbehaviour: laziness on the job, unexcused absence from work and feigned illness. Outbreaks of *Bummelei* normally followed pay-days or on Mondays. Here, then, was a contagious malady which must not be allowed to spread! Unfortunately, it was not easy to quarantine. 'Labour idealism', such as DAF had hoped to instill, was conspicuously absent at the mines. Disciplinary sanctions were of only limited usefulness so long as severe shortages of labour prevailed, and initially they were quite mild: Concordia Mine docked one half-day's pay for an initial offence; a repeated *Bummelant* (shirker) would forfeit an entire day's pay; a three-time offender would be fired.[21] These penalties were completely ineffective, because 'Those recently hired were often glad to get the sack'.[22] Soon, additional measures were taken, but they also accomplished little. In July 1937 Director Dechamps of Concordia convinced the Treuhänder der Arbeit to deduct unexcused absences from vacation leave, but this would soon cease to exist in all but name. Another approach, withholding heavy labour rations *(Schwerstarbeiterzulage)* from 'malingerers', was self-defeating since it reduced physical strength still further. Beginning in early 1939 resort was made to exemplary punishment. In early 1939 a Gestapo agent named Lewinski began a secret investigation of malingering at Concordia. In December several victims were singled out and sent to Dachau.[23] Similar actions took place at other mines as well.[24]

There was agreement among all authorities concerned with eliminating *Bummelei* that results could not be achieved by external interventions but would hinge on the ability of the 'basic labour force' *(Stammbelegschaft)* to discipline new arrivals. Thanks to the effectiveness of the councils of trust, whose members time and again denounced those who did not work productively, the malady did not spread. As a result, pre-war rates of both sickness and absence, excused and unexcused, did not differ significantly from those of 1929, the last previous year of full employment. On the average day in 1929 5.91 per cent of the work force reported sick and another 1.69 per cent were absent. The corresponding figures for 1938 were 5.58 per cent and 1.69 per cent.[25]

But the effort to raise production succeeded only marginally because the fall in man-shift productivity made incremental output gains costly (see Table 4). To some extent this was inevitable. According to the coal expert Rudolf Regul,

> productivity is always lowest when demand is greatest, and reverse. This contrariness is explained by the fact that with the rise in production necessary preparatory work must be postponed to meet immediate demand. To meet a subsequent demand in increase therefore becomes increasingly difficult.[26]

Table 4 Daily man–shift productivity and annual output in the Ruhr, 1932–1944

	Total work force	*Underground*	*Output (tons)*
1932	1628	2093	114,567,000
1936	1711	2199	107,478,000
1937	1627	2054	127,752,000
1938	1547	1970	127,284,000
1939	1611	2064	130,184,000
1940	1568	2013	129,188,000
1941	1527	1959	129,971,000
1942	1529	1848	128,490,000
1943*	1258	1656	127,515,000
1944*	1208	1617	110,851,000

Source: Länderrat des Amerikanischen Besatzungsgebiets (ed.) *Statistisches Handbuch von Deutschland 1928–1944* (München, 1948), 279.

Note: * First six months.

But the decline in productivity was also due to the depletion of labour reserves, fatigue, the working of less productive seams and the bad supply situation.

The Bergassessoren never ceased to complain about the inadequacy of iron and steel provisions. This situation stems directly from the lack of Ruhr coal influence at the Four Year Plan office which regulated production by allocating steel on a priority basis. New construction, Four Year Plan projects, and military requirements naturally got priority. As for Ruhr coal, in July 1937 it estimated total monthly steel consumption at 95,700 tons, of which some 50,000 tons was for current requirements, the rest being for new construction. It was allotted a quota of only 45,000 monthly tons, and actually received only half this amount during the first half of 1937. As of October, stocks were depleted and both surface and subsurface construction came to a halt.[27] In addition,

> The lack of conveyors *(Schüttelrutschen)* [prevented] complete exploitation of working points . . . and the lack of coal cars caused bottlenecks in movement through tunnels. . . . The result [was] that . . . in spite of the engagement of thousands of new miners in the past few months, there has been no increase in output.[28]

In January 1938 Plenipotentiary for Iron and Steel Allocation von Hanneken imposed a fixed rate for current requirements of 3.2 kg of iron and steel for every ton of coal output. While this system ended the most severe shortages, it still left a very tight supply situation. It did nothing, however, to stem the unending flow of complaints from the operators.[29] While difficult to estimate, shortages of iron and steel may have been responsible for one-half of the fall in man-shift productivity, and therefore also partly for the disappointing rise in outputs.[30] They increased from 127,752 million tons in 1937 to 130,184 million tons in 1939, while actually declining to 127,284 million tons in 1938 (Table 5).

Table 5 German coal output, 1928–1944* (000 tons)

Year	*Ruhr*	*Aachen*	*Saar*	*Upper Silesia*	*Total***
1928	114,567	5509	13,107	19,698	150,871
1929	123,603	6040	13,579	21,996	163,441
1930	107,183	7721	13,236	17,961	142,695
1931	85,627	7094	11,367	16,792	118,634
1932	73,275	7447	10,438	15,277	104,731
1933	77,801	5558	10,561	15,640	109,905
1934	90,388	7528	11,318	17,392	124,891
1935	97,668	7478	10,623	19,042	143,013*
1936	107,478	7634	11,684	21,065	158,407
1937	127,752	7835	13,365	24,481	184,489
1938	127,284	7754	14,389	25,983	186,186
1939	130,184	7382	13,258	26,552	187,956
1940	129,188	7125	11,293	26,390	184,354
1941	129,971	7294	14,431	24,961	186,531
1942	128,490	7215	15,290	27,125	187,920
1943	127,515	7469	16,152	29,375	190,482
1944	110,851	4667	12,404	28,572	166,059

Source: Statistisches Handbuch von Deutschland (München, 1948), 279.

Notes: * Including Saar after March 1935; ** 1937 borders.

But such minor overall gains did not come even close to meeting supply requirements. The industry came under unexpectedly strong pressures to export until mid-1938, due partly to a rise in foreign demand but also to considerations of Reich policy such as a desire to supply foreign allies and a need to gain foreign exchange earnings to counterbalance higher imports. Ruhr coal exports jumped from 27,655,866 tons in 1936 to 39,023,273 tons in 1937. At the same time, the coal appetites of the new Four Year Plan projects proved to be unexpectedly large. The synthetic petroleum plants alone devoured 6.5 million annual tons. The Reichswerke Hermann Göring under construction in Salzgitter consumed at an annual rate of about 5.7 million tons. These new requirements could be met only in small part from other coal districts such as Silesia because of differences in combustion qualities and high transportation costs. Savings might have been made by reducing supplies to households but the considerable power of the party apparatus stood in the way of drastic action. Mining experts estimated shortages of industrial coal at anywhere between 7.5 million and 11.5 million annual tons.[31] Hitler's own wild guess (of January 1937) was that the Reich would require 20–30 million additional annual tons of output.[32]

Coal shortages were in fact felt more or less across the board. Although the weakness in export markets in the second half of 1938 provided some measure of relief, matters reached a crisis point in spring 1939, when, in spite of its effects on steel output, a reduction of 5 per cent was ordered in coke-making to relieve the coal supply situation at gas works, cement plants and a number of other industries.[33] Weeks later Director Oskar Gabel of the Mining Section of the Ministry of Economics none the less described the coal supply situation as still 'catastrophic', since only 50,000 tons of the Reichsbahn's daily consumption requirement of 70,000 tons could be delivered. He also pointed to the likelihood of further difficulties, since 'at the most important factories, which normally hold three months' reserves, stocks have been reduced to levels sufficient only for a day or two'.[34]

These shortages led to an intense struggle over the coal supply. It pitted RWKS against all other main claimants: customers dissatisfied with delivery conditions, dealers angry about volumes and margins, the officials from the Foreign Office advocating the use of coal as a diplomatic tool, bureaucrats intent on maximizing the hard currency yield on exports, and the bosses of party-sponsored industrial projects such as the Reichswerke Hermann Göring demanding priority treatment. The syndicate recognized only late in the day that it was in an impossible situation. While protesting that shortages were due to supply problems RWKS made none of the tactical concessions necessary to stave off the regime's attempt to assert control over coal marketing.

While it is difficult to gain more than glimpses into the disputes that occurred between RWKS and its customers, the bitter disagreement with the city of Hamburg provides one revealing case. On 17 April 1937, meeting at the Rohstoff-Amt, its representative accused RWKS of price-gouging: instead of the customary fine coal the syndicate had delivered the 40 per cent more expensive large kernels (*Nusskohle* I/III). Dr Rixfähren of RWKS, citing attempts to narrow differentials between the two grades, rejected sarcastically imputations that the coal industry distinguished between 'first- and second-class consumers' and that the syndicate intended to 'sabotage' its customers. He added that, the cheaper grade being unavailable, Hamburg had better accept the offer than do without, insisting in the face of an objection that the syndicate had every right to withhold a portion of output for consumption at the mines *(Selbstverbrauch)* regardless of grade. To this remark, President Lange of the Rohstoff-Amt, 'expressing in extraordinarily frank language his astonishment and disgust', promised to 'appeal the dispute to higher authority'.[35]

As for the dealers, they felt 'sand-bagged' by the syndicate. Although rebates had been increased from 2.3 to 4 per cent, they were (except in Aachen) still required to buy through syndicate middlemen and, once shortages had begun to appear, accept low grades of coal with narrow price-spreads. Nor had their overall share in retail sales increased. In short, they had made very little progress towards the 'parity' with producers they had demanded since 1933.[36]

In the export field, RWKS was the victim of the regime's own confusion. On the one hand, the syndicate was ordered to make unwanted deliveries to political allies. This happened in March 1939 when RWKS attempted to slip out of a contract with Italy, a distant market, on the grounds that poor railway scheduling was delaying deliveries by 25–30 per cent. The Italian coal import monopoly, by this time down to a ten-days' supply, rejected the RWKS suggestion that it purchase from Britain since 'the Rome–Berlin Axis should have a coal dimension in addition to a [diplomatic and military one]'.[37] The Ministry of Economics ordered the syndicate to execute the contract. But it also ordered simultaneously that higher priority be given to deliveries to hard currency countries (France, Belgium/Luxembourg, Holland). In February 1939 Minister of Economics Funk not only directed an increase of 20 per cent in foreign coal sales in order to raise them to 1937 levels but also that preference in domestic deliveries be given to firms manufacturing for export. These additional demands intensified the already bitter conflict between Ruhr coal and the Reichswerke Hermann Göring, which consumed no less than 25 per cent of the total Reich output of coking coal.[38]

This dispute put the very existence of RWKS into jeopardy. The disagreement grew out of Göring's well-known confrontation with the steel industry, sparked off when the foundrymen refused to smelt the low-grade German ores of the Salzgitter field of Vereinigte Stahlwerke. The consumption of this raw material would have required doubling blast furnace capacity, conveyancing and coke consumption rates. It would therefore also have required either sharp price increases or the acceptance of huge subsidies from Berlin. Unable to force the steel industry to submit to his demand, Göring announced the formation of the firm named after himself which, he assured his enemies, would erect the largest blast furnaces in history.[39]

The Reichswerke did not play by the usual rules. As Göring made 'unmistakably clear', the enterprise was founded to serve as an instrument of national policy: his company would not be a slave to the 'bottom line', but would require subsidies, indeed exact them from the rest of industry as necessary. Its growth, moreover, would not depend on success in the marketplace but on the political fortunes of the Reich. The Reichswerke thus were financed by forcible contributions in the form of stock swaps, first with steel producers, then coal, and finally industries in territories conquered or annexed by the Reich. Pessimists from the Ruhr feared that, as Göring proclaimed, the new Konzern would serve as a model for the 'German socialism' of the future, but as Göring's girth expanded his attention span diminished, and he no more ran the complex bearing his name than he did the Four Year Plan. Management of the Reichswerke was in the hands of the

Krauch-like figure Paul Pleiger and it was with him that the operators would have to contend.[40]

One of Pleiger's main objectives was to secure a reliable coal supply, if possible through direct participation in the industry. While RWKS remained steadfastly opposed to allowing this, there were limits to its powers of resistance. One of them was posed by the presence in their midst of Friedrich Flick. He was an anomaly in the industry, a financier rather than a mining engineer. Flick owned two of the choicest Ruhr collieries, Harpener Bergbau and Essener Steinkohle AG, but since the Reich acquisition of his shares in Vereinigte Stahlwerke in 1931 he had lacked a Ruhr foundry. The Aryanization of the Julius and Ignaz Petschek brown coal properties of Werschen–Weissenfelder Braunkohlen AG and Anhaltische Kohlenwerke AG, which came under control of the Reichswerke, gave Flick an opportunity to make a profitable trade. It also gave Pleiger an opportunity to acquire a hard coal base for his future foundry.[41] This was done by means of a 'commissarial order' from Pleiger declaring the Petschek properties as forfeit. He then swapped them with Flick for a 40 per cent share in the Harpen mine. This made it possible, as Flick cynically remarked to his shareholders, to deal remuneratively and, at the same time, 'emerge with our moral credentials intact'.[42]

But since the two mines provided only a fraction of the Reichswerke's consumption requirements, Pleiger also sought to secure preferential delivery terms, specifically the *Umlage* exemption enjoyed by tied-in foundries, and reduced freight rates. On 21 February 1938, Iron and Steel Plenipotentiary von Hanneken responded to repeated RWKS objections in exceptionally harsh language:

> I cannot understand how it is possible after what has happened to the steel industry that the leaders of coal mining are so shortsighted as not to recognize what is at stake, even though they have seen as in the case of the automobile industry the setting up of the DAF-run Volkswagen project to compete with independent manufacturers that the national leadership and the Four Year Plan are more than ready to take the necessary steps.

Hermann von Hanneken, the report goes on, made these remarks 'fully aware of their seriousness', and to emphasize this concluded that 'if the syndicate does not agree to the conditions of the Reichswerke it will face an extremely harsh *fait accompli*'.[43]

By June 1939 the diffuse resentments felt against RWKS had focused into an organized opposition led by the Four Year Plan. On the fifth of that month von Hanneken took aside Director Buskühl of Preussag and informed him 'in the most sharply critical language' that 'RWKS shows no understanding whatsoever of allocating according to consumption priorities. More and more, it clings to sterile old forms . . . preferring deliveries to toilet paper factories than to important Four Year Plan plants'.[44] An official of the Ministry of Economics put the matter still more bluntly: 'syndicates and cartels no longer have a place'. Hanneken, however, eventually relented, declaring himself willing to give the RWKS a final chance to 'set up a monthly delivery programme . . . which, if drafted and executed properly, . . . would spare it from interventions by third parties'.[45]

This ultimatum elicited a desperate and long-overdue response. At a 29 June 1939 meeting of the syndicate's general assembly, RWKS Chairman Hermann Kellermann (Gutehoffnungshütte) demanded that he be granted the necessary powers to prevent the imposition of a coal commissar and a quota system for distribution. He wanted a broad mandate to 'direct the necessary amounts to the Reichsbahn, safeguard adequate provisioning in the countryside, . . . and deliver on a preferential basis factories of special national-political importance at the expense of those less essential *(lebenswichtig)*'.[46]

These powers were granted but proved inadequate, due to the intervention of Paul Walter. He was first appointed Plenipotentiary for Productivity Increases in the Coal Mines (Beauftragter für die Leistungssteigerung im Bergbau), then in December 1939 promoted to head of Reichsstelle Kohle, and finally in April 1940 raised to the dignity of Reich Coal Commissar (Reichskohlenkommissar). Walter was a throwback to the kind of economic primitive who flocked to the party before 1933 but whose influence had since dwindled. But the one-time DAF official's admitted ignorance of both the financial and technical sides of the coal business was no obstacle to his intention of making a policy for the industry. His plans were very grand indeed. At the mines, the name Walter became an anathema. His reforms, if enacted, would have destroyed the power of RWKS.[47]

Walter rose as coal policy failed. As Productivity Plenipotentiary his job was to make the 'Göring–Verordnung' work. When by mid-summer 1939 it had become apparent that lengthening the work day could not bring about corresponding increases in output, he acquired a vast new array of powers with which to overcome shortages. In theory they were to enable him to overcome supply bottlenecks as well as increase outputs. But not even the correspondent of the *Frankfurter Zeitung* could quite understand how his office was to operate:

> it seems as if the new functions will emphasize the importance of coal allocation *(Bewirtschaftung)* while also including those for stepping up productivity. The new office will therefore combine the marketing and production responsibilities of General Hanneken's office (in the Four Year Plan) with the social policy tasks of DAF. The new organization may also extend to the district level and below. Up to now the representatives of RWKS [and the other regional coal cartels] have been responsible for allocation at these levels. It has long been . . . foreseen that management responsibility for coal production should be shifted away from the Ministry

of Economics, whose responsibilities are in any case essentially supervisory, and placed elsewhere. The change that has come about is not due to onset of war conditions.[48]

The evident vagueness of Walter's mandate, together with an apparent licence to interfere with coal allocation at the regional level provided a ready-made formula for conflict with the syndicates.

But soon Walter's mandate broadened still further because of the increasing unmanageability of coal supply problems. This was the result of the exceptional harshness of the winter of 1939–40. In November train loadings were down 50–60 per cent and coal shortages had become acute at gas and electricity works as well as in households. In December the waterways began to freeze. Exports from North Sea harbours came to a standstill, as did deliveries of essential mine supplies, such as pit-props. By 23 January 1940 the marshalling yards of the Ruhr were at a total standstill, with some 450 coal trains unable to move. In a frantic attempt to break the log jam, trains were sent off randomly to discharge coal at the nearest destination; at the same time, rail traffic was restricted to coal and foodstuffs. The latter were by then in such short supply that municipalities were forced to commandeer buses for potato-digging forays to the countryside and the Wehrmacht to help out with emergency truck transport. Thanks to Walter's 'drastic cure' of forming convoys of coal-cars *(Ganzzüge)* the tide began to turn on 27 January and by the end of February daily loadings had returned to normal levels. In April 1940 Walter, whose drastic cure encountered heated RWKS protests, was appointed Reich Coal Commissar.[49]

While still Productivity Plenipotentiary, Walter spelled out in no uncertain terms his vision of the future. Although declining to make 'programmatic statements', he expressed astonishment that

leading coal circles still have notions about cartels *(Syndikatswesen)* which might have been discussable ten years ago but today have not the slightest justification. Sales of output quotas still take place. . . . One can only ask: what kind of world do the operators think they're living in? For the rest, they're simply too complacent.[50]

Walter's eventual 'programmatic statements' were indeed anything but reassuring. He proposed a total break-up of the distribution system. In his view, Germany should be divided into twenty-six districts corresponding to *Gauen* and sales be conducted through no more than twelve to fifteen wholesalers, dealing with the gamut of solid fuel products, including brown coal. He admitted that this would require the elimination of many independent firms. To his mind, these were mere 'telephone-traders'. When asked about 'a matter to which he had obviously given no thought, namely the fate of such old and well-respected [trading] firms as Stinnes, Haniel, Klöckner, and Raab

Karcher', all of which had close ties with the mines, Walter could only reply with anodyne reassurances that they could somehow be worked into his plans. Emphasizing in conclusion that the purpose of the proposed change was to increase profit margins at pithead (by decreasing those of the marketing machinery), he admitted to being perplexed at the evident lack of enthusiasm exhibited by his audience of Bergassessoren.[51]

While Walter's dilettantism presented the most immediate threat to the industry, the increasingly unrealistic output targets set by the Four Year Plan in the months before the war posed a greater if slightly more remote one. Table 6 summarizes the three production plans of 1939.

Table 6 1939 Coal production plans

	Quota of 22 Jan. 1939	*Quota of 13 June 1939*	*% inc. over 1937*	*Quota of 14 Aug. 1939*
1939	147.0	—	—	147.4
1940	153.0	154.3	20.8	158.3
1941	156.5	159.7	25.0	160.2
1942	161.0	163.0	27.6	164.8
1943	—	166.9	30.0	—
1944	—	169.9	33.0	—
1945	—	170.4	33.4	—
1946	—	171.5	34.3	—

Source: Hans Spethmann, *The Mining Industry of the Ruhr and World War II* (unpublished ms.), ch. 1, 10, 11, 12.

The figures in Table 6 require but little comment. To arrive at the 23 January 1939 quotas technocrats in the Four Year Plan added together daily historical output maxima at each mine without taking into account either transportation or supply factors. The two revisions were based merely on the anticipated requirements of the coal-consuming industries. It was a mystery how the industry would be able to supply the 170.4 million tons called for by 1945 in the 13 June 1939 production plan unless by means of a yet to be discovered wonder weapon *(Wunderwaffe)*. But the leaders of the industry were in no position to take the absurd figures of 23 June lightly. On the same day the Ministry of Economics declared the industry collectively, and the unfortunate General Director Buskühl personally responsible for attaining the output targets.[52]

As the period of 'neither peace nor war', whose piecemeal gains began with the annexation of Austria, moved by phases into the Europe-wide assault on civilization launched with the Western Campaign of May 1940, the survival of the Ruhr mining industry as a private enterprise appeared increasingly doubtful. The collieries had few friends in Berlin influential enough to protect them from the political consequences of almost certain future fuel supply shortages. Yet the industry gained an unexpected reprieve. It won a powerful convert in Reichswerke managing director Paul Pleiger. It came into possession of a grotesque and unrequested *Wunderwaffe* in the form of slave labour. Finally, the conquest of France and the Low Countries created new management needs which only German businessmen could satisfy. To them fell the task of organizing and administering the economies of Hitler-dominated Europe, without whose productive resources the German cause could not prevail. The unwanted burden of war would make possible the survival of the Ruhr coal industry.

Notes

1 Bundesarchiv (BA) R3/1930 Rheinisch-Westfälisches Institut für Wirtschaftsforschung (Heft 9), 'Der Ruhrbergbau. Vergleich der Entwicklung im ersten Weltkrieg'. (Essen, 1944).
2 Tim Mason, *Arbeiterklasse und Volksgemeinschaft* (Opladen, 1975).
3 Dietmar Petzina, 'Germany and the Great Depression', *Journal of Contemporary History*, 4 (4), October 1969.
4 ibid., 27; Wolfgang Birkenfeld, *Der synthetische Treibstoff 1933–1945. Ein Beitrag zur nationalsozialistischen Wirstschafts- und Rüstungspolitik* (Göttingen, 1964), 31.
5 Birkenfeld, op. cit., 102.
6 ibid., 49 f.
7 ibid., 83.
8 Ministry of Economic Warfare, 'The Oil Industry', *Economic Survey of Germany* 7 f.
9 Westfälisches Wirtschaftsarchiv, Dortmund (WWA) F26/358 '6. Sitzung des Hauptausschusses für Forschungswesen', 12 January 1937.
10 BA R26I/a 'Aufgabenverteilung im Vierjahresplan', 26 June 1937.
11 Gutehoffnungshütte (GHH) 400101320/16 'Gremium', 10 August 1937.
12 WWA F26/93 'Besprechung mit den Herrn Dr. Berkemeyer und Dr. Bie', 4 April 1936; '. . . Besprechung mit Dr. Berkemeyer und Dr. Bie', 20 January 1937; BM 58/12400 Nr. 12 (GBAG) 'Betriebsbericht 1938/9'.
13 Bergbau Museum (BM) B13/1753 'Sitzung des Beirats der Bezirksgruppe Ruhr', 22 December 1936; GHH 400101320/100 'Besprechung über die Kohlenversorgungslage', 20 July 1939; USNA OMGUS 26–2/1 Hans Spethmann, *The Mining Industry of the Ruhr and World War II* (unpub. ms.): vol. I *Between the two world wars*, 3 f.
14 WWA F26/24–1 'Jahresbericht der Concordia Bergbau', 1937; BA R41/174 Untitled note, July 1939.
15 WWA F26/365 'Zur Nachwuchserwerbung. Bericht von Bergrat Ziekursch', 5 July 1942; GHH 400101330/13 'Nebelung durch v.d. Linden', 28 December 1936.
16 WWA F26/365 'Sogemaier an Herren Mitglieder des Beirats', 5 March 1942; BM 55/12400 Nr. 13 (GBAG) 'Betriebsberichte 1939/40, 1940/1, 1941/2; BM B13/1205 NSDAP 'Kreisleitung Recklinghausen. Sonderbericht über die wirtschaftliche Lage des Bergmanns'; BA R261/1 'Gesundheitszustand der Bergmänner, Dez. 1938'; B 13/1205 'Bericht Dr. Steckelberg, Marl', 26 August 1938; GBAG to Schlattmann, 16 November 1937, Doc. 85 in Mason, op. cit.

17 BM B13/1057 'Besprechung betreffend Krankfeiern und Unfallfeierschichten', 8 October 1938.
18 GHH 400101305/9 'Statistische Angaben aus dem Ruhrkohlenbergbau', September 1943; Länderrat des Amerikanischen Besatzungsgebiets (ed.) *Statistisches Handbuch von Deutschland* (München, 1948), 279.
19 BM B13/1204 'Zur Lage des Bergarbeiters. Denkschrift erstellt im Auftrag des Gauleiters', November 1938; WWA F26/393 'Vertrauensratssitzung', 3 February 1939; F26/359 'Sitzung des Beirats der Bezirksgruppe Steinkohlenbergbau Ruhr', 7 July 1939; GHH 400101330/5 'Auswirkung der Erhöhung der Förderleistung und des Leistungslohnes im Bergbau vom März 1939'; 400101330/5 Kellermann to Vögler, 21 October 1938; 400101330/5 Kauert to Buskühl, 24 October 1938.
20 WWA F25/24–1 'Jahresbericht der Concordia Bergbau AG . . . für das Geschäftsjahr 1940'.
21 ibid.
22 WWA F26/26/391 'Telefongespräch mit Kreisobmann Staubach', 21 November 1939.
23 WWA 'Vertrauensratsitzungen', 20 February 1939, 13 April 1939, 12 May 1939, 14 July 1939, 1 November 1939.
24 GHH 4001026/10 'Vertrauensratssitzung', 9 September 1937.
25 *Statistisches Heft. Produktions- und wirtschaftsstatistische Angaben aus der Montanindustrie* (Essen, 1939), 93, 100.
26 WWA F26/358 Rudolf Regul, 'Technik, Forschung, und Leistung . . .' (ms.).
27 GHH 400101303/1 'Besprechung im Amt für deutsche Roh – und Werkstoff', 28 May 1937; 400101303/1 Buskühl to Göring, 19 July 1937; 400101303/1 Winkhaus to Vogelsang, 20 September 1938.
28 GHH 400101303/1 Winkhaus to Göring, 1 October 1937.
29 GHH 400101303/1 'Aktennotiz Vogelsang', 25 September 1937; 400101303/1 Hanneken to Wirtschaftsgruppe Bergbau, 6 September 1937.
30 GHH 400101320/100 'Kohlenversorgungslage', 20 July 1939; GBAG to Schlattmann, 16 November 1937, Doc. 85 in Mason, op. cit.; BA R7/590 RWM to Göring, 2 May 1939; WWA F26/358 6 'Sitzung des Hauptausschusses', 12 January 1937.
31 GHH 400101303/1 Buskühl to Göring, 19 July 1937; BA R7/590 RWM to Göring, 'Mangel an Bergarbeitern', 2 May 1939.
32 Bundesarchiv Spethmann V, 24.
33 GHH 400101320/99 'Besprechung', 5 June 1939.
34 Ibid., 19 June 1939.
35 GHH 400101320/134 'Sitzung beim Rohstoff-Amt', 17 April 1937.
36 GHH 101320/33 'Besprechung Kleiner Handelsausschuss', 3 July 1939; BA R7/2017 'Beiratssitzung der Wirtschaftsgruppe Vermilttler Gewerbe', 20 December 1940.
37 GHH 400101320/17 'Gremium', 20 March 1939.
38 ibid., 13 February 1939; 400101520/100 'Allgemeinen Erlass Nr. 95/39 P. St.', 15 June 1939.
39 Arthur Schweitzer, 'Business Power under the Nazi Regime', *Zeitschrift für Nationalökonomie*, 20 (3–4), 1960, 425.
40 US National Archives OMGUS (Legal Division) 58–2/2 39 German Industrial Complexes, 'The Hermann Göring complex'; M. Riedel, *Eisen und Kohle für das Dritte Reich. Paul Pleigers Stellung in der NS-Wirtschaft* (Göttingen, 1973); GHH 400101303/1 'Vortrag (Göring) über die deutsche Eisenwirtschaft', 23 July 1937.
41 NI 31 Annex 2 'Biography of Dr Flick'; USNA OMGUS Legal German Industrial Complexes, 'The Flick complex', RG 260 Box 27–2/11.

42 NI 5274, 784, 900, 3878, 3245, 3226, 3309, 5588, 3397, 3291, 3287, 3276, 3274, 3281, 3363, 3375, 3376, 3383/84, 3377, 10,138, 5304, 3345.
43 GHH 400101300/0 'Aktennotiz', 23 February 1939.
44 GHH 400101320/99 'Besprechung', 5 June 1939.
45 GHH 400101320/99 'Kleiner Handelsausschuss', 3 July 1939.
46 GHH 400101320/17 'Gremium', 29 June 1939.
47 Nürnberg Industrialists (NI) 11,228 'Erklarüng Paul Pleiger', 31 July 1947.
48 GHH 400101320/96 'Der Umbau in der Kohlenwirtschaft, FAZ', 19 December 1939.
49 BA Nachlass Spethmann III, 41 f.
50 GHH 400101330/6 'Paul Walter über seine Aufgaben', 8 August 1939.
51 GHH 400101320/96 '(Walters) Besprechung mit Herrn Dr. Obst', 20 December 1940.
52 Ernst Buskühl, 'Leistung und Aufgaben der Rurhkohlenbergbaues im Rahmen der neuen kohlen- und energiewirtschaftlichen Entwicklung', *Glückauf*, 19 June 1919.

4

RUHR COAL AND THE ENERGY BUSINESS

The 1930s witnessed the unfolding under quite different circumstances of the business strategies laid down by the Ruhr mines in the previous decade. They involved asserting market control, reducing costs, and increasing yield on output through investment in processing. While in some respects a success, this strategy could not prevent the long-term decline of the coal business. In the 1930s Ruhr collieries also missed a chance to diversify into more competitive energy fields such as oil, electricity and gas. Thus the decline of coal-mining reduced the power of the industrial complex known as 'The Ruhr' as well as that of the region it dominated.

A strange combination of constraint and opportunity shaped the business environment of national socialist Germany. On the one hand, numerous controls had been imposed to gear industrial output to rearmament policies. The Reich dominated financial markets. Strategic necessity and foreign exchange requirements partly regulated exports and imports. Prices and wages were officially frozen. On the other hand, dynamic economic growth occurred, the inefficient planning process created numerous opportunities to expand profitably, and beneath the official veneer of life in the Third Reich, Germany continued to experience social and economic changes similar to those taking place in other industrial nations. Business inevitably responded to movements in population, shifts in consumer demand, as well as to alterations in habit, taste and expectation. Germany of the late 1930s witnessed major industrial reorganizations and the creation of whole new branches of production. These developments took place both outside and inside the armaments sector.[1]

While such economic and political forces pulled Ruhr coal into new markets, it was pushed in the same direction by the traditional strategy of promoting by-product sales in order to increase yield on output. By 1933 the Benzol-Verband, a mine-owned syndicate, had become an important force on the German petroleum market. The Ruhrgas net (which piped the by-products of coke- and steel-making) extended to Hannover and, through affiliates, down the left bank of the Rhein to Bonn.

Finally, the industry had attempted since the late 1920s to set up an electric utility company to provide markets for unsaleable coal. The business conditions of the 1930s were propitious to expansion in each of these fields, but for Ruhr coal the results were disappointing. In petroleum the regime was committed to motorization, 'recovering' the retail market from the domination of the Anglo-American multinationals and increasing domestic outputs especially of synthetic fuel. Yet, while all these aims were to some extent realized, the Benzol-Verband derived only modest benefit from them. Results were a little better in the other fields. Rearmament and the construction of the Hermann Göring complex at Watenstedt necessitated huge increases in coke supply and therefore also the renovation and expansion of cokeries. This increased gas outputs. Unfortunately, the hyper-intensive *Interessenpolitik* of national socialist communities and regions complicated attempts to extend the gas grid. Thus markets remained elusive. In the electric power field, the mines built a number of new on-site thermal generating plants to provide an outlet for otherwise useless ballast coal. In this case the industry succeeded in exploiting the regime's failures in the field of energy planning, which extended to electricity as well as coal. After 1937 shortages of publicly distributed current prevailed; only the Ruhr mines, which had large surpluses of their own power, could offset them. The result was coal's greatest triumph of the 1930s, the founding of STEAG (Steinkohleelektrizitätsgesellschaft), a company set up in 1937 to supply electricity to public utilities. Yet the operators never regarded STEAG as anything more than a useful market for unsaleable quantities of coal and gas, fearing that it might develop into a competitor. As previously, coal would not get its share of benefits from the long-term growth in electrical power consumption.

The 1930s witnessed a remarkable lack of development in the getting and marketing Ruhr coal. This was due only in part to the policies of the Four Year Plan. Management preferred to seek profit-making opportunities from surface operations while simply maintaining existing plant below ground, as reflected in Table 7. As indicated, one-half of the total investment undertaken in connection with the Four Year Plan was related to the production of synthetic fuel. Of this amount, some RM 195 million went into the improvement of underground operations. But quite large additional amounts were reserved for new cokery construction (RM 120 million) as well as new power plant (RM 110 million). The heavy investment in these areas was determined as much by business as by the regime.

Numerous considerations influenced the decision to direct resources away from coal-mining and marketing: the 'mature' character of the basic industry, the workings of the regulatory machinery, and general market conditions. For these reasons, themes important in the earlier history of the Ruhr coal business were all but absent after 1933. Except for the Reichswerke Hermann Göring, there was no rush on the part of outsiders to acquire coal properties. Thus

Table 7 The financing of expansion undertaken on behalf of the Four Year Plan, March 1937

			RM *million*
I	Synthetic fuel plants under construction (Scholven Rheinpreussen, Ruhrchemie, Klöckner-Werke)		
	– hydrogenation and Fischer–Tropsch plants	=	100
	– coking facilities	=	11
	– power plants	=	16
	– mining installations (surface)	=	36
			163
II	Synthetic fuel plants called for by 18-Month Plan (Gelsenberg, Scholven, Stinnes, Essener Steinkohle, Krupp, Hoesch, Rheinpreussen, Ruhrchemie, de Wendel)		
	– hydrogenation and Fischer–Tropsch plants	=	270
	– coking facilities	=	30
	– power plants	=	53
	– mining installations (surface)	=	115
			468
III	Increased coke productions	=	120
IV	Mines (underground)	=	400
V	Power plants	=	110
	(III—V)	=	630
	(+I—II)		
		=	1261

Source: Hans Spethmann, *The Mining Industry of the Ruhr and World War II* (unpublished ms.).

disagreement did not arise within the RWKS and the other cartels as a result of changes in quota distribution. The inclusion of Aachen and the Saar districts in the RWKS counted for little in this respect. Another dispute which had at times threatened the survival of the cartel, over the relative *Umlage* shares of 'independents' as opposed to mines tied in to foundries, faded into history as the amount of the levy was reduced. This occurred less because of the slight recovery of export prices than because the Reich took over the major share of the subsidy burden through the *Zusatzausfuhrförderungsbgabe*. The famous RWKS tonnage levy decreased steadily as follows: RM3.7/ton in 1934/5, RM3.71/ton in 1935/6, RM3.45/ton in 1936/7, RM2.81/ton in 1937/8, RM2.12/ton in 1938/9.[2] Nor did the methods and machinery of marketing the industry had pioneered undergo any important changes in the 1930s. The inclusion of the Saar and Aachen districts ended the underbidding of the 1920s and the high coal demand after 1937 nearly eliminated competition with the east Elbian districts.

As indicated by the wholesale price index (Table 8), the Reich tariffs in effect as of 1933 held until 1939. Prices were stable. Production methods, the central concern of the 'rationalizers' of the late 1920s, remained much the same. An increase in yield per working point continued, but far less dramatically than before.[3] From the beginning of 1927 to the beginning of 1936 this figure more than quadrupled from 23 tons to 106 tons. By the end of 1938 it had reached only 122 tons (Table 9). Although there was some replacement of steam by electric power, technologies (as indicated in Table 10 by the lack of increase in the number of machines in operation underground) remained essentially static: digging was done with the pneumatic pick, propping with timber, back-filling with shovel, and conveyancing by hand to moving belt or shuttle. Finally, there was but little scope for decision-making regarding the business aspects of mine management.

Wage rates were officially frozen, and in practice highly regulated, as were costs for mine supplies such as timber, steel and machinery. 'Spreads' could be increased by forcing buyers to accept expensive grades of coal or through the occasional cut in freight rates. At the same time, they could be eliminated by events effectively beyond the control of factory managers such as delivery delays, transportation snarl-ups and other supply difficulties. Because of financial controls and the rationing of raw materials and production goods 'profit' itself had very little significance; it could neither be freely distributed nor reinvested without official authorization.[4] Business success depended heavily on securing permission to expand or at least maintain existing operations. This had little to do with sound plant management and much to do with politics.

The stagnant character of coal-mining and marketing stood in sharp contrast to developments in other German energy fields in the 1930s. Petroleum was the most dynamic of them. It presented the coal industry with a unique opportunity to expand. Developments in other industrial nations clearly pointed the way for Germany. Reich per capita automobile ownership in 1933 (1 per 90 inhabitants) lagged far behind French (1 per 22) and British (1 per 27), not to mention American (1 per 3.5). Relatively speaking, this put Germany at the level of the USA in the year prior to the introduction of the Model T. Ford.[5]

Hitler's policies provided strong impetus to increasing the production, refining and distribution of petroleum products. The Führer's love affair with the automobile is well-known: the motorization of the Reich figured in even his earliest plans for economic recovery and indeed became a constant of policy. As a result, by 1939, 2500 miles of Autobahn had been constructed; between 1928 and 1938 vehicle production tripled and during the same years total consumption of petroleum products increased from 3.5 million to 7 million metric tons.[6] Hitler was also committed to reducing the share of the Anglo-American petroleum multinationals in German fuel markets. This was considerable. As of 1928 DAPG (Deutsch-Amerikanische Petroleum

Table 8 German wholesale coal prices (1913 = 100)

1925 = 132.90	1935 = 114.38
1930 = 136.00	1936 = 113.98
1931 = 129.00	1937 = 113.94
1932 = 115.50	1938 = 113.91
1933 = 115.28	1939 = 112.00 (to June)
1934 = 114.53	

Source: Bergbau Verein, *Statistisches Heft. Produktions- und wirtschaftsstatistische Angaben aus der Montanindustrie* (Essen, 1939), 79.

Table 9 Consolidation of working points in the Ruhr, 1927–1939

	Working points	*(1927 = 100)*	*Production per working point (+)*	*(1927 = 100)*
Beginning of 1927	16,700	100	23	100
1929	12,500	75	30	130
1931	7,460	45	47	203
1932	5,111	31	59	257
1933	4,075	24	73	317
End of 1934	3,669	22	94	408
Beginning of 1936	3,172	19	106	461
End of 1936	3,416	20	110	478
1937	3,551	21	116	504
1939	3,280	20	122	530

Source: Bergbau Verein, *Statistisches Heft. Produktions- und wirtschaftsstatistische Angaben aus der Montanindustrie* (Essen, 1939), 117

Table 10 Subsurface machines in operation 1926–1938

	Total number	*Horsepower*	*Electric*	*Horsepower*
1926	131,083	1,127,199	2,894	471,479
1932	112,027	995,613	3,203	517,566
1933	103,381	891,071	2,904	495,688
1934	107,294	896,623	3,032	506,234
1935	110,745	918,450	3,081	504,201
1936	120,279	972,724	3,191	531,773
1937	137,163	1,039,946	3,516	539,275
1938	137,071	1,075,958	3,690	548,887

Source: Bergbau Verein, *Statistisches Heft. Produktions- und wirtschaftsstatistische Angaben aus der Montanindustrie* (Essen, 1939), 117.

Gesellschaft), owned by Standard of New Jersey, controlled 28 per cent of the total civilian market; Rhenania (Rhenania-Ossag Mineralölwerke AG), owned by Shell, controlled another 22 per cent and Olex ('Olex' Deutsche Benzin-und-Petroleum Gesellschaft), owned by Anglo-Iranian, controlled an additional 17 per cent. With the exception of a 13 per cent share held by the Benzol-Verband and another 3 per cent held by IG Farben's Deutsche Gasolin AG, smaller foreign-held companies controlled the remainder of the German market.[7] The lack of German participation was an opening which the Benzol-Verband could have easily exploited. The Führer provided the means for this to be done. He imposed controls over imports while promoting synthetic petroleum production. Table 11 depicts the rising share of German, especially synthetic, output in total Reich petroleum consumption.

Table 11 Gasoline supply, 1934–1938 (000 tons)

	Total	*German production*	*Synthetic production as % of total*
1934	2613	815	31.2
1936	3836	1430	37.3
1938	5040	2215	43.9

Source: Statistisches Handbuch von Deutschland (München, 1948), 111.

Although beginnings were promising, the Ruhr coal industry made but disappointing progress in new petroleum markets. It is clear in retrospect that it should have appropriated a portion of the distributing and refining operations of the multinationals in return for granting the right of future access to artificial petroleum. But IG Farben, not Ruhr Coal, succeeded in making this trade-off. The Benzol-Verband tried a modest variation of it and failed. The obstacles to success were the mining industry's inability to conceive of petroleum markets as anything but an extension of the coal business, the prior connection of IG Farben with oil producers, and miscalculation.

The petroleum-related operations of the coal industry were sizeable but never co-ordinated. Pride of place belonged to the Benzol-Verband (BV). In 1933 it controlled some 6000 petrol stations in the Reich (one-fifth of the Reich total). This cartel was, however, 'conceived to serve the needs of benzole for a market', and it made no serious attempt to incorporate the other diverse petroleum-related activities of the coal industry.[8] The development and sale of rights for the Fischer–Tropsch process fell under the purview of Ruhrchemie, a separate mine-owned cartel. The synthetic fuel process was used only belatedly as a bargaining tool in the petroleum field. This was a valuable card if played well. By 1938 patent rights to Fischer–Tropsch were sold to Société de Produits Chimiques Courrières-Kuhlmann of France, the

Anglo-Transvaal Consolidated Investment Co. Ltd, Johannesburg, Mutsui Bussan Kaisha Ltd, Tokyo, and Glavnoe Uprarlenie Gazovaj Promyšlennosti, Moscow, among others.[9]

In addition, because of the versatility of the process, other opportunities for licensing (for instance in the transformation of natural gas to petroleum) were available. A third mine-owned company, Ruhrbenzin, was responsible for marketing Fischer petroleum. But Ruhrbenzin led an unhappy existence. Founded in 1935 'solely to prevent lignite from pushing hard coal completely out of the synthetic fuels market and despite the poor commercial prospects facing it', the company was dissatisfied with prices received from BV and wanted new customers. Ruhrbenzin was never able to operate at a profit.[10] The output of the hydrogenation plant built at GBAG was sold through a curious entity, Gelsenberg Benzin AG. Formed because GBAG lacked the necessary time to construct Fischer–Tropsch installations, IG Farben blocked Gelsenkirchen's sales through BV.[11] Thus it had to found its own distribution company in spite of its low outputs.

BV, the mining industry's standard bearer, was eager to seize the growth opportunities opened by the Nazi seizure of power but did so in a foolish way, namely trying to profit from the regime's bullying of its Soviet partner, DEROP. This did force the Russians to hand over their retail operations to BV. But supplies of crude from the USSR soon stopped and BV had little choice but to acquire this from the 'multis' and their ally, IG Farben. BV was thus not able to mount a successful challenge to their domination of the growing German petroleum market, and failed even to increase its market share over the decade.

From the first day of the national socialist takeover BV enjoyed substantial support from the regime.[12] The minutes of syndicate meetings are thus replete with such statements as 'the government is energetically attempting to increase German motor vehicle traffic . . . and will exercise considerable influence on the petroleum market, especially as regards the business of the Benzol-Verband, the most prominent German producer of motor fuels'.[13] The regime's attempt to build up the national petroleum industry was a groping one. It first tried to reduce 'middle men' and retail outlets, although the former was of slight importance and the latter were too few even for present needs. The regime also tried to compel other petroleum interests to increase BV's quota in the Leichtstoff-Konvention, which since 1928 had governed petroleum distribution on the German market, threatening at one point to impose a *Zwangskartell* (government-ordered syndicate). But BV had already begun to 'cheat' on its partners. According to the 12 January 1934 minutes of the syndicate, a 'strong wave of national feeling [which] has increased customers for German producers such as BV and [IG Farben's] Deutsche Gasolin, and this has led to our exceeding authorized sales allowances'.[14] BV none the less depended too heavily on Anglo-American controlled sources of supply to risk wrecking the convention by 'cheating' too often.

The takeover of 2500 of DEROP's petrol stations offered a second growth strategy and considerable pressure was applied in pursuing it. In early 1934 USSR petroleum import allowances were cut in half. Next, DEROP personnel were subjected to official harassment *(Säuberungsaktionen)*.[15] BV did not object to these actions. As put in an official report of 7 December 1934,

> The German government has long been intent on restoring order to the German fuel market. It has been suggested that the Benzol-Verband take over DEROP, thus clearing out a wasp's nest *(Unruheherd)* while increasing market share . . . BV now has 18 per cent. With the acquisition of DEROP . . . this will increase to 25 per cent. At stake is less prestige than the prospect of a co-operative venture with the government to build the German fuel market on German foundations.[16]

In January 1935 BV took over DEROP. For RM13.5 million it acquired 2500 filling stations, which increased its network by half to 16 per cent of the German total, and raised its total sales quota in the petrol cartel to 26 per cent. The Soviet Union also agreed under duress to continue supplying BV with the amount of crude previously sold through its German distribution net. In February 1936, however, deliveries suddenly stopped because of 'difficulties with foreign payments'. They did not resume.[17]

After the DEROP débâcle, the lack of a dependable source of supply hindered BV's growth. To compound its problems, increases in the importation of Romanian crude were necessary to alleviate shortages. This product was marketed not by BV but by new independent distributors. Through price-cutting they increased their share of total petrol sales from 6 to 15 per cent over the space of a few months. BV was then forced to sell at a loss, but it did manage to gain a measure of support from the regime as compensation. Although previously the distribution of synthetic output had been based on the quotas of the fuel cartel, BV was designated sole retailer of the new output from BRABAG.[18] However neither BV nor the regime could assert control over the much larger amounts produced by IG Farben or imported by the Anglo-American multinationals.

It might have been possible for BV to control imports by constructing massive new refineries as was being done in France and Italy. There was ample room for development in this field. Reich refineries normally processed only a fifth of imported crude. From 1933 to 1935 such a policy found vigorous advocates among those concerned with foreign exchange and work-creation *(Arbeitsbeschaffung)* policy. But interest in refinery development faded away with the adoption of the synthetic fuels programme.[19] Without a large position in refining BV proved unable to break the ties between IG Farben and Standard Oil. Their partnership had two consequences: it eliminated BV as a distributor of the IG Farben product and provided political protection for the German operations of foreign petroleum interests.

The terms of the IG Farben–Standard Oil relationship are by this time well-known. In 1929, as the result of a pooling agreement, IG Farben sold to Standard Oil its patents for synthetic fuel and the right to market the product outside of Germany. In return it received $30 million of Standard Oil stock, a 20 per cent share in the proceeds from Standard Oil's synthetic fuel sales, the right to exploit certain Standard Oil patents in Germany, and Standard Oil's agreement not to enter certain fields of the chemical business without its consent. The US firm further agreed to market as much IG Farben synthetic petroleum output as the chemical firm could produce.

This was a key provision. It meant that Standard Oil, not BV, sold the rising outputs of hydrogenation-produced petrol, which actually tripled from 1936 to 1942. In 1935, Shell, through Rhenania-Ossag, reached a similar agreement with IG Farben. As 'reinsurance' against future competition from synthetic fuel, both Standard Oil and Shell took 25 per cent shareholdings in IG Farben's Deutsche Gasolin. This provided a barrier to any BV takeover attempt.[20]

The Ruhr mining industry was drawn only belatedly into the oil–chemical *Interessengemeinschaft*, and even then in a manner that had no immediate relevance for developments on the German petroleum market. In late 1937 the American Kellogg Co., a manufacturer of refinery equipment interested in the *gas* (as opposed to petroleum) refining properties of the Fischer–Tropsch process, approached Standard Oil to suggest bringing Ruhrchemie into the arrangement with IG Farben. Standard Oil soon proposed that BV set up a number of companies with IG Farben for the joint foreign sales of their patents, adding that success would depend on similar co-operative agreements for the German market. Bergassessor Knepper overcame Ruhrchemie's initial objections, with the argument that 'We have learned only a little about processing and refining primary products and lack the time to solve these problems.'[21] On 20 July 1938 Krauch presented the mines his terms. They were very tough: Ruhrchemie should concentrate on primary products; Fischer–Tropsch capacities should be *doubled* in order to provide a reserve for times of high demand; and the mine-controlled association would not 'get an insight into overall IGF planning'.[22] Although the IGF–Ruhrchemie agreement may never actually have taken effect, it did provide the necessary basis for the latter's entrance into the framework of the worldwide IGF–Standard Oil arrangement.

BV did not particularly profit from the war. With the introduction of rationing at its outbreak, the so-called Zentralbüro für Mineralöl (which had counterparts for other primary petroleum products) took over responsibilities for distributing all liquid motor fuels in the Reich. Thereupon brand names disappeared as well. The new 'war company' operated through its component organizations, whose facilities, stocks and personnel it took over. It also respected the quota system of the old Leichtstoff-Kartell. But the civilian market for petroleum shrank steadily. To supply the growing *military* fuel market, the government set up its own organization under the Ministry of Economics. This was WIFO (Wirtschaftliche Forschungsgesellschaft). WIFO became a giant with assets of over RM1 billion consisting principally of bomb-proof depots, pipelines and transport equipment. Finally, BV was not invited to participate in the huge exploration company organized in early 1941 to exploit the petroleum reserves of German-occupied Europe, Kontinentale Öl AG. Its sponsors fully expected it to become an equivalent of Standard Oil or Shell. Founded with a nominal capital of RM80 million subscribed by the government, big banks and German oil-producing companies, the new company entered a number of large-scale ventures: drilling in the south of France, operating a refinery in Trieste, exploring (through seven subsidiaries) in south-eastern Europe, operating wells in the Caucasus and Estonia, and entering a 50:50 partnership with Shell in Greece. The net worth of Kontinentale Öl AG in 1943 was about RM200 million. The new company dwarfed BV (net assets RM155 million) and clearly was intended to be *the* German oil company. BV had missed its chance to dominate the petroleum field by the mid-1930s.[23]

While a combination of rising demand and government policy pulled the mining industry into liquid fuels, output increases also pushed it into gas and electric power. At work was the *Sortenproblem*: increased coal production meant more hard-to-sell grades of too little value to transport. As a result, proposals to construct on-site thermal generating plants and coal-gas retorts, which could consume this material, gained a new immediacy. So too did the search for new gas and electricity markets. In the case of gas, the huge increase in supply made possible by the expansion of coke output also impelled the industry forward (Table 12). The industry therefore tried to create a coal-gas analogue to the electric power grid of RWE.

The large-scale cokery construction sponsored by the Four Year Plan

Table 12 Outputs of coke oven gas in the Ruhr, 1934–1938

	Ruhr coke output (000 tons)	*Coke oven gas* (000 m^3)
1934	19,975,000	8,290,421
1935	22,958,000	9,748,852
1936	27,411,000	11,650,748
1937	31,566,000	13,314,054
1938	33,634,000	14,227,320

Sources: Bergbau Verein, *Statistisches Heft. Produktions- und wirtschaftsstatistische Angaben aus der Montanindustrie* (Essen, 1939), 30; United States Strategic Bombing Survey, *The Coking Industry of Germany* (Washington, 1946), 8.

proved to be more useful to the mining industry than to the Reich. There was no shortage of coking capacity. The funds provided by the plan went into modernization. The industry had long practised systematic replacement of small and outdated operating units. The collapse of the coke markets during the Great Depression accelerated this process: some 2000 ovens were broken up, another 9000 put out of service, and only 6900 left operating at low levels. New construction began in 1935, apparently in anticipation of the future needs of the armaments economy. By 1936, average output per unit was 10 per cent above that of 1929 and Ruhr coking capacity was estimated at 40 million tons annually. But such outputs would never be necessary. There were no shortages of coke in 1937 even though cokery construction all but came to a halt because of inadequate supplies of structural steel to the mines. Still, the Four Year Plan decided in 1938 to add 4.5 million annual tons of capacity per year even in the face of severe shortages of coking coal. The new cokeries made possible steady increases not only in the output of coke but of coke oven gas, only some of which could be consumed in the steel-making process. The remainder was put up for sale to city gas distributing companies as a fuel for street lighting and home heaters.[24]

This was a huge market. In 1933 coke gas sales were three times as large as total German petroleum sales. By 1935 the anticipated availability of large amounts of surplus coking gas rekindled the interest of both industry and regime in exanding Ruhrgas operations into a national grid, creating what had been dubbed in the 1920s the *Grossraumgaswirtschaft*. As one enthusiast put the matter,

> Where during World War I a high voltage map of Germany was drawn up, we must now begin work on a high pressure gas map. This will provide the foundation for a project which will incorporate thousands of kilometres of main lines, as well as numerous pumping and pressure stations, and be of such grand dimensions that it can be realized only over considerable time.[25]

This expansion was to be accomplished similarly to RWE's, through acquisition of local production units, in this case municipal gas cokeries. The coal industry was keen to embark on distribution to households, a market relatively invulnerable to economic slowdowns. Minister of Economics Schacht strongly supported Ruhrgas as did Schlattmann, his deputy for coal, and Keppler of the raw materials staff in the Four Year Plan. The industry also received backing from Gauleiter Fritz Terboven of Essen. At the same time, it encountered tenacious opposition from the cities whose nets it had hoped to take over. The local gas works of Köln, Bonn, Mainz and Frankfurt, the most immediate objects of Ruhrgas interest, faced severe competition from RWE in the electric lighting field. They also had plans of their own to build new cokeries. While coke made as a by-product of gas generation was normally suitable only for domestic heating purposes, this was a profitable business. According to an official of Ruhrgas, the expansion plans of the municipal gas works would cost the mines more than RM30 million per year. Unfortunately, the municipalities could also count on strong political backing from the *Städtetag* (League of Cities) as well as the Leader of the Commission for Economic Policy of the NSDAP, Bernard Kohler.[26]

The Electro-Energy Conference of 10–17 January 1935 brought the confrontation of the two parties to an impasse. The municipal gas works presented their case in several position papers arguing that new cokery construction should take place mainly under their auspices and the mining industry be restricted to the supply of industry and exportation. Grounds for opposing an extension of the Ruhrgas grid included the ideological undesirability of promoting monopolies, the economic good sense (greater flexibility, improved reliability and lower cost) of maintaining diverse sources of gas supply, and the strategic soundness of dispersing generating units. The Ruhr countered initially with protests of its need to hold on to profitable markets to offset losses in metallurgical coke and subsequently with threats to raise the effective price of coal deliveries to the gas works by changing their composition while at the same time undercutting them by reducing the price of domestic heating coke. Terboven also travelled to Köln and Bonn in order to 'promote' the conclusion of delivery contracts between the cities and the Thyssen net, an affiliate of Ruhrgas. These efforts were only partially successful. Sales of coking gas to Köln increased, and the grid was extended to Frankfurt and Rüsselsheim. But this was only one small step towards the realization of a *Grossraumgaswirtschaft.*[27] As indicated in Figure 2, the main increases in coke-gas sales during the late 1930s resulted from purchasing by traditional industrial consumers in the Ruhr.

In the electric power field, the Ruhr mining industry enjoyed far greater relative success than in gas or electricity. It was due above all to mistakes in planning for which RWE must assume a portion of the blame. Their occurrence comes as a surprise. The electrical power industry was often praised as an exemplar of German organizational genius. Indeed a report compiled on RWE by the decartelization branch of the post-war French occupation government waxed rhapsodic in describing

> the famous chain of hydro-electric and thermal power created to serve the interests not of particular localities but the Reich as a whole . . . (it) allows movement of almost unlimited amounts of current from one corner of the Reich to the other . . . presenting a true parallel to Hitler's Autobahns . . . and like them, the appearance of serving peaceful purposes while, as so eloquently explained by its planner, the prophetic Arthur Koepchen, doing service equally as an instrument of national power.[28]

Planned in the First World War, the national grid *(Verbundwirtschaft)* was organized during the 1920s. At the Second World Power Conference of 1930

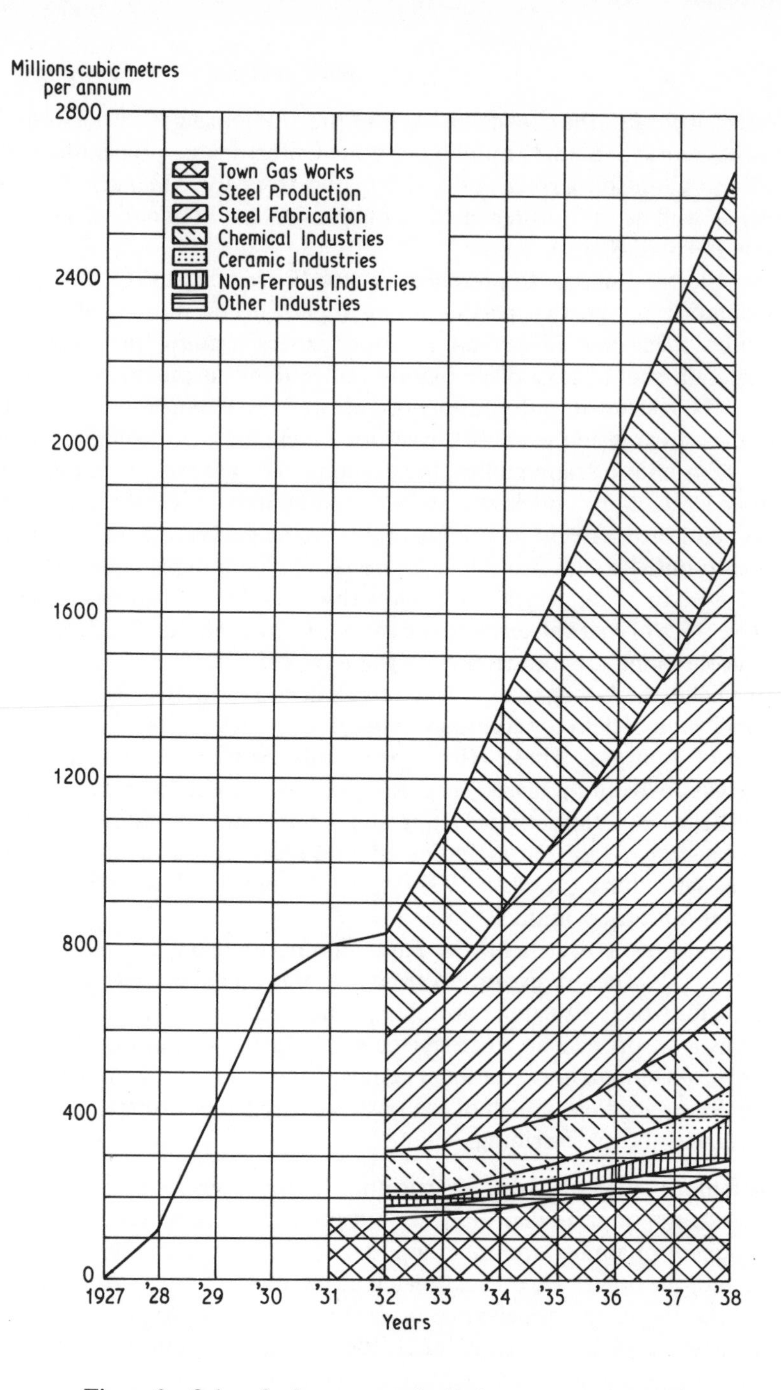

Figure 2 Sales of coke oven gas by Ruhrgas AG, 1927–1938
Source: Ministry of Economic Warfare 'Section D', Fuel, power and public utilities services. London 1944, 72.

in Berlin the German representative, Oskar Oliven, proposed in visionary language the spread of the German net throughout western Europe, thus creating an 'electric Paneuropa'. He advocated specifically the immediate construction of a new line to Luxembourg and three much larger ones to France, while adding to the capacity of those carrying current to Belgium and the Netherlands.[29] Planning mistakes in the electric field are also surprising because of the close ties between RWE's management and the regime. They were due to two special circumstances: as a result of the *Gleichschaltung* of municipalities, the shares of those which had been incorporated into the RWE grid were controlled by local party figures; and the Board of Supervisors had been reduced from 108 members to 17 in order to eliminate the Jewish members representing the two large Rhenish lignite companies, Rheinbraun and Roddergrube. Albert Vögler, a party member of long standing, took over the representation of their interests.[30]

Unlike coal, there was a form of central direction in electric power. The energy law of 1935 authorized Schacht to supervise the entire industry, promote extensions of the grid and authorize the erection, extension and operation of power stations. But he made scant use of this authority. The post-1936 expansion of the industry occurred along lines laid down by a company policy paper of 1930 which predicted little need to increase generating capacity and assigned priority to filling out the grid. As late as early 1936 managing director Koepchen anticipated a future fall in demand for electrical current.[31] Three-quarters of the RM100 million invested in the years from 1933 to 1937 went to extending the grid, and 'only a fraction' to building power plants. The US Bombing Survey summed up the results as follows:

> In 1934 the reserve capacity of the German integrated system amounted to approximately 35 per cent. This reserve capacity became smaller and smaller and was practically used up at the beginning of the war. Despite every effort it was found impossible to increase generating station capacity in keeping with the increased demand for electricity. Curtailment or rationing of electric energy to industrial consumers was necessary on occasions even before the war and such curtailments became more frequent, more severe, and more prolonged as the war continued. . . . The extensive transmission system was valueless in this general capacity shortage.[32]

This situation provided a long-awaited opportunity for the Ruhr coal industry to enter the electric power field. The mine directors considered their absence from this growth area a matter of historic injustice: 'In the years when the modern grid was built, the mines laboured under the export burdens imposed by the Versailles *Diktat*, and therefore the government promoted hydraulic power and RWE greatly stepped up its consumption of lignite.'[33] RWKS made a serious attempt to change this situation in 1928. In negotiations with RWE,

> the syndicate first attempted to erect its own power plants, leaving transmission to the electric companies. But it soon became obvious that [we] could do nothing to break the power of the [transmission] monopoly. RWE, and the lignite industry which stood behind it, had no intention whatsoever of compromising. They maintained that power plants should rely mainly on water power and lignite, using hard coal only during peaks.[34]

RWE also refused the syndicate's offer to drop its construction plans if the utility would agree to build a new plant designed to consume mainly hard coal. Instead RWE concluded long-term supply contracts with several important Ruhr Konzerne which, because of the fall in demand caused by the Depression, it could meet without difficulty. When reserves became thin in 1936, however, the coal producers resumed the attempt to break into the public power net.[35]

Some time towards the end of 1936, Krauch and Pleiger decided that the Four Year Plan should erect both a buna plant at Hüls and an aluminium works at Lünen. To meet their anticipated electricity requirements would have required RWE's affiliate which generated power in the eastern portion of the Ruhr area, VEW (Vereinigte Elektrizitätswerke Westfalens), to double its output. The operators 'recognized at once this altogether exceptional development as a last chance for the mines to get into the electricity business'.[36] RWKS soon founded a new mine-owned entity called Ruhr-Elektrizitäts-Gesellschaft to force the coal industry's entrance into the electrical power field. 'What we want,' RWKS director Kellermann wrote to managing director Koepchen,

> is for coal to participate in far greater measure [than now] and over a long period of time in providing general public consumption requirements for electricity so that it will be protected from economic crises and able to deal more effectively with the grade problem.[37]

Coal's terms were straightforward. It agreed to build plants of 150,000 kwh capacity to supply the Four Year Plan virtually at cost on the condition that it be allowed to supply 'general public needs' *(allgemeine Landesversorgung)* as well as be granted a fixed share in the increase of power consumption. The mines could meet such requirements without immediate new investment because surpluses of mine-generated current were already on hand. RWKS estimated that mine deliveries to RWE, in 1937 running at a rate of 70 million kwh per year, could be raised to 100 million kwh per year and that approximately equal amounts could be gained by linking additional existing mine power plants to the grid.[38]

In the first half of 1937 war raged between RWKS and RWE/VEW concerning the terms of the coal industry's entrance into the electrical utility business. Even in the face of severe temporary local shortages of current, the mines refused to increase deliveries to the RWE net until its demands were accepted.

The utilities countered with evasion, complicated arguments against the suitability of coal as a fuel for power generation, an offer of prices far below the break-even point for coal-generated current, and the insistence that as a 'garbage current' *(Abfallstrom)*, coal-mine electricity could only be considered for use during peak load periods.[39] But the issue was never seriously in doubt: the Four Year Plan had the need, the mines the means to supply it. At a 4 August meeting chaired by Pleiger VEW agreed that brown coal-generated current would no longer be distributed in the eastern half of the Ruhr area. This meant that VEW would draw from STEAG an amount equal to that generated in its own plants, agree to shut down one power plant, Kraftwerk Krukel, and desist from erecting any others. VEW also agreed 'to allow the mines to build [new] generating plants, locating them as dictated by coal needs'. STEAG was founded 10 September 1937 to supply current to the VEW net and construct the two new power plants for the plan.[40]

This success merely whetted the ambition of the industry. Its plans were laid out in a July 1938 position paper from Bezirksgruppe Ruhr. It argued that the new synthetics plants would increase electric power consumption requirements in the Ruhr 15 per cent annually over the coming four years, adding that shortages of manpower would further increase needs. It criticized RWE's continued failure to meet existing requirements, which had increased 64 per cent between 1929 and 1937, while generating capacity growth had followed far behind at about 15 per cent. Available RWE/VEW reserves had fallen 79 per cent, and it was impossible to construct new turbines fast enough to prevent a further widening of the gap between requirements and capacity. By contrast, the *Ruhrbergbau* forecast an increase in available mine-generated power in the VEW area from 29,400 in 1938 to 234,200 in 1940, and in the RWE area from 45,000 to 68,000 in 1940. Taking the offensive, the coal industry spokesmen protested against the 'monopolistic' RWE/VEW practice of maintaining a demarcation line between the regions served by the two allied utilities. This, they argued, aggravated shortages since it was impossible to transfer current along the 5kv connection line between the surplus Westphalian and the deficit Rhenish sides of the district. The coal industry then sought the legal rights both to send current along the existing line and construct a new one.[41] This would increase the coal-generated power available for distribution, threaten RWE/VEW's parent with a competitor, and force it to enter an agreement similar to the one with its affiliate. But reality soon intruded: by the beginning of 1939 shortages of even the low-value grades of coal normally used to fuel the power plants had become so severe that to meet its existing supply obligations to VEW, STEAG had to consume higher grades than stipulated in the contract price for current. The coal-owned producer thereupon attempted to raise basic sales prices to VEW. This marked the end of STEAG's offensive. Except for the construction of a line between Hüls to the GBAG synthetic petroleum plant, its plans had to be shelved until after 1945.

Table 13 Coal-generated electric power, 1928–1943

Year	*Current* (millions of kwh)		
	Total	*Solid fuel*	*Hard coal*
1925	27,870	21,301	10,540
1929	30,661	23,581	11,239
1930	29,104	22,073	10,517
1931	25,787	19,485	9,542
1932	23,460	17,978	8,478
1933	25,655	19,864	9,260
1934	30,662	23,598	10,890
1935	36,710	27,592	13,001
1936	42,487	31,910	15,013
1937	48,969	37,788	17,539
1938	55,333	43,370	20,466
1939	61,380	48,230	22,517
1940	62,964	50,632	23,866
1941	69,999	56,000	26,922
1942	71,500	—	—
1943	73,943	62,100	31,409

Source: Länderrat, *Statistisches Handbuch für Deutschland* (München, 1949), 335.

Still, gains had been made and a foothold secured for the future. As indicated by Table 13, there was a substantial increase in coal-generated electric power from 1936 to 1943.[42]

This was not accomplished without costs. The ambitions and miscalculations of STEAG on the one hand and the monopolistic attitudes of RWE/VEW on the other contributed to a situation in which Berlin's power in the electricity business grew at the expense of both parties. This was clearly recognized by director Dechamps of Concordia mine, a lawyer rather than engineer by training, who often represented the coal industry in negotiations with outside parties. When VEW attempted to pull out of the July 1937 contract, in retaliation for STEAG's threat to build an east–west connecting link, Dechamps appealed to the Ministry of Economics to block this under the terms of the energy law of 1935. At the same time he warned his mine colleagues that 'the power of Berlin grows whenever private interests call it in to settle disputes which formerly were handled privately by businessmen themselves'.[43] But neither Dechamps nor any other figure from either of the feuding industries could stem the breakdown that occurred when coal sought to renegotiate delivery prices for current. VEW's refusal to discuss the matter elicited an accusation from Dr Schilt, the managing director of STEAG, that VEW's chairman of the board, Dr Vosberg, 'behaved like a Jew'. VEW refused to discuss price without a prior retraction of the remark, Vosberg in the meantime filing a civil suit. The two related matters were dragged before the Plenipotentiary for Energy, the Office of Technology, the chief of Reichsgruppe Industrie, the Reich Office for Economic Morality, the Ninth Civil State Court in Essen, the Upper State Court in Hamm, and the Reich Court in Leipzig. They also resulted in a full-scale confrontation between Pleiger (coal) and Dr Todt (power) before being settled in June 1940 on the basis of a compromise satisfactory to neither party. This unedifying spectacle concluded Ruhr coal's forays into the energy field during the Hitler years.[44]

For the Ruhr collieries, the financial results of the six years between the seizure of power and the outbreak of the war were disappointing, particularly in light of developments in other sectors of production. The industry did not expand its operations on a substantial scale during the boom years from 1936 to 1939. IG Farben received no less than 72.7 per cent of total Four Year Plan investments. This left very little for the coal industry. It grew by only 11.5 per cent in the years between 1936 and 1939.[45] Nor did the traditional businesses of the Ruhr collieries become profitable. The mining of coal, still by far the most important field of activity, continued to be a losing proposition. In a detailed 1940 survey of twelve companies which mined 48 per cent of total output, the auditors of Bezirksgruppe Steinkohlenbergbau Ruhr concluded that the mines produced at a loss of 70 pfennige per ton. These estimates made assumptions about requirements for capital costs, risk and depreciation which could be challenged. But it seems unlikely that depreciation was used to conceal profits. The Schmalenbach Commission estimated necessary depreciation at RM1.74/t. As indicated by Table 14 this rate was never even approached during the 1930s. The cokeries operated consistently at losses: 1932 RM−19.6 million; 1933 RM−15.3 million; 1934, RM−16 million; 1935, RM−10.8 million; 1936, RM−16.8 million; 1937, RM−17.7 million; 1938, RM−17.8 million. The yield from total by-product sales (including coke, tar,

Table 14 Depreciation (RM/ton): selected mines, 1933, 1937

	1933	*1937*	+/−
Essener Steinkohlenwerke	1.29	1.22	−.07
Preussengrube AG	0.44	0.73	+.29
Bergbau Lothringen	1.10	1.53	+.43
Bergwerksges. Dahlbusch	1.03	1.58	+.55
Concordia Bergbau	1.22	1.24	+.02
Harpener Bergbau	1.22	1.46	+.24
Mühlheimer Bergwerksverein	1.02	0.90	−.12
Bergwerksgesellschaft Hibernia und Recklinghausen	1.95	1.05	−.90
Average	1.18	1.23	.05

Source: Arbeitswissenschaftliches Institut der DAF, 'Preise und Kosten im Kohlenbergbau', *Jahrbuch 1938* (Berlin, n.d.), 433.

Table 15 Tonnage yields, 1929–1938

	Tonnage value of mined coal	*Total yield per ton**
1929	15.56	17.66
1932	11.30	12.45
1933	10.65	12.03
1934	10.40	11.77
1935	10.37	11.86
1936	10.54	11.96
1937	11.10	12.51
1938	11.96	13.53

Source: Arbeitswissenschaftliches Institut der DAF, 'Preise und Kosten im Kohlenbergbau,' *Jahrbuch 1938* (Berlin, n.d.), 450.

Note: *Includes coking, the processing of tar, benzole, ammonia, gas and the manufacture of briquettes.

benzol, ammonia, gas and briquettes) raised tonnage values only slightly (Table 15).[46]

These mediocre results have several causes. According to one Bezirksgruppe report,

> The special situation of the mines is due to having fixed sales prices for its own products since 1936, at least those sold on domestic markets, while other industries have benefited from increases because of cost-plus contracting (*LSÖ-Berechnungen*). This has meant higher costs for everything the mines buy.[47]

Prices for the most important mine provisions rose between 1933 (= 100) and 1937: wood to 133, metal to 128, construction material to 113 and iron to 102. The pits also faced increased labour costs due to the fall in productivity. As indicated in Table 16 rises in labour cost ran consistently ahead of those in both syndicate prices and the wholesale price index. Neither was the export trade ever profitable: it could only be conducted thanks to subsidies.[48]

But these financial results must not be judged too harshly. A high rate of profitability might have attracted an undesirable amount of attention from Berlin. Despite their poor performance, the mines did earn enough to keep underground operations essentially intact and even modernize cokeries and processing installations. The underlying strengths of the industry were not substantially reduced. It remained the chief energy supplier to industry in Germany and western Europe. But success in this role also involved the regulation, organization and cartelization of international markets for both coal and steel products. This activity would be crucial to its survival through depression, war, and the period of defeat which followed it.

Table 16 Wage costs, syndicate prices and the wholesale price index, 1913–1938

	Wages	*Syndicate prices*	*Wholesale price index*
1913	100	100	100.0
1932	126	118	115.5
1933	127	117	115.3
1934	128	117	114.5
1935	128	117	114.4
1936	128	117	114.0
1937	129	117	113.4
1938	130	117	114.7

Source: Arbeitswissenschaftliches Institut der DAF, 'Preise und Kosten im Kohlenbergbau,' *Jahrbuch 1938* (Berlin, n.d.), 428.

Notes

1 Arthur Schweitzer, *Big Business in the Third Reich* (Bloomington, 1964), 420 f; Claude W. Guillebaud, *The Economic Recovery of Germany. From 1933 to the Incorporation of Austria in March 1938* (London, 1939), 158; Dietmar Petzina, 'Germany and the Great Depression', *Journal of Contemporary History*, 4 (4), October 1969, 154 f; David Schoenbaum, *Hitler's Social Revolution* (New York, 1966).
2 Gutehoffnungshütte 400101320/10 'Entwicklung der Grundumlage nach Beitritt der Aachener Zechen'.
3 Bergbau Verein, *Statistisches Heft. Produktions- und wirtschaftsstatistische Angaben aus der Montanindustrie* (Essen, 1939), 117.
4 Schweitzer, op. cit., 461.
5 Gérard Nauwelaerts, *Petroleum: Macht der Erde* (Tilburg, 1931), 96.
6 R.J. Overy, 'Cars, Roads, and Economic Recovery in Germany, 1933–1938', *Economic History Review*, no. 3, 1975 466 f.
7 Nauwalaerts, op. cit., 196.
8 Benzolverband, *Vierzig Jahre Benzolverband, 1898–1938.* (Bochum, 1939), 28.
9 Westfälisches Wirtschaftsarchiv, Dortmund (WWA) F26/325 'Entwurf eines Vertrages zwischen IHP und Ruhr-Chemie', 8 August 1938.
10 GHH 400101320/9 'Gründung der Ruhrbenzin AG', 25 September 1935.
11 Bergbau Museum (BM) 55/12400 No. 12 (GBAG) 'Die Stellung der Vereinigten Stahlwerke AG zu der Frage der Erzeugung von flüssigen Treibstoffen aus Kohle', August 1936.
12 WWA F35/3356 'Gesellschafter Versammlung', 12 January 1934.
13 ibid., 16 June 1933.
14 ibid., 12 January 1934.
15 US National Archives (USNA) RG151/1503 'Special Report No. 71. German Benzol Association absorbs Russian DEROP'.
16 WWA F35/3355 'Übernahme der DEROP AG', 7 December 1934.
17 WWA F35/3356 'Gesellschafts Versammlung', 6 June 1936.

18 WWA F35/3357 'Gesellschaftliches Bericht Nr. 3', 5 August 1935; Benzolverband, op. cit.
19 USNA RG 151/1407 'Special report. Opposition to German oil refinery expansion', 25 May 1933; Thérèse Rox, *Mineralölwirtschaft und Mineralölpolitik in Deutschland unter besonderer Berücksichtigung des Erdöls* (München, 1937), 66; 'Deutschlands Treibstoffwirtschaft: Autarkie oder Umstellung der Wirtschaft?', *Die deutsche Volkswirtschaft*, Nr. 26, 1939, 812–15.
20 Tom Bower, *Blind Eye to Murder. Britain, America, and the Purging of Nazi Germany – A Pledge Betrayed* (London, 1981), 309 f.; James S. Martin, *All Honorable Men* (Boston, 1950), 77–81; Joseph Borkin, *The Crime and Punishment of I.G. Farben*, New York 1978), 76 f.
21 OMGUS (Decartelization Branch) 'Report on cartels and combines VII', op. cit.; WWA F26/293 'Präsidialsitzungen der Ruhrchemie AG', 13 October 1937, 18 March 1938.
22 WWA F26/293 'Präsidialsitzung der Ruhrchemie AG', 20 July 1938.
23 Ministry of Economic Warfare, 'Fuel, power and public utility services', *Economic Survey of Germany*; BIOS, Final Report No. 513, Item No. 30 'Notes on the organization of the German petroleum industry during the war'.
24 Bundesarchiv (BA) Nachlass Spethmann, 59 f.; Burton H. Klein, *Germany's Economic Preparations for War* (Cambridge, 1959), 124.
25 Erich Weister, *Ausbau der deutschen Triebwirtschaft* (Dortmund, 1935), 5; GHH 400101303/0 'W. Roelen, Grossraumgaswirtschaft (1937)'; 400101320/136 'Besprechung mit Ruhrgas', (n.d.).
26 (BM) 55/12400 (GBAG) 'Die wirtschaftlichen und betrieblichen Grundlagen für den Ausbau der Gaswirtschaft', 11 July 1935.
27 GHH 400101320/106 'Elektro-Energie Tagung, 10–17 January 1935'; 400101320/136 'Aktennotiz (Herbig) über eine mit Baum gehabte Unterredung'; 400101322/6 Ruhrgas to Kellermann, 2 March 1937; 400101322/6 'Neuer Finanzbedarf der Ruhrgas', November 1937; US Strategic Bombing Survey (USSBS), Munitions Division, 'The coking industry of Germany (January 1947)'; 400101320/116 'Entgegnung auf dem von Seiten der kommunalen Gaswerk gebrachten Vorschlag, die Kokserzeugung für den Inlandsbedarf von den Zechen auf die Gaswerke zu ver legen'.
28 'Etude le groupe "Rheinisch-Westfälisches Elektrizitätswerke AG (RWE)" Essen' (Etude no. 7), GFCC, 1947.
29 Werner Kittler, *Der internationale elektrische Energieverkehr in Europa* (München/Berlin, 1933), 9.
30 USNA RG 260 OMGUS (Legal Division), German Industrial Complexes, Box 27-3/11 'The RWE complex'.
31 US Strategic Bombing Survey (USSBS) 'German electric utilities industry report', January 1943; Ministry of Economic Warfare, op. cit., 43 f; USSBS, *The effects of strategic bombings on the German war economy* (Washington, 1945), 114.
32 USSBS, 'German electric utilities industry report', 2.
33 GHH 400101320/136 'Bergbauliche Äusserungen zu der Tagung betr. Elektro-Energie', 16–17 January 1936.
34 W. Tengelmann, *Die Steinkohle in der Elektrowirtschaft* (Herne, 1936), 11.
35 WWA F26/269 Discussions RWE–Schlattmann, 3 January 1937; GHH 400101320/13 'Gremium', 11 February 1936; WWA F26/270 'Entwurf', 2 June 1937.
36 GHH 400101320/9 'Gremium', 23 August 1937.
37 WWA F 26/269 Kellermann to Koepchen, 15 January 1938.

38 GHH 400101320/9 'Mitgliederversammlung', 23 August 1937; BM F26/269 Holle to Kellermann, 15 October 1932.
39 WWA F26/269 'Verhandlungen mit der RWE', 14 January 1938; F 26/269 'Verhandlungen', 17 June 1937; F 26/269 'Entwurf', 5 July 1937.
40 WWA F26/274 'VEW-STEAG, 1. Zeuge Paul Pleiger', 15 November 1939.
41 WWA F26/271 'Zusammenfassung der wichtigsten Stromversorgung im Ruhrkohlengebe it und Einschaltung in die Landesversorgung', 'Bemerkung zur Stellungnahme der VEW vom 18. August 1938'.
42 WWA F26/269 'Besprechung mit Koepchen', 17 November 1938; F26/261 'Besprechung', 4 August 1938; BM 55/12400 Nr. 12 (GBAG) 'Betriebsbericht 1937/8'.
43 WWA F26/275 'Rechtstreit . . . VEW–STEAG', (n.d.).
44 WWA F26/271 'Klage der VEW gegen Steag', 4 July 1939; F26/276 'Streitsache VEW/Steag', 14 June 1940; F26/276 Pietzch to Todt, 4 June 1940; F26/279 'Urteil in Sachen der VEW Dortmund gegen Steag, Essen', 22 January 1940; F26/271 Müller to Kellermann, 13 March 1937; F26/276 'Angelegenheit Pleiger und Rheinländer', 26 June 1940.
45 Borkin, op. cit., 71.; Petzina, op. cit., 181.
46 WWA F26/365 'Sitzung des Beirats der Bezirksgruppe Steinkohlenbergbau Ruhr', 20 January 1941; Arbeitswissenschaftliches Institut der DAF, 'Preise und Kosten im Kohlenbergbau', *Jahrbuch 1938* (Berlin n.d.), 417–63.
47 WWA F26/365 'Sitzung des Beirats der Bezirksgruppe Steinkohlenbergbau Ruhr', 20 January 1941.
48 Arbeitswissenschaftliches Institut der DAF, op. cit., 449, 453.

5

TOWARDS THE UNIFICATION OF WEST EUROPEAN HEAVY INDUSTRY

The 1930s were a dismal decade in international commerce. In this sphere the Depression lasted until the war. The 1930s were years of 'beggar-thy-neighbour', competitive devaluations, export subsidies, high tariffs and import quotas; of defaults, the barter trade, officially sponsored dumping, and 'funny-money'. But while inviting censure and even ridicule, such methods were indispensable as props for recovery. All attempts to restore international commerce through liberalization, even after domestic economies had begun to revive, failed dismally. There are two main reasons for this. First, the free trade cause lacked effective leadership: Britain, the traditional champion, went protectionist in late 1931 and the USA, which, after 1945, would attempt to impose free trade on the world, immured itself during the 1930s behind insurmountable tariff barriers. The Depression also engendered universal disillusionment with traditional liberal economics and a search for alternative approaches.[1]

For Europe, only the Reich might have filled the moral and material vacuum left by discredited liberal economies. Germany was the third largest world trading nation and the leader in Europe. Its rate of growth over the decade was phenomenal. The Reich was also the home of 'organized capitalism', the only available non-socialist alternative to the theory and practices blamed for the Depression. Not surprisingly, Germany became an economic model for its neighbours. During the 1930s Belgium, the Netherlands, France and even Great Britain enacted laws promoting the organization of industry to encourage producers to work together co-operatively as in the Reich, instead of competing with each other. They did this to solve business problems but also to strengthen links between business and the state. These partnerships, it was hoped, would provide the bases for more prosperous and, above all, more stable societies.[2]

But there were limits to Germany's ability to serve as a motor of recovery.

One of them was its weak financial situation, the product of high foreign indebtedness. At no point during the decade was the Reich strong enough economically or politically to repudiate the payments obligations stemming ultimately from defeat in the First World War. Nor were the governments of the Reich's west European trading partners – who, along with the USA, were also its main creditors – prepared to forgive German debts. They gave priority to the interests of bondholders, even if this meant retarding the recovery of trade. They faced the following situation. To service creditors in western Europe the Reich needed an export surplus, provision for which was made in each of the bilateral commercial conventions concluded between Germany and its trading partners after 1931. These agreements normally required that the Reich's trading partner restrain exports to Germany in spite of high unemployment levels. If, however, German export surpluses increased above the agreed upon levels, the trading partners would restrict them. Such restraints effectively nipped in the bud the chances for a German-led trade recovery.

The Reich's own policies were an even more formidable restraint on its ability to serve as motor of recovery. After 1936 the regime was officially committed to *Autarkiepolitik* in order to reduce dependence on foreign supplies. The workings of this policy have to be properly understood. *Autarkiepolitik* was in some ways less a new programme than a propaganda response to hard currency shortages and it did not actually reduce German imports but increased them. *Autarkiepolitik* had a political rather than economic aim: to prepare Germany for war. This was Hitler's sole objective. There is nothing to suggest that he ever entertained the idea of promoting a German-led recovery in Europe, even as a component of an expansionist strategy. Such ideas did, however, occur to figures at the ministerial level, such as Schacht and his successor at both the Ministry of Economics and the Reichsbank, Funk, and also found some favour among German businessmen.

Many prominent figures in the western democracies, looking to Germany for solutions to the economic problems faced by their own nations, were encouraged to believe by the prominence of 'moderates' such as Schacht and Funk in the regime that one could 'do business with Hitler'. British and French attempts to effect an economic reconciliation with the Reich, which ran through the decade, reached a crescendo after the Munich Agreement of 15 September 1938. In the following months the diplomats of the Foreign Office and the Quai d'Orsay tried to work German industry into giant 'communities of interest' *(Interessengemeinschaften)* with their own producers in the hope that such associations could be made remunerative and powerful enough to rule out any economic rationale for starting a war. These appeasement efforts were in high gear when, as a result of the German annexation of rump Czechoslovakia on 15 March 1939, they were overwhelmed by the tide of events.[3]

It is easy to criticize these initiatives as having rested on a thorough misunderstanding of the national socialist political system. A genuine economic reconciliation with the Reich would surely also have required a much more radical break with the post-Versailles settlement than any contemplated between the wars in either Paris or London. But 'business appeasement' was not a chimera. It followed the precedent set in 1926, when the ISC agreement ushered in four years of *détente* and Franco-German trade expansion. During the 1930s as well, western Europe's coal and steel producers would work together to overcome the Depression. The governments of the area also joined in the effort. Yet this co-operation was exceptional. In the rest of industry it was more difficult to restore trade relationships broken off by the collapse of the early 1930s. The heavy industry arrangement indeed provided the only foundation upon which to build a policy of economic appeasement.

A steel agreement was once again the first step towards an overall heavy industry settlement. In June 1933, the ISC (which had collapsed earlier as a result of the sharp contraction in export markets during 1931 and 1932) was revived, this time in a stronger and wider form. By the end of 1938 the cartel controlled no less than 85 per cent of the world trade in steel.[4] Although run jointly by its 'founder members' (Germany, France and Belgium–Luxembourg), its membership also included the producers of central Europe. British and American producers affiliated with the ISC. The cartel successfully increased both product prices and western Europe's share of the world steel export trade during the 1930s. Its steadily mounting strength indicates conclusively that it worked to the satisfaction of its membership.[5]

A coal settlement in western Europe was much more difficult to arrive at. The main steel producers were all from the same area and competed on the same third country export markets whereas arrangements in coal involved different principles and problems. The important European exporters were Great Britain, Poland and the Netherlands as well as Germany, Belgium and France and the main issue in coal was the regulation of supply from the Ruhr. It therefore involved interests other than those of the producing industries.

To resolve them commercial diplomacy came into play. The delegates on the several bilateral commissions which regulated German trade with western Europe had to find compromise solutions to a number of quite different coal supply problems. The Reich's main concern was to secure foreign exchange, the Netherlands' to safeguard its huge carrying trade, Belgium's to protect its port of Antwerp as well as its own uncompetitive mines, and France's to secure reliable deliveries to the foundries of Lorraine. On the whole, the bargains struck by the bilateral commissions did protect each of these vital interests. Over time, western European confidence grew in the 'reasonableness' of the Reich in matters relating to the coal trade. It peaked with the Franco-German ore–coal treaty of 10 July 1937, which was intended to make the Reich virtually the sole supplier of coking coal to French industry. Expected to usher in a period of *détente* similar to that after 1926, this treaty was the immediate forerunner of the policy of economic appeasement devised by Georges Bonnet. The economic collaboration of the war was but an extension of this approach.

Progress was also made during the 1930s in increasing the strength of coal producer organizations. In 1936 a syndicate was set up for coke, in 1939 one for coal. The British took the initiative in both cases. The National Government wanted a kind of partnership with the Ruhr through which British mines could learn German methods of industrial organization. The British also wanted to increase coal exports. The Ruhr's sole pre-condition which met few objections, was acceptance of the *Gruppenschutz* principle banning competition in established markets.

Cartelization of coal did not go as far as in steel. The coke cartel operated informally, as an 'understanding', because of the weakness of the British syndicates, and the coal cartel was never really tested. These arrangements were none the less important. They encouraged the British to envisage the possibility of an alliance on a world scale with Reich business interests and they led RWKS to believe that even after German military victory there would be room for a Europe-wide producer syndicate run in partnership with Britain.

Several circumstances account for the remarkable strength of the ISC during the 1930s: organizational improvements; general receptivity to the adoption of German approaches; favourable operating results; and the statesmanship of the Ruhr steel industry, whose influence in its affairs was almost inevitably the largest of any national group. The organizational improvements were partly technical, partly political in character. Their successful operation required a new readiness to co-operate and compromise. Whereas the ISC agreement of 1926 had merely assigned export quotas to each member, relying on domestic markets to absorb surpluses, the new one required signatories to organize effective syndicates to regulate national production as well. Domestic and foreign sales could then be coupled to insure the 'founder-members', whose export-dependence varied greatly, roughly similar levels of operation. This was done by adopting a sliding scale which, as exports increased, favoured France and Germany (nations with large domestic economies) but, as they fell, assigned larger shares to Belgium and Luxembourg, whose steel industries depended overwhelmingly on foreign sales. The enforcement of this provision made it necessary for Belgium to organize a strong syndicate similar to the German Stahlwerksverband and the French Comptoir Sidérurgique. On 31 May 1933, 'COSIBEL' (Comptoir de Vente de la Sidérurgie Belge) was created. Its success would depend on the readiness of its members to adopt German methods.[6]

Britain had still further to go towards 'Germanizing' its business organizations. British steel producers had been disqualified for affiliation with the ISC in 1926 on the grounds that its high state of disorganization rendered it *kartellunfähig* – unsuited to cartel membership. But the Depression brought about a fundamental change in outlook at the top. At the Board of Trade, Foreign Office, Treasury and the Bank of England 'industrial self-government' became the word of the day; through protection and self-regulation, Britain would modernize its factories. Britain was to have a cheap pound (export advantage), empire preference (protectionism), administrative restraints on imports and industrial associations to work out plans for regulating production and sales. The National Government tried to promote their formation by encouraging British producers to enter international cartel agreements.[7]

In March 1935 the National Government provoked a trade crisis in order to effect British entry into the ISC by imposing a temporary 30 per cent increase in the steel tariff. The measure threatened the three-quarters of a million tons continental producers normally exported to Britain annually. But the crisis was soon resolved. The British were granted a satisfactory export quota in the ISC but more importantly continental producers were assigned annual import quotas ranging from 525,000–670,000 tons. Critical from the National Government's standpoint, the newly created British Iron and Steel Federation was assigned sole responsibility for distributing this imported material. The earnings of the wholesale monopoly, it was hoped, would protect the profit margins of the least efficient producer, at the same time leaving a surplus that could be ploughed back into renovation of plant.[8] These arrangements worked out satisfactorily from the British standpoint.

The ISC deserves at least some credit for restoring the health of the west European steel industry. World steel production, stimulated by the rearmament boom of the late 1930s, increased from 66.73 million long tons in 1933 to 133.28 million long tons in 1938, an historic high. Although the export trade never fully recovered by 1938, reaching only 80 per cent of 1929 levels, the four European founder-members enjoyed a disproportionate share in this increase. Their exports doubled from 3.5 million tons of steel in 1933 to 7.1 million tons in 1938. The ISC also deserves credit for the improvement in steel export prices after 1933. Thanks to them, the German and British industries enjoyed several years of continuous prosperity and those of France and Belgium–Luxembourg at least occasional ones.[9]

These accomplishments owed a good deal to the rough tactics of the cartel. Examples abound. In April 1938 the members agreed unanimously to take every necessary measure to force the Dutch re-rollers DEMKA and Van Lier – each then in the midst of ambitious expansion plans – out of business. The ISC also wrecked the plans of an English consortium led by Hermann Brassert (designer of the Reichswerke Hermann Göring) to construct a steel complex in Bulgaria. The ISC's continued refusal to deliver girders prevented the completion of a mill in Karakük, Turkey. In 1938–9, the cartel did 'everything in its power' to frustrate the erection of a rolling mill by A. Bergens Bliktrykkeri, Norway.[10]

But the success of the ISC owed a good deal to diplomacy as well. The leaders of Ruhr steel recognized in the late 1920s that over the long run it would be impossible to compete against the USA on a national basis. There was no choice but to join producers in neighbouring countries in creating common marketing organizations, co-ordinated production programmes, overall investment plans, and eventually similar business environments. There was also no alternative to Ruhr leadership or to a long-term learning process *(Lernprozesz)* with German steel as instructor and its partners as pupils. To secure its position the Ruhr was prepared to make short-term sacrifices. In 1926 the Ruhr ceded a generous share in the domestic steel market to the exporters of France and Luxembourg *(contingent franco-luxembourgeois)*. In 1933 the Ruhr made a series of concessions to the Société Générale (including the grant of a quota on the German market) in order to strengthen the hand of the giant holding company in disciplining the many independent-minded Belgian steel firms.[11]

The national socialist seizure of power strengthened the conviction of Ruhr steel in the correctness of its course. The chief German representative to the ISC, Ernst Poensgen of VS, won the assent of industry to the June 1933 agreement with the argument that the only alternative to membership was a high steel tariff which would put the industry at the regime's mercy.[12] The dispute over the Hermann Göring Werke provided an unpleasant reminder that the Ruhr's international ties were an important safeguard of its independence. The Ruhr therefore did not demand larger shares in the ISC as a consequence of German expansion after 1937. Instead, it dealt out export quota increases to the French, Belgians and Luxembourgers in the readjustments following *Anschluss*, the occupation of the Sudetenland, and the 'March on Prague'.[13] Thereby the Ruhr gained a measure of good will by 'relinquishing' quotas which, because of the rearmament boom then prevailing in the Reich, it could not in any case have filled. This was a sound and far-sighted move; German territorial expansion, it seemed, paid handsome dividends not only to the producers of the Reich but those allied with them.

The National Government's coal policy was similar to that for steel. Coal was much the more important field for British co-operation with Germany since the two were the leading European exporters. Creation of an Anglo-German coal axis was also favoured by the commercial convention in effect between the two nations. It gave British collieries a large quota on the German market for sales in the areas of Hamburg, Bremen, and their hinterlands, a possible equivalent to the *contingent franco-luxembourgeois* of the 1926 steel agreement. Between 1934 and 1937 British coal exports to the Reich increased from 2.5 million tons to 3.6 million tons in 1938[14] (Table 17).

Unfortunately, these results contrasted sharply to the overall trend in 1930s British coal exports (Table 18). To reverse their fall, the British initiated

Table 17 German coal imports from Great Britain, 1930–1939 (000 tons)

1930	4786	1935	2961
1931	3733	1936	3113
1932	2222	1937	3336
1933	2102	1938	3695
1934	2541	1939 (1st quarter)	1069

Source: Bergbau Verein, *Statistisches Heft. Produktions- und wirtschaftstatistische Angaben aus der Montanindustrie* (Essen, 1939), 64.

Table 18 Percentages of European coal exports, 1913–1938

	1913	*1929*	*1932*	*1936*	*1937*	*1938 (6 months)*
Great Britain	61.9	53.6	50.8	42.7	40.3	39.9
Germany	28.7	23.4	23.5	37.9	37.9	36.5
Poland	—	12.2	13.1	10.2	10.9	11.9
Belgium–Luxembourg	4.7	3.3	4.5	5.8	4.2	4.4
Holland	4.2	3.2	4.4	3.8	3.9	3.9
Czechoslovakia	—	1.6	1.8	1.6	2.2	2.4
France	1.1	2.7*	1.9	1.0	0.6	1.0
Total (millions of ton)	120.6	114.2	77.8	82.2	101.8	44.6

Source: Gutshoffnungshütte (GHH) 400101320/88 'G. Trinkhaus', 23 September 1938.
Note: * Including Saar.

discussions for a coal agreement with Germany which, they hoped, would have wider implications. In proposing that negotiations begin, the chief of economic policy at the Foreign Office, Sir Frederick Leith-Ross, dangled visions of Anglo-German joint ventures in third countries financed over the City before Dufour of the *Auswärtiges Amt*. Piggott, of the Board of Trade, went even further. He suggested that 'the real purpose of the coal discussions was to bring Germany within the framework of the Ottawa Convention'.[15] At Leith-Ross's suggestion, negotiations for a 'world coal convention' began in August 1935.[16]

The RWKS representative, Ernst Russel, none the less soon attached a number of conditions which defined the scope of the negotiations much more closely. Discussion was to be limited to coke but would include continental as well as maritime markets and involve the western European steel partners (France, Belgium and the Netherlands) as well as the Poles. Above all, the Germans insisted on imposing group responsibility *(Gruppenverantwortlichkeit)*, in other words, required that the British set up a much stronger marketing organization.[17]

This was no easy matter: 'Each of the British districts', as the *Deutsche Bergwerkszeitung* put it, 'produces different grades of coal under different geological conditions using different methods of production and sells in different markets with different price elasticities.'[18] There were also great variations in the age, financial strength, technological levels, size of plant and character of ownership of British coal-mines. Any effort to 'rationalize' production or marketing would be complicated and likely to encounter heated objections from many sides. Several official commissions had recently contended with these problems and, with the support of one faction in the coal industry, had begun to move in the direction insisted upon by RWKS. In 1927 the Central Collieries Commercial Association was formed as a first step towards the setting up of a national sales syndicate. Only the Midlands districts joined, however. Their so-called 'Five Counties Scheme' established quotas and provided for an export subsidy but could not control prices and by 1930 had ceased to function. The Coal Mines Act of 1930 renamed this body the Central Council and vested in it the authority to impose compulsory rationalization and marketing schemes. From the standpoint of such men as A.W. Archer (chairman of the Export Committee of the Midland District) and R.A. Burrows (chairman of Lancaster Associated Collieries) the prospect of a future agreement with RWKS provided a carrot with which to entice, or a stick with which to menace, independent-minded producers.[19] These methods had to be liberally applied, for as the governor of the Bank of England, Montague Norman, informed Paul Reusch privately, 'productive discussions can only resume after the English mining industry has organized itself'.[20]

The announcement in March 1936 of the Central Council's plans to set up district selling syndicates provided the necessary impetus to resume serious talks. By July agreement had been reached concerning markets, quotas and penalties. Political complications delayed the entry of other exporters into the convention. The necessary protocols were signed in December 1936.[21] They established export quotas of 5.6 million tons or 48.4 per cent of the total for Germany and 2.4 million tons or 20.88 per cent for Great Britain, the remainder to be divided later between the Netherlands, Belgium and Poland. The agreement also empowered a business committee to administer prices and arbitrate disputes. It was composed of three delegates from Germany, two from Britain, two from the Netherlands, one from Belgium and one from Poland.[22]

HM government looked upon this arrangement as an important move towards a closer relationship with the Reich. On 3 November 1936 Leith-Ross wrote to Poensgen with excessive optimism: 'opinion in all sections of industry is now . . . strongly in favour of international agreements, and the Government would be glad to see broader discussions with Germany brought to a satisfactory conclusion'. On 5 December Poensgen responded that RWKS was prepared to enter negotiations for a general coal understanding. This time, it was mutually agreed, the talks would be conducted on a strict bilateral basis; other national producer groups would be included only after prior Anglo-German agreement had been reached.[23]

Coal talks between industrialists of the two nations dragged on for two years before being forced to a conclusion by the National Government. On 7 November 1938 the British Ministry of Mines submitted to its negotiators a memorandum entitled 'The problem of the coal export trade'. It blamed the fall in exports on German subsidies and threatened to impose a tax on production and use it to subsidize British coal in order to offset the Reich export advantage. Such a move would have undone the recent coke agreement and wrecked the coal negotiations under way. Bargaining began at once over quotas, the Germans, demanding 1937 as a base, offered the British 48 per cent as opposed to 31 per cent for themselves. The British countered with 1929 as a base and quotas of 53.1 and 25.5 per cent. On 28 January 1939 compromise was reached on a ratio of 50:30. With the inclusion of coke, briquettes and bunker coal, this worked out at 32.08 and 46.27 per cent respectively. Poland, Belgium, the Netherlands and France divided up the remaining 22 per cent of the total quota. The Foreign Office hailed the Anglo-German agreement as the predecessor to an eventual international sales organization for coal that would assure 'just allocation to all European exporters'. The British, in other words, looked forward to a mine version of the ISC turning on an Anglo-German axis.[24]

In the coal agreement the Ruhr adopted strategies long familiar in steel. While RWKS ceded the British a quota that would have enabled their ailing industry to increase output should demand rise, it received pledges that in return British producers would organize themselves in the manner of German syndicates.

The Ruhr's concessions were a shrewd and realistic response to conditions on coal export markets in 1937 and 1938. The sharp increases in French and British military spending announced in March 1937, the Italian Five Year Rearmament Plan and the widespread fears that labour unrest in Belgium and France would hobble production there, brought about 'frenzied stockpiling' in the spring, which created an upsurge in demand lasting for over a year. Already labouring under the strains of the domestic armaments boom, RWKS was obliged to slow down foreign shipments in the summer of 1937. On 11 October it suspended certain deliveries to Scandinavia until 1938 and suffered an 'embarrassing' failure to meet contract commitments in Belgium and France. On 11 March 1938 RWKS foreign trade expert Ernst Russel admitted to 'a distressing inability to supply our large Belgian quota'.[25] In spring 1938 the syndicate fell increasingly behind in its deliveries to Italy. To cope with the shortages, RWKS tried to ally with syndicates through which it could 'displace' orders. The Belgian and Dutch sales organizations were thus 'invited' to discharge certain RWKS contracts in Luxembourg and France. In Baltic and Mediterranean markets, where Britain had been the main competitor, mechanisms for displacement did not exist. It made good sense for RWKS to give the British strong incentives to organize so that it could delegate some of this business to them.[26]

The British response to the coal agreement was desperately over-enthusiastic. The appeasers in the cabinet viewed it as a springboard to an inter-industry pact between Britain and the Reich which would lead the way to a co-operative exploitation of world markets and European *détente*. The president of the Board of Trade, Oliver Stanley, said at a gala dinner arranged to commemorate their conclusion,

> The coal trade talks have been valuable precursors to the wider talks now [scheduled] to start. From them we can draw many lessons and much encouragement. . . . It might be possible to look back upon their conclusion as a turning point, not only in the methods of Anglo-German industrial relations, but also in the history and hopes of the world.[27]

Accordingly, the Foreign Office proceeded with plans for a mammoth meeting between the two 'peak organizations' for business, the Federation of British Industry and Reichsgruppe Industrie. On 16 March 1939 the famous Düsseldorf Agreement was concluded between the two organizations. A joint public statement noted concurrence on twelve points. Some of them were banal: existing co-operative efforts should be built on, exports raise living standards and be profitable, and destructive competition be banned. But the agreement envisaged much more, a world economic partnership between the business communities of the two countries. It was agreed that British producers should organize themselves as desired by the National Government and also, as with coal, that outsiders should be invited to enter Anglo-German conventions only after the two parties had worked out matters between themselves. Individual branches of industry in the two countries were to be encouraged to begin negotiations at once to form bilateral cartels. Finally, the two 'peak' industry associations pledged themselves to invoke the powers of their governments when necessary to force third country industries into compliance with the terms of the bilateral arrangement.[28] How Britain's obligations under this understanding were to be reconciled with those to her allies is a question best left open.

With the conclusion of the Düsseldorf Agreement British economic appeasement overreached itself: the treaty was a dead letter even before formally signed. The strength of the reaction in the British public to the German 'March on Prague' of 15 March was too strong to permit the government to make economic bargains with Hitler. Official encouragement of business-to-business contacts ceased abruptly. The British delegates to Düsseldorf returned home to discover that the policy they had pursued with such apparent success had been dropped.[29]

For economic reasons as well, the Düsseldorf Agreement had little chance to succeed. The ties that developed between German and British heavy industry during the 1930s were unique and due in part due to the workings of the Anglo-German commercial convention of 1 November 1934. Because of the large amount of British-held German debt and the political power of the City, an 'iron ratio' of 100:55 governed German and British exports. This was the most favourable of all commercial agreements enjoyed by the Reich from the standpoint of trade balance (Table 19). The understanding incorporated into

Table 19 Anglo-German trade, 1929–1938 (RM million)

	Exports to Germany	*Imports from Germany*
1929	865	1305
1930	639	1218
1931	453	1113
1932	258	446
1933	238	405
1934	205	382
1935	256	374
1936	263	405
1937	308	432
1938	283	352

Source: Allen A. Bonnell, *German Control over International Economic Relations, 1930–1940* (Urbana, Ill., 1960), 128, 136.

this convention, that coal would be the main export product to Germany crowded other British goods out of that market. The share of the combustible in total UK exports to Germany therefore increased from 45.7 per cent to 60.3 per cent from 1934 to 1937. British *manufacturers*, in contrast, had virtually no stake to protect on the German market. Beyond this, they enjoyed protection in the Commonwealth and had no reason to discuss opening this vast market to German competitors. In response to an FBI circular, representatives of the most important branches of British industry such as engineering and textiles expressed disinterest in negotiating bilateral agreements. In fact the main British organizer of the Düsseldorf meeting, Parliamentary Under Secretary at the Board of Trade Hudson, had great difficulty drumming up a delegation of sufficient size and prestige to attend it.[30]

But the coal talks had an important sequel. Although with the outbreak of war, direct contacts ended between British and German mines operators, RWKS's conviction that it had reached an understanding with its most important competitor lived on, indeed led the syndicate to adopt as the primary aim of its 'foreign policy' the creation of a common market for coal. This objective is stated clearly, and Britain's relationship to it underscored, in one of the

RWKS 'war aims' studies of summer 1940. Compiled at the request of Minister of Economics Funk, these reports were supposed to spell out the demands of each industrial sector in the light of recent military victories and provide suggestions for the European peace treaty believed to be close at hand.

The RWKS paper posited that European coal should turn on a future Anglo-German axis: 'The [recent] agreement,' it emphasized, 'should provide the basis for a European arrangement to regulate the export trade of Germany, England, Holland, Belgium, France, Poland, and Czechoslovakia in coal, briquettes, and coke.' The report adds that this understanding need not be anchored in an international coal statute incorporated in a peace treaty if the British government could be persuaded to strengthen the Coal Mines Act. Once the organization of Britain's mines had been improved, the report continued, producers in the Netherlands, Belgium and France could easily be brought in line. It would then be possible to form a European coal syndicate to regulate domestic as well as foreign sales. The Ruhr would run it as a 'natural consequence' of both geology and victory, but no new coal districts need be annexed to the Reich. The British were expected to aid the Ruhr in directing the future syndicate, the less important members to conduct domestic sales autonomously. Thanks to the strong 'inner control' to be exercised by the component national producer organizations, it would be possible to avoid both the Scylla of 'destructive competition' and the Charybdis of tariffs and quotas. The report concludes that common pricing and sales policies would be the rule.[31] Such expectations guided RWKS policy towards occupied Europe even in the absence of Britain. The mines of Belgium, the Netherlands and France were the main beneficiaries of the Anglo-German coal and coke arrangements of the 1930s.

In France there had existed a strong lobby for closer trade relationships with the Reich since 1926. In the 1930s those businessmen and technocrats joined it, who, as in the UK, found German economic methods praiseworthy. The fortress of the pro-German faction was the Comité des Forges, the steel directorate controlled by the Laurent and de Wendel families of Lorraine. Prominent figures from other branches of industry (Henri de Peyremhoff of the comité des houillières and René Duchemin of Ets. Kuhlmann), the administration (the 'X'-graduates Coutrot and Branger), and the world of opinion-making (the publicist Vladimir d'Ormesson, the historian Lucien Romer and the sociologist André Siegfried) were associated with it. This party could count on favourable treatment from an influential section of the press. Big industrialists owned four Paris dailies outright, *Le Temps*, *Le Journal des Débâts*, *L'Information* and *La Journée Industrielle*. They paid subsidies to ten others. From September 1931 to October 1938 Ambassador André François-Poncet, himself a well-connected foundryman, represented the interests of this group in Berlin. His maiden speech was an impassioned plea for Franco-

German industrial cooperation. It sounded the *Leitmotiv* of 'Hitler's favourite ambassador'.[32]

To prevail this group had somehow to change official policy towards Germany from military containment to economic collaboration. This shift began in spring 1937 and culminated between mid-summer 1938 and March 1939 under Foreign Minister Georges Bonnet. In the months between Munich and the 'March on Prague', 'economic appeasement' was *the* French strategy for coping with the German problem. To succeed, this policy had to overcome not only public enmity towards most things German but a complex of severe economic problems growing out of the Depression. For why speak of political reconciliation if collaboration had not, or demonstrably could not, work even in the more limited realm of economic affairs?

Between 1929 and 1936 French exports to Germany fell to one-fifth and German exports to France to one-seventh of their 1929 levels. Neither government could take the essential step to restore this trade, a moratorium on all German debt payments to France. Instead, as Pierre Mendès-France put it, 'L'équilibre par le bas' was the rule in Franco-German commerce. In a process of uninterrupted ratcheting downwards, protectionism led to payments imbalance, and this to export restraint. By the end of 1936 coal was virtually the only German good being exported to France, and French exports to Germany had nearly ground to a halt. But thanks to this braking the Reich could work up a sufficient franc balance to meet its commitments to Dawes and Young Plan bondholders. The stage was set for a new beginning.[33]

It coincided with the French decision to re-equip the armed forces. This would inevitably bring sharp increases in the coke consumption requirements of the Lorraine steel industry which only the Ruhr was in a position to supply. Britain had no inclination to compete for this business. Indeed, France's most important military ally was punctiliously loyal to the negotiations under way with Germany for the coke and coal conventions and refused to provide any information concerning their progress. In France, Britain's reliability as a coal supplier was understandably suspect.[34]

Because of the payments situation, France had no choice but to step up ore exports to offset the increase of German coke imports. This encountered two problems. One was public opposition to shipping a strategic good to a presumptive enemy, the other a Germany far less dependent on ore than France on coking coal. To solve them the government had to broaden the terms of the trade agreement with the Reich to include other products (including those from the French Colonies) then 'sell' the package to the public as a first step in the process of reconciliation with the Reich.

Unfortunately, *minette* was no longer able to compete in the Ruhr with the higher grade of ores imported from Sweden. By the mid-1930s three-quarters of German foundry consumption (by iron content) came from there, and this would increase because of the greater suitability of these ores for armaments grades steels. On 2 July 1935 Schacht told the Fuhrer in a private conversation that 'eventually we can replace Lorraine ore with Swedish. Under the circumstances there is no reason to accommodate France and we should not send an economic delegation to Paris'.[35] To 'sweeten' the deal, French trade negotiators had to agree to export colonial goods such as the hardwoods used in airframe manufacture.

As for public opposition, the German reoccupation of the Rheinland on 7 March 1936 touched off a spontaneous boycott of German goods.[36] On 12 August 1936 Prime Minister Léon Blum, succumbing to public pressure, banned *minette* exports to the Reich. When the subject of increasing coke–ore commerce came before the inter-governmental trade commissions on 15 September, Minister of Commerce Bastid informed Schacht 'that the French public would hardly understand it if France began to deliver Germany ore which would be used wholly for armaments purposes'.[37]

Still, a counter-offensive began almost at once. It involved a co-ordinated official protest of mine employers and the union representing some 30,000 employees followed by a formal request to the Germans to increase purchases of French ore which Ambassador François-Poncet delivered in person to the Wilhelmstrasse. Blum eventually accepted the need for this. On 1 November he declared a readiness to supply ore if Germany would renounce its 'aggressive intentions towards other nations' and deliver coke in return. Blum reportedly also said that such a transaction could take place

> without harming our foundries and benefiting of those of the Ruhr . . . since a precondition of [a coal–ore trade agreement] was the maintenance of the International Steel Cartel, the prototype of international economic organization, and one appropriate to all branches of industry in that it assures equilibrium, order, economic prosperity, and, consequently political peace.[38]

Soon, a delegation headed by the Mayor of Nancy arrived in Berlin to meet with Schacht and Göring. According to the reporter of *Paris-Midi*,

> the interview with Göring was of greatest significance. He gave us the impression that Germany is predisposed to collaborate economically with France in the closest possible way and proposed to his visitors a return pure and simple to normal commercial exchanges.[39]

A coal/ore agreement, the basis for a new commercial convention, was concluded 10 July 1937 and signed with great fanfare by Minister of Economics Schacht at the opening of the Paris Exposition. The deal called for an increase in German imports of French iron ore from a monthly average of 490,000 tons to 600,000 tons, it being understood that these amounts could be raised once 'labour difficulties' had been overcome. German coke deliveries to France were to be raised even more substantially, from 116,000 to 275,000 monthly tons, it being agreed that 'The French will fill all of their coke import requirements from the Reich.'[40]

The deal was heralded by many in both government and industry as the dawn of a new era in Franco-German relations. Minister of Commerce Chapsal, the leader of the French negotiating team, declared that

> [it] went far beyond usual trade agreements and would result in the settlement of many outstanding questions . . . The French government and its citizens celebrate the conclusion of the treaty as an opportunity to inaugurate a period of trust and closer relations. The agreement provides an opportunity to create a smoother, more amicable, and calm atmosphere.[41]

Foreign Minister Delbos, echoing these sentiments, was more specific in remarks to the German commercial delegate Hemmen. He viewed the deal as a point of departure for 'joint co-operation and the conclusion of further agreements, above all for *collaboration plus large* on the international level', or what he termed 'a "pact of mutual understanding" '.[42] The Deputy Paul Elbel took a still broader view. 'Once satisfied,' he declaimed in the Chamber,

> Germany will cease to appear 'a nation of dispossessed' and, with prosperity, shall return a love of calm and a will to collaborate. Thus the question of raw material, its distribution and transformation moves out of the limited technical realm to determine, in truth, the question of war or peace.[43]

According to the political analysts of the German Embassy, such sentiments were widely shared. With one exception, press reaction to the treaty was very favourable and it 'received a highly sympathetic welcome in industry as a whole'.[44]

But French hopes for the coke-ore agreement and the July 1937 trade treaty were not to be realized. Both of them were political as well as economic failures. Total exports to the Reich, which rose to RM154 million in 1937, actually fell to RM141 million the following year. The results of the coke–ore exchange were still more meagre. German deliveries of coke, targeted at 275,000 tons per month, fell to 113,000 tons per month in the first four months of 1938 and to 90,000 tons per month a year later. This reduction can be traced directly to continued labour unrest, economic slowdowns, and the idling of blast furnace capacity in France. The maintenance of continued demand in the Reich during the same months created severe strains on the agreement. To supply what the Germans demanded would have opened the French government to accusations of fuelling the German war economy and eliminated the franc balance needed to service bondholders.[45]

The July 1937 agreement benefited the Reich rather than France. It enabled the steel industry to fulfil its *minette* requirements because the French government was unwilling to reduce exports for fear of increasing unemployment. It preferred to swallow hard when accused of aiding the German rearmament effort. Though unable to admit so publicly the French also made uncompensated franc payments on a temporary basis from the 'Office franco-allemand des paiements commerciaux' lest Germany's Dawes and Young Plan creditors not be serviced punctually. At the same time, the government had to restrain the exportation of manufactured goods, opening itself to still more criticism. Not surprisingly, the French renewed the treaty of 1937 with a pronounced lack of enthusiasm: 'In spite of our concessions,' a trade delegate reported, 'we are satisfied with the conclusion of the new agreement. In economic matters even the most mediocre arrangement is better than quarrelling.'[46]

But the lack of progress concerning trade did not end the quest for closer relations with Germany and German business. It was pursued even more actively after the Munich conference than before. Karl Lindemann, a director of North-German Lloyd, was pleasantly surprised to discover during an October meeting of the International Chamber of Commerce in Paris that 'the adverse effects of the Czech crisis were not evident. . . . I was received not with the usual cool French politeness but with open respect'.[47] He left with an 'overall impression' that 'French colleagues without exception feel both a pressing need and the strongest desire for a Franco-German understanding'. An editorial in *Le Temps* was more explicit about the matter. It held that,

> The time has indeed come to give real substance to the Munich accords and to the . . . declarations that accompanied it. The development of commercial relations between Germany and the two western Great Powers as well as co-operation of the sort to enable the Reich to return progressively to normal economic practices will mark the beginning of . . . a reduction in armaments. This should provide an occasion for reflection: no purely political solution will bring about the reduction of arms that is the essential step to the maintenance of peace. This will only occur by way of economic collaboration *(la collaboration économique)*.[48]

But how was this to be achieved given the tenuousness of commercial relations between the two countries? This job fell to a protégé of Foreign Minister Bonnet, Count de la Baume. He headed the Commercial Relations Section at the Quai d'Orsay. The numerous initiatives of autumn and winter 1938–9 that originated in his office can be grouped under three different headings. First, there were those for *an increase in trade*. In exchange for a German readiness to accept increased agricultural exports, France promised to import 50 million francs-worth of synthetic nitrogen and to provide German firms with public contracts (machine tools, diverse machinery, scientific instruments, etc.) in the value of 95 million francs. De la Baume's proposals also include *joint ventures*. He suggested 'in a general way' setting them up for harbour improvements in South America, bridge and road building in the Balkans, and railway construction in Africa and proposed the creation of a

Franco-German consortium to handle reconstruction projects in Spain, where the civil war was then drawing to a close. A note of 11 March 1939 contains specific proposals for mutual undertakings in the French empire. These were the opening of a new mine in Conakry, the setting up of a large-scale paper mill, and the expansion of the Moroccan manganese mines. Further, de la Baume worked out a barter contract between the Société française de Chatillon-Commentry and VS, which required the German firm to deliver 10 million francs-worth of machine tools over a two and a half year period in return for half the ore output from the French firm's mine at Halouze.[49]

But a proposal of a third type was the most critical. It was for a business pact with Reichsgruppe Industrie anchored in industry-to-industry cartels. In late January the Confédération Générale du Patronat Français and the Chambre de Commerce de Paris were instructed to propose ideas 'to adapt existing cartels to present circumstances and extend them to new categories of production'. Although a first step, this would, according to de la Baume, 'serve as an example for the conclusion of additional business'.[50] He added that direct discussions with the government and industry in the Reich, expected to begin soon, would 'establish the basis for collaboration on a vast scale [and] promote the economic interests of both countries'. On 22 February 1939 a 'Centre Economique Franco-Allemand' was founded by leading parliamentarians and business leaders to 'promote Franco-German economic relations by all practical means'.[51]

In the short run, virtually nothing came of these initiatives for two very good reasons. The first, as noted in a 2 March 1939 letter from the business manager of Reichsgruppe Industrie, was that

> after circularizing all branches of industry, I must report that we received no serious expressions of interest in entering negotiations with the French. Where on the German side market agreements are felt to be necessary they already exist and are working well. As for the rest, we will have little to contribute to the discussions with French industry.[52]

The results of the survey, grouped under four headings, showed specifically that: 'co-operation' existed in steel and such specialty products as sheet, wire, needles and enamel ware but outside this area only in buttons; 'co-operation was desired' by the electrical industry (sales on third markets), machine tools (German firms as subcontractors on turnkey projects), railway equipment (French public works contracts), sanitary ceramics, hand tools and certain specialty castings; 'special wishes' of slight importance were expressed for deals in the woodworking, fur and tin-can industries; finally, 'no interest in co-operation' was expressed by several important groups – clothing, textiles, iron and steel tools, paper, iron ware and steel home products – all of which had had 'bad experiences' with earlier arrangements. Industries not included apparently did not think it worthwhile to respond.[53]

The second reason for the failure of 'economic appeasement' is still more obvious. The public reaction in France to the 'March on Prague' was if anything even stronger than in Britain. As one German importer in Paris reported,

> The March events, which led to the disappearance of the Czech state, took the French completely by surprise. The reaction, while slower in coming than to earlier crises, promises to be more long-lasting. The catchword 'boycott' does not begin to express its consequences.[54]

He cited case after case in which customers in trade and industry had cancelled German orders, concluding that 'the Spring Season is a total loss and, since nothing happens here in July and August, we will have to wait for autumn before things get going again'.[55]

The lack of German business interest in entering closer relationships with French producers and the continued wariness, even hostility, of the French public to 'economic appeasement' have a common origin in the almost total failure to stimulate a trade revival outside of the coal–ore sphere. In 1929 Franco-German trade totalled RM1575 million, in 1938 RM386 million, a fall of over three-quarters in total volume (Table 20). The bilateral export of

Table 20 Franco-German trade, 1929–1938 (RM million)

	Exports to France	*Exports to Germany*
1929	934	641
1930	1148	518
1931	834	341
1932	482	189
1933	395	184
1934	281	176
1935	252	154
1936	254	98
1937	313	154
1938	215	141

Source: Allen A. Bonnell, *German Control over International Economic Relations, 1930–1940* (Urbana, Ill., 1960), 128, 130.

manufactures fell by nine-tenths over the same period. Thus the attempt at political reconciliation with Germany by means of 'economic collaboration' never got beyond the stage of projects and plans.

Heavy industry was the exception. While it is true that the ore-coke agreement did not live up to its expectations, German exports of the combustible remained at a high level during the 1930s at annual averages of about 5 million tons, only slightly less than 5.3 of the record year, 1929 (Table 21).

Table 21 German coal exports to France, 1930–1938 (000 tons)

1930	*1931*	*1932*	*1933*	*1934*	*1935*	*1936*	*1937*	*1938*
5359	5141	4147	3782	3557	4963	5941	8045	5409

Source: Bergbau Verein, *Statistisches Heft. Produktions- und wirtschaftsstatistische Angaben aus der Montanindustrie* (Essen, 1939), 64.

In addition, the Ruhr substantially increased its share of the French coal import market during the decade. As for the traffic in the other direction, the slight increase in French exports after the catastrophic year of 1936 (RM98 million to the RM131 million of 1938) was due almost entirely to the increase in ore shipments. During the same years the ISC continued to operate in an 'exemplary' manner. Together, the supply relationship in coal and the producer relationship in steel kept alive hopes that 'economic appeasement' could work.

But in early summer 1939 when the trade treaty came up for renewal even these hopes faded. The German delegation restricted coal deliveries to 141,000 tons per month instead of the 275,000 agreed upon earlier, which the French now 'desperately' needed for their foundries. The RWKS representative at the meeting in London of the Coke Cartel confirmed this refusal. To aggravate matters, RWKS insisted in a letter to Comité des Forges that henceforth deliveries to France would be taken out of the 'self-consumption' quota of the de Wendel-owned mines in the Ruhr. In retaliation, the French government dispatched the de Monzie coal mission to the USA.[56] On the very eve of the war the structures built up painstakingly during the decade threatened to come down with shocking suddenness. But, according to the German delegation leader Hemmen, 'Both parties without qualification were unanimous that in spite of the catastrophic fall in trade, which has both economic and political causes, the contractual basis of the commercial relationship between the two nations must remain in place'.[57]

While war and occupation would indeed change the 'contractual' basis of the Franco-German relationship, in significant ways it was an extension of the developments of the 1930s. Between 1936 and 1939 'economic collaboration' was fully developed as a rationale for a policy of reconciliation with the Reich. It would be revived in a new setting after the events of May and June 1940. So too would be the tradition that made it plausible, heavy industry co-operation in western Europe as led by the Ruhr. The 'war aims' study concerning Britain's place after German victory reveals that the Ruhr viewed the problems arising from the war as continuations of those preceding it. Thanks to this conservative approach progress made towards the unification of west European heavy industry would continue during the years from 1940 to 1945.

Notes

1 H.W. Arndt, *The Economic Lessons of the 1930s* (London, 1963), 225 f.; Charles Kindleberger, *The World in Depression* (Berkeley, 1973), 199 f.; Joseph S. Davis, *The World Between the Wars 1919–39: An Economist's View* (Baltimore, 1975), 302 f.

2 John Gillingham, 'Business diplomacy in the 1930s: west European heavy industry cartels, Hitler's foreign policy and economic appeasement' (unpublished ms); Herbert von Beckerath, *Grossindustrie und Gesellschaftsordnung* (Tübingen, 1954).

3 Ervin Hexner, *The International Steel Cartel* (Chapel Hill, 1943), ch. 1.

4 Ministry of Economic Warfare, 'Foreign Trade', *Economic Survey of Germany* (ESG) (London 1944), 16.

5 US Federal Trade Commission, 'Report (of the FTC) on international steel cartels' (Washington, 1948).

6 Hexner, op. cit., 110 f.

7 Sidney Pollard, *The Development of the British Economy* (London, 1962), 166 f.; A.J. Youngson, *The British Economy, 1920–1957* (Cambridge, Mass., 1960), 9.9 f.; Bernd-Jürgen Wendt, *Economic Appeasement: Handel und Finanz in der britischen Deutschlandpolitik* (Düsseldorf, 1971).

8 Bundesarchiv (BA) R13I/272/259 'Der europäische Eisenpakt', *Die deutsche Volkswirtschaft*, 2 December 1935; Gutehoffnungschütte (GHH) 4000090/11 'Kürzbericht über die Sitzung der Verbändekommission', 10 March 1936.

9 Hexner, op. cit., 325; 'Steel shares in war-time', *The Economist*, 4 November 1939, 173 f.

10 BA R13I/270 'Sitzung des Joint Coordinating Committee', 18 April 1939; R 13I/270 'Sitzung des Joint Coordinating Committee', 8 May 1939; Hearings, Sub-Committee on Study of Monopoly Power, House of Representatives, 81st Congress, 2nd Session, Serial No 14, Part 4-B 'Steel exhibits, Bulgaria 156–61; Turkey 162–5, Norway 177–182.'

11 Hexner, op. cit., 120 f.; US National Archives (USNA) T501/102/1096 'Gesamtbericht über die Tätigkeit auf den wichtigsten Industriegebieten', 31-8-1940; GHH 400101320/16 'Gremium', October 1937.

12 GHH 40000090/11 'Reusch. Internationale Eisenverhandlungen', 6 March 1933.

13 BA R/13I/273 'Sitzung des Verwaltungsausschusses der IRG', 15 June 1938; R13I/270 'Sitzung des Joint Coordinating Committee', 15 February 1939.

14 Wendt, op. cit., 301.

15 Politisches Archiv des Auswärtiges Amtes (AA) Sonderreferat W. Kohle Bd. 10, 'Anfzeichungen Dufour', 17 March.

16 GHH 400101320/88 'Grossbritannien und das europäische Kohlenproblem', *Deutsche Bergbau Zeitung*, 4 August 1935.

17 GHH 400101320/88 Russel note, 3 November 1935.

18 GHH 400101320/88 'Der Bergbauingeneur hat seine Pflicht getan!', *Deutsche Berwerkszeitung*, 31 September 1935.

19 GHH 400101320/88 'Vor Neuordnung des britischen Kohlenbergbaus', 31 December 1935.

20 GHH 400101320/13 'Gremium', 12 August 1935; 400101320/13 'Gremium', 11 December 1935.

21 GHH 400101320/14 'Gremium', 10 March 1936; BA R7/622 'Internationale Koks-Konvention'; USNA T120/1988/E65521 'Notiz Aelardt', 3 October 1936.

22 GHH 400101320/88 'Gremium', 10 August 1938.

23 GHH 400101320/88 Leith-Ross to Poensgen, 3 November 1936; Poensgen to Leith-Ross, 5 December 1936.
24 GHH 400101320/15 'Gremium', 12 March 1937; DGFP (Series D) No. 263 German Economic Mission to the Foreign Ministry, 7 November 1938; Wendt, op. cit., 545; DGFP (Series D) No. 303 Ambassador in Great Britain to Foreign Ministry, 28 January 1939; GHH 400101320/88 'Internationale Kohlenverständnis'.
25 GHH 400101320/15 'Gremium', 12 March 1937; BA R7/621 RWKS to RWM, 25 March 1937; GHH 400101320/16, 'Gremium', 11 October 1937; 400101320/16 'Gremium', 11 March 1938.
26 GHH 400101320/88 'Gremium', 10 August 1938; 400101320/17 'Gremium', 10 March 1939.
27 'Anglo-German Trade', *The Times*, 22 February 1939.
28 Wendt, op. cit., 574.
29 DGFP (Series D.v.V) No. 11. 'Memorandum by the Director of the Economic Policy Department', 16 March 1939.
30 Wendt, op. cit., 63, 267; DGFP (Series D) No. 134 'Memorandum', 2 February 1939.
31 BA R7/592 'RWKS. Kohlenwirtschaft und deutsch–englische Kohlenverständigung', 3 September 1960.
32 Anthony Adamthwaite, *France and the Coming of the Second World War* (London, 1980), 281 f.; Franklin L. Ford, 'Three observers in Berlin: Rumbold, Dodd, and François-Poncet', in Gordon Craig and Felix Gilbert (eds) *The Diplomats, 1919–1939*: vol. II *The Thirties* (Princeton, 1953), 437–76.; Alfred Sauvy, *Histoire économique de France entre les deux guerres*: vol. II *Les idées économiques* (Paris, 1965), 248 f.; US National Archives RG9122/29 Norman Bursler, 'Aspects of German Economic Warfare as a Prelude to Aggression' (US Department of Justice, 30 October 1944).
33 AA Botschaft Paris 890b/Bd.13 'Les rélations commerciales franco-allemandes', *Petit Matin*, 22 February 1935; Anita Hirsch, 'La politique commerciale', in Sauvy, op. cit., IV, 1–48; Allen Bonnell, *German Control over International Economic Relations* (Urbana, 1940), 136; Ministry of Economic Warfare, op. cit., 23.
34 BA R7/621 'Aktenvermerk Ritter', 5 June 1937.
35 USNA T120/2610/E410115 'Atkenvermerk Ritter', 2 July 1935.
36 AA Paris Botschaft 892[a]/Bd. 19 'Vermerk Heyden', 18 March 1936; USNA T120/1638/E021592 'Frankreich und Sanktionen'.
37 AA Botschaft Paris 892[a]/Bd. 19 'Besprechung Dr. Schacht mit Bastid'.
38 AA Paris Botschaft 892[a]/2 Bd. 20 C. Allera, 'La Paix par le minerai?', 'La France va désormais livrer à l'allemagne 600,000 tonnes de minerai de fer par mois', 8 August 1937.
39 AA Botschaft Paris 892[a]/Bd. 19 'Une délegation d'industriels est l'object d'attention officielles multiples', *Paris-Midi*, 19 December 1930.
40 USNA RG151/1575 'Special Report No. 6. New Franco-German trade agreement', 16 July 1937; AA T120/1638/E 021741 'Die deutsch-französischen Wirtschaftsverhandlungen',; AA Botschaft Paris 892[a]/2 Bd. 21 'Lothringische Minette und Ruhrkoks', 2 July 1937.
41 AA Botschaft Paris 892[a]/Bd. 21 'Brieftelegramm W 912', 9 July 1937.
42 AA Botschaft Paris 892/3 'Aufzeichnung Hemmen', 13 July 1937.
43 AA Botschaft Paris 892/3 Paul Elbel, 'France-Allemagne', *L'Oeuvre*, 10 November 1937.
44 AA Botschaft Paris 892[a]/2 Bd. 20 'Pressestimmen zu den neuen deutsch-französischen Vertragswerk', 15 July 1937.

45 AA Botschaft Paris 892[a]/Bd. 19 'Il faut engager des négotiations commerciales avec l'Allemagne', USNA T 120/1638E/021538 f. 'Aufzeichnung', 8 August 1939.
46 AA Botschaft Paris 'L'accord commercial Franco-Allemagne', *L'Usine*, 11 August 1938.
47 USNA T120/1638E/021454 'Meine Eindrücke anlässlich der Tagung des Verwaltungsrats des IHKs', 21 October 1938.
48 AA Botschaft Paris 892[c]/1 'Les Négotiations économiques avec Allemagne', *Le Temps*, 20 February 1939.
49 DGFP (Series D) Docs 371 'The Franco-German Economic Discussions in Paris on 7 December 1938, 388 Campe to Wiehl, 22 February 1939', 389 Memorandum: Co-operation in the reconstruction of Spain, 391 'Memorandum: Kreutzwald, 1 March 1939'; AA. Botschaft Paris 892[c]/Bd. 1 'Note, 11 March 1939'; Botschaft Paris 892[c]/Bd. 1 'Aufzeichnung (Campe) über eine deutsch-französische Zusammenarbeit beim Wiederaufbau Spaniens', 1 February 1939.
50 AA Botschaft Paris 892[c]/1 'Aufzeichnung Campe', 21 February 1939.
51 AA Botschaft Paris 'Bevorstehende Gründung eines "Centre Economique Franco-Allemand" ', 22 February 1939.
52 AA Botschaft Paris 892[c]/Bd. 1 Koppen to Campe, 2 March 1939.
53 USNA T120/16381E/021511 'Industrielle Zusammenarbeit zwischen deutschen und französischen Industriegruppen (zu W.II.1589)'.
54 AA Botschaft Paris 892[c]/Bd. 1 'Die wirtschaftlichen Rückwirkungen der März-Ereignisse auf den deutsch-französischen Handel', 8 May 1939.
55 USNA T120/1638/E021542 'Telegramm, Paris', 8 June 1939; Botschaft Paris 892[c]/Bd. 3 'L'accord commercial franco-allemand', 29 July 1939.
56 T120/1638/E021543 'Sitzung des HPA', 8 June 1939.
57 USNA T120/138/E21566 'Verlängerung des deutsch-französischen Wirtschaftsvertrags vom 10 Juli 1937', 14 July 1939.

6

RUHR COAL AND THE WAR

The subject of this chapter is the Ruhr collieries' attempt to meet the rising fuel requirements of the German war economy. Given the inadequacy of investment in subsurface operations after 1936, this was no easy matter. To be sure, several developments of the early war years relieved pressure on the mines: the rich seams of Polish Silesia came under German control in September 1939, defeat reduced demand in western Europe in summer and autumn 1940, and tighter controls over consumption imposed after coal commissioner Paul Walter's dismissal created one-time savings in March 1941. Still, these were mere palliatives. In the long run, shortages of Ruhr coal could only have been overcome by raising outputs and this never occurred. The record year for the Ruhr was 1939, with total production reaching 130,184,000 tons. Thereafter it decreased to 129,188,000 in 1940, 129,971,000 in 1941, 128,490,000 in 1942, 127,515,000 in 1943 and 110,851,000 in 1944.

Only one 'solution' was available to the wartime coal problem: to increase labour inputs by lengthening work days and weeks and adding to mine employment. But the problem was easier to identify than to solve. Even before the war the work day had been increased by forty-five minutes, some twenty-five days per month were being worked, and employees were approaching exhaustion. Furthermore, the operators were ill-positioned to compete against other claimants for scarce labour. Still, there were untapped resources outside of Germany's borders. The recruitment of foreigners began in earnest after the campaign in western Europe but proved to be difficult: most of those who came soon left. In a national socialist variant of policies adopted in the First World War, an army of eastern European slaves mainly from PoW camps was conscripted for toil in the mines. But even this drastic expedient, which added over 120,000 to the workforce, was not enough. Though willing to work, these miserable wretches could do no more than temporarily stave off the fall in output resulting from the progressive exhaustion of mine labour and machinery (Figure 3). Coal shortages persisted during 1943, preventing increases in steel outputs and causing breakdowns in production and transportation at many points. It took the destruction of the rail system in the middle months of 1944 to improve the fuel balance. For the mines this

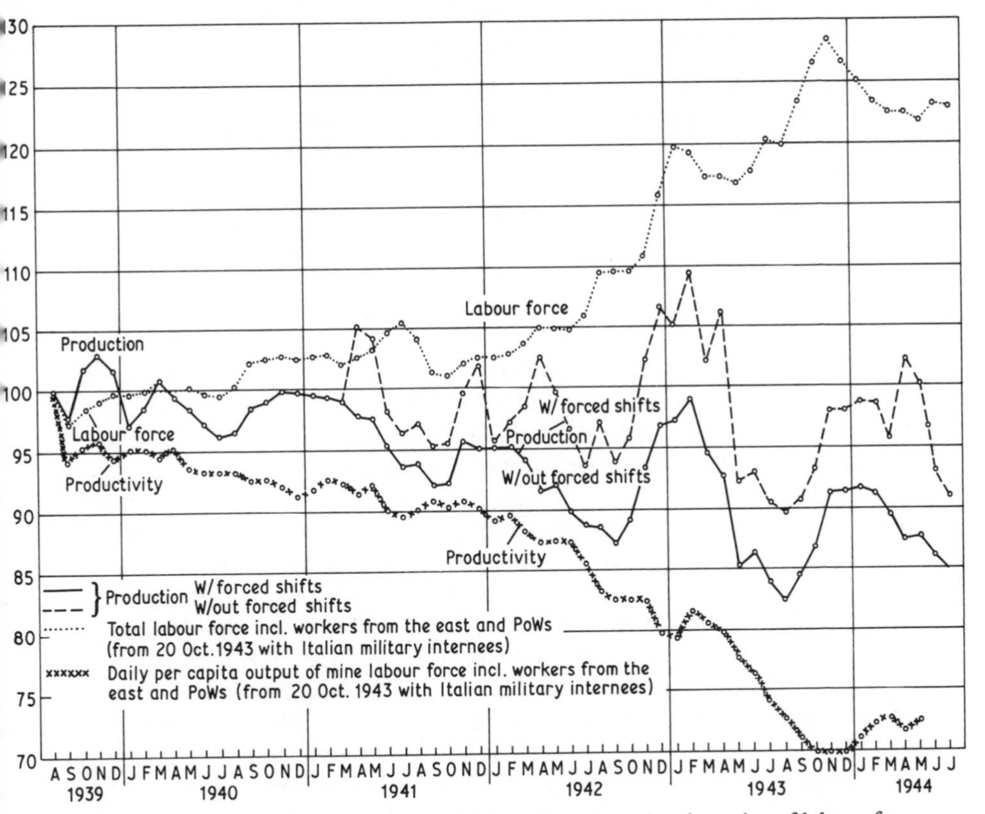

Figure 3 Comparative development of daily average production, size of labour force and productivity, 1939–1944

Source: Gutehoffnungshütte 400101305/9, 'Statistische Angaben aus den Ruhrkohlenbergbau', (n.d.).

event came as a blessing in disguise, as the first respite in over seven years, and thanks to this, a collapse did not occur. The coal industry of the Ruhr emerged from the war in terrible shape but still intact.

The inadequacies in coal policy were no less serious during the war than before it. Germany entered the fray without knowing either how much coal the economy would need or how much of it could be hewed and raised without destroying the productivity of the mines. As Minister of Armaments and Munitions Albert Speer admitted in the famous Linz speech of 24 June 1944,

> Unfortunately, we did not pay enough attention to coal before the war. We built up production in coal-devouring branches such as chemistry, while at the same time [pretending] that the coal industry could remain about the same. Today we are suffering enormously as a result.[1]

Although the prediction of future coal consumption requirements involved both political imponderables and daunting technical variables, the same cannot be said, with regard to the production side: here limits were well-known. The lack of coal planning was due to continued administrative weakness. The conflict between Walter and the industry got worse during the war. Walter wanted to reorganize coal administration along the lines of the *Reichsnährstand*, (Reich's Food Estate), which had entailed a thorough overhaul of structures. Existing syndicates, he believed, should be eliminated and marketing areas redefined to coincide with the administration boundaries of the 'organizations of industry'. Coal retailing by firms (*Werkshandel*) should be ended. To sabotage such plans RWKS and the other coal cartels waged guerrilla warfare and thus crippled policy-making.[2] Coal Commissioner Walter's planning efforts were confined to setting output targets high enough to please his bosses. These the industry, which 'knew better', accepted as attainable rather than opposing openly. At the same time, it attached so many conditions that responsibility for failure to meet the output targets could be evaded. Official coal planning was totally unrealistic and provides a poor guide for judging mine performance. Still, the output targets are worth noting because they figured in political discussions. With production running at daily levels of 420,000–430,000 tons in early summer 1939, the Ministry of Economics ordered increases by the end of the year to 485,000 tons, and by the end of the following two months to 521,000 and 527,000 tons. The Ruhr's official counter-estimate was that with eight-hour shifts it could produce 462,408 tons, 489,531 tons and 519,205 tons respectively and, with the addition of a further forty-five minutes to the work day, 485,528 tons, 513,819 tons and 544,531 tons. In the 1940 revision of the coal programme Walter 'urged' the Ruhr to produce 460,000–470,000 tons per day. The industry however again demurred, setting target ranges of 425,0000–450,000 daily tons. In December 1940 the Ministry of Economics, without prior consultation, ordered RWKS to produce 450,000 tons per day. The 1941 plan reiterated the previous one. The 'optimum conditions' that both industry and officialdom postulated for the attainment of their targets were fanciful. Wartime daily outputs never again approached the levels of autumn 1939.[3]

In March 1941 the 'organizational problem' was essentially solved: Walter was 'dumped' and Paul Pleiger, who had risen to prominence as the chief executive officer of Reichswerke Hermann Göring, designated chief of the new Reichsvereinigung Kohle (RVK) – Reich's Coal Association. This was a prototype for the 'organizations of self-responsibility' championed by Albert Speer after his appointment as Minister of Armaments and Munitions in February 1942. RVK's authority superseded that of all other coal industry associations. The Bergassessoren administered the new body under the direction of a figure representing the interests of the state. In spite of the long-standing conflict between Göring and Ruhr coal, Pleiger proved to be an effective guardian of the industry. He protected the mines from 'irresponsible' political attacks and persuasively defended their special needs and concerns. Within limits, he also 'protected the industry against itself', by ending some of the restrictive practices which had made it the object of jealousy and aversion.[4] But Pleiger and RVK came too late to change the basic coal picture. By 1942 shortages were desperate and growing worse. His job was to force production to the maximum, the mines be damned.

The first problem facing the operators at the outset of hostilities was to protect miners in the most productive age groups from the military draft.[5] This proved to be very difficult. In the third quarter of 1939 6.6 per cent of the mine labour force was conscripted. The numbers of miners in military service held fairly steady until early 1943 but then tripled over the next eighteen months (Table 22).

Table 22 Conscripted Ruhr miners (net number and as percentage of mine labour force), 1939–1944

	Quarter	*Net number*	*As percentage of total German mine labour force*		*Quarter*	*Net number*	*As percentage of total German mine labour force*
1939	III	21,904	6.63	1943	I	30,097	9.13
	IV				II	35,933	10.18
1940	I				III	36,335	11.12
	II	24,373	7.20		IV	55,663	16.72
	III	20,338	5.99	1944	I	62,408	18.85
	IV	19,668	5.73		II	63,749	19.36
1941	I	17,473	5.17		III	73,373	21.55
	II	32,735	7.05		IV	76,595	22.85
	III	24,466	7.12				
	IV	23,519	6.78				
1942	I	19,209	5.56				
	II	20,391	6.11				
	III	18,442	5.62				
	IV	20,505	6.30				

Source: Bundesarchiv Nachlass Spethmann VI, 786.

As indicated in Figure 4, the loss of manpower from the draftable cohorts – in particular that of 45,000 underground workers from the critical 25–35 age groups – brought deterioration of the age structure. A fall in labour productivity was for this reason alone a virtual certainty.

Another circumstance also played a role. There was a further decline in the calibre of mine recruits because it was necessary 'to employ all persons who are such that they cannot otherwise be employed'.[6] They included the physically unfit, juvenile delinquents and the emotionally disabled. The increase in 'mine-unsuitable' workers was responsible for the rise in unexcused absences from 2.92 per thousand shifts in January 1940 to a high of 5.30 in October of

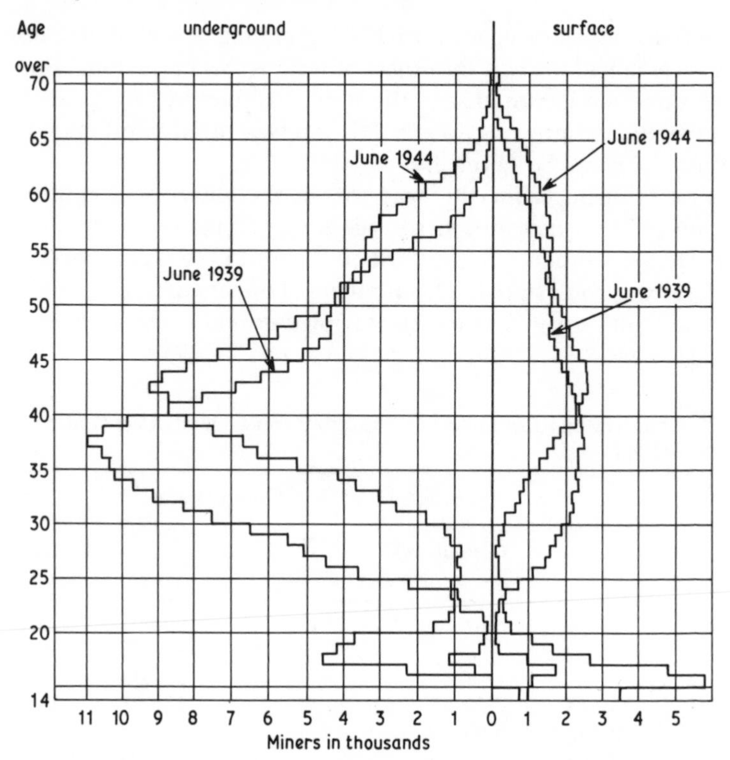

Figure 4 Age structure in the Ruhr mining industry, June 1939 and June 1944
Source: Headquarters North German Coal Control. Interim Report on the General Economic and Financial Situation of the Ruhr Mining Industry (September 1945).

that year and contributed to a decline in daily miner output from 2058 tons in the second half of 1939 to 2014 tons in 1940 and 1959 tons in 1941.[7] The operators and party attempted to reverse this trend by tightening discipline. Procedures for dealing with 'recalcitrants' had been revised on the eve of the war. They involved fines followed by summonses to appear before formations and, as a last resort, referrals to civil authorities for punishment. At the first indication of a *Bummelei* contagion, the authorities shifted to 'hard measures'. Here they could count on the co-operation of the basic labour force (*Stammbelegschaft*).[8] The recent arrivals, untrained and likely also unfit for the hard work of the mines, were unpopular. According to the affidavit of a Harpener Bergbau miner-apprentice who had been an inmate at an institution for juveniles in Dortmund-Lundtrop, he and others formerly in detention were ridiculed as 'SS, bandits, and Sing-Sings', subjected to numerous forms of petty persecution, kicked in the seat of the pants, slapped around and even urinated on. Such treatment could only have aggravated the morale problem. In December and November 1939, partly as a result of discussions held in councils of trust, eight 'slackers' in the district received sentences ranging from four weeks to eight months, the most severe of which was handed out to a miner who was absent from the job twenty-three times in the months of May and June.[9]

Even after hiring 'undesirables' and foreign volunteers, it was impossible to maintain pre-war levels of mine employment, as indicated in Table 23.

Table 23 Non-conscripted miner employment levels, 1939–1944

	Underground	*Total*
Aug. 2/39	229,886	313,202
Dec. /39	230,660	313,202
Aug. 6/40	230,226	314,466
Dec. 12/40	236,014	
Aug. 6/41	240,847	326,119
Dec. 12/41	235,099	320,090
6/42	228,626	313,692
12/42	222,322	304,782
6/43	212,155	291,078
12/43	296,388	276,891
6/44	187,465	266,028

Source: Gutehoffnungshütte 400101305/9 'Statistische Angaben aus dem Ruhrkohlenbergbau. Zusammenfassende Darstellung seit Kriegsausbruch bis Juli 1944' (n.d.).

There were theoretically two ways to overcome the shortage of potential able-bodied miner-recruits, but one of them was politically unacceptable. The idea of German women working in close proximity with men, some foreign, in unsupervised places deep in the earth was intolerable to national socialists, even though women had long since proved to be a valuable adjunct to the mine labour force in Poland.[10] The remaining alternative, one also subject to ideological objections, was to recruit from abroad, where labour supplies were plentiful. Coal Commissioner Walter, military planners and civil authorities in Berlin urged such a course on the industry but met head-on opposition, backed by the local *Gauleiter*, and, after that failed, the usual foot-dragging. The operators had reasons for opposing the employment of foreign labour in addition to the obvious ones of cost and productivity; they feared that this use of foreigners in the pits would lower the prestige of mining as a career and undermine the long-term campaign to increase its appeal. It seemed doubtful, moreover, that foreign recruits could be retained.[11]

The introduction of manpower from abroad began on a small scale in April 1940 with 996 Poles and then increased sharply in July to include miners hired in the districts of Belgium and North France, many of whom were also

Polish-speaking. By the end of the month some 7475 men had been brought in. The new arrivals made a poor impression. The Harpener mine reported to the Bezirksgruppe that

> those sent here look really weak . . . A considerable number [of them] is undernourished and . . . unsuitable for mine labour. An examination of arms has revealed severe muscle deficiencies and bodies are equally undeveloped. Most of the Poles go to work looking stupid (*stumpfsinnig*) and apathetic. The susceptibility to illness is just as great as one would expect it to be.[12]

The new arrivals were also unpopular with their German work mates. The head of the council of trust at Concordia, complained that 'the Poles are allowed to run around unrestricted after work . . . and need to be supervised more carefully . . . Nor should anything be "given away" to them on the job. Slackers must be severely punished'.[13]

Differences on the foreign labour question came to a head in summer 1940. At a 19 June meeting of the Defence Commissioner in Münster, Bergassessor Emil Stein refused outright even to discuss the question of large-scale recruitment. At a second session six weeks later, Wilhelm Tengelmann, a politically well-connected mine manager who often handled negotiations with the regime, insisted on racial grounds that the collieries accept 'No more Poles! . . . because they are inferior and can be disciplined only by using the most severe measures.'[14] Although the industry thought it had 'secured full recognition that in the future, just as the German peasant will work the German soil, only German comrades will be allowed to mine our coal', in reality, it had sustained a grave defeat.[15] On 4 September Marshall Göring ordered the immediate step-up in foreign manpower recruitment and assigned the task to DAF. The policing and supervision of foreign employees except when 'on the job' – tasks incidentally unwelcome to management – also fell to DAF. The assignment of these responsibilities to the pseudo-union provided a guarantee of management dissatisfaction.[16] The programme was a failure. Although enough foreigners were brought in to offset the decrease in the number of German miners, their productivity was so low that outputs could not be raised. Worse yet, costs were excessive because of high training and housing expenses and rapid turnover. Table 24 summarizes turnover in the final stages of the foreign labour recruitment programme.

Another reason for the failure of the programme was the ineptitude of the recruiters. The Croats engaged for the Osterfeld mine of Gutehoffnungshütte, 'while willing to work', were 'not only . . . untrained' but had 'never actually seen coal before.'[17] Of the 5000 Dutch workers promised by DAF, only 155 ever arrived, and most of them deserted the mines within a space of a few weeks.[18] But the Italians were the greatest fiasco. Although hand-picked under DAF supervision by the Confederazione Fascista, they proved to be, according

Table 24 Foreign mine labour recruitment as of 31 December 1941

Country of origin	*Total allocated*	*Number present*	*Percentage of departures*
Poland (Kattowitz and Litzmannstadt)	5,310	2,298	56.73
Italy	14,040	4,938	64.83
Denmark	1,040	242	76.86
Belgium and northern France	18,473	7,292	60.55
Croatia	13,828	7,447	46.15
Holland	155	54	65.16
Galicia	11,299	10,692	5.37
Total	64,145	32,963	48.62

Source: Bundesarchiv Nachlass Spethmann V, 16.

to Pleiger, 'utterly worthless at the mines'. Of the approximately 5000 who arrived in May and June of 1940 one-half walked off the job over the following eight months. A second action of April 1941 brought in another 8000 Italians, nine-tenths of whom similarly disappeared. On October 1941 the industry formally requested the repatriation of those still employed. In despair, both coal management and officialdom concluded apparently on racial grounds that 'Italians are temperamentally unfit for mine labour' – utter nonsense considering the large numbers of them who both then and since have worked productively at Belgian and French pits.[19]

A more fundamental reason for the failure of the foreign recruitment programme was national socialist racialism. In theory the newcomers were to be treated more or less 'like our German workers', since many of them came from allied nations, others (Danes and Dutch) were considered to be Aryans, and still others (the Poles from Belgium and North France) were skilled and experienced.[20] This proved to be easier said than done. Problems began at the moment of arrival. The recruits, housed in barracks, were issued no more than one thin blanket, one 'coarse' blanket, two towels and one straw mattress. The Bezirksgruppe, after raising considerable protest on hygienic grounds (spread of vermin), managed to secure the issuance to each man of a bedsheet. Recreational opportunities were minimal, since the foreigners were to be kept physically isolated from the population. To ensure this, they were issued uniforms with the designating letters ('P' for Poles, for example) stitched over the breast pocket. Further, they were expressly forbidden to attend mass with Germans. As if for consolation, Himmler issued an emergency order in March 1941 decreeing the erection of brothels for foreign miners. This occasioned initial opposition from the Bezirksgruppe, which preferred a giant single unit ('bordello-barracks') to the several smaller ones proposed, and argued that the community rather than the mines should bear the costs. This objection was turned away with the rejoinder that only initial expenses were involved in the planned construction: the bordello was expected to be almost immediately self-financing. Later DAF *did* launch a campaign to recruit priests for the various national groups. In addition, the setting up of libraries and sports clubs received official consideration as possible morale boosters.[21] While the bestowal of cigarettes, sweets or the occasional bauble may have had at least some 'positive' psychological effect, the provision of food rations, adequate though meagre, provided the primary work incentive. But niggling distinctions were maintained here as well. While 'west-workers' officially received German rations, Poles got 15 g less butter per week, 7 g less bread but additional potatoes when available. The Italians, while also to receive German rations, could employ their own cooks.[22] Such cosmetics could not disguise the general resemblance of the volunteers' camps to penal 'honour farms'.

The integration of foreign civilians into the production process presented great difficulties. One was the babble of tongues, but this was at least partly the unnecessary result of a deliberate policy choice. It was decided specifically *not* to recruit from the occupied regions of the USSR Jews, 'Asiatics' or any Poles or Ukrainians with even the most rudimentary knowledge of German out of a fear that they would serve as vectors of communist propaganda.[23] The same concern ruled out the formation of work parties of Polish-speakers which might have included those engaged from eastern and western Europe being headed by those who had long resided and laboured in the Ruhr. In fact, only two possibilities existed: the organization of separate national contingents or the integration of foreign workers into German-run labour units.

The former was the preferred national socialist approach. In July 1940, the Gestapo warned that in Oberhausen

> several mines have for economic reasons organized small formations of Poles with which German work parties have been forced into contact. The German miners, among whom are many party members and SA men, consider it very degrading to share the same washrooms and sanitary facilities . . . They believe that unless separation is practised, morale will be hurt and productivity fall.[24]

But *apartheid* was not technically feasible. To be sure, it was easy to direct that German miners be allowed to use the changing rooms before the others, even to provide separate water canisters. Poles could also be given 'priority assignment to jobs that were either or harmful to health, such as work in cokeries, cleaning ashes out of boilers, and loading coal'.[25] Still, mine operations forced Germans to come into contact with foreigners. To sweeten the pill, the Bezirksgruppe directed that this necessity be presented in a favourable light: 'Employment of Poles is intended to provide relief [from drudgery] for the German worker and increase his opportunities for promotion. If our guidelines are followed, the engagement of these [new workers] will prove to be highly advantageous.'[26]

Authority to discipline foreign labourers was exercised by their Aryan work mates, sometimes with undue force. German miners were fed up. At the Concordia Mine the council of trust received frequent complaints that the low productivity of foreigners forced Germans to work harder but penalized them for the failure of their work groups to meet output norms. While hinting to the angry miners that inexperience rather than 'slacking' was at the heart of the problem, Managing Director Dechamps declared his readiness 'to go farther if necessary than directed by the instructions of the labour authorities in dealing with cases of resistance'.[27] This was promising quite a lot: since 4 September 1940 it had been policy that 'Foreign workers who demonstrate ill-will or passive resistance are to be registered with the Bezirksgruppe. After agreement between the Coal Commissar and the Reichsführer-SS, they are then to be sent to a concentration camp in order to learn how to work.'[28] Whether because of or in spite of shabby treatment, foreigner-recruit productivity varied from 80–90 per cent of German (Polish civilians) to less than 25 per cent (Italians). Annual Ruhr coal output fell from 130,184,000 tons in 1939 to 129,188,000 tons and 129,971,000 tons in the two years during which the recruitment of foreign labour featured prominently.[29] But in the same months, demand increased sharply. The sale of domestic coal mounted by 30 per cent, in large part because of additional consumption by the Wehrmacht. Allocations to the railroad system were up by a quarter and those to public utilities (electricity, gas and water) by 15 per cent. General industrial consumption increased by 12 per cent. Although winter 1940–1 witnessed many of the same temporary shortages as in the previous year, significant bottlenecks in the supply of coal to industry were prevented until mid-summer 1941. These results were attained thanks partly by drawing down stocks and increasing outputs of lignite, but thanks also to military and organizational developments.[30]

The defeat and dismemberment of Poland brought the rich and productive seams of east Upper Silesia under German control. In the brief period from October 1939 to March 1940 19.8 million tons of coal were mined in the district, and in 1940–1 a further 49 million tons. Reich coal outputs increased from 204.8 million tons in 1939–1940 to 247.9 million tons in 1940–1. But only a small amount of Silesian coal is cokable and the costs of transport west of the Elbe are heavy. The substitutability of Silesian material for Ruhr coal was thus limited.[31]

The formal commencement of hostilities between France and Germany, along with the British blockade, reduced the Ruhr's export burden substantially. Sales of coal and coke to the foundries of Lorraine, in 1937 totalling 8.0 million and 2.3 million tons respectively, virtually came to a halt. The movement of Ruhr coal on waterways to the Netherlands and Belgium dropped from 9,347,507 tons and 1,700,400 tons in 1938, to 5,591,275 tons and 922,867 tons in 1939, and 732,265 tons and 69,060 tons in 1940. The low figure for 1940 was also due in part to the disruptions caused by the Western Campaign. Because of low industrial demand both at home and in France, the Belgian mines were even able to export coal to the Reich for a few months.[32]

Finally, the organization of Reichsvereinigung Kohle (RVK) in March 1941 made possible savings in domestic coal consumption. After the shortages of winter 1939–40 Commissioner Walter set up a 'point system' for coal rationing devised to benefit 'small consumers'. It was based on their own assessments of future requirements. One of Pleiger's first acts as RVK chief was to substitute a system based on amounts previously allocated by dealers who, like producers, were required to belong to the new coal association. The Pleiger reform was responsible for savings of about 6 million annual tons.[33]

Except for the new system of domestic coal allocation, these improvements were ephemeral. It soon became obvious that the lack of adequate means of transport would make it impossible to benefit fully from the Silesian mines. Where the waterways of the Ruhr could carry 120,000–130,000 tons daily from the pithead, the loading capacity of those in Silesia was a mere 20,000–25,000 tons. The overburdened rail system in the eastern district began to break down at an early date, and the process would continue inexorably for the remainder of the war. By early 1942 this bottleneck was restricting mine output by 100,000 daily tons, an amount about equal to a quarter of that produced in the Ruhr. As Pleiger pointed out at a 15 July 1942 meeting of Zentrale Planung, Silesian rail problems increased pressure on the Ruhr mines, which he 'had already called upon for over a year to pull through the entire coal industry'.[34]

The onset of Pax Germanica in western and northern Europe together with the continuation of war elsewhere meant that the Ruhr was called upon more and more frequently to supply either reluctant allies or the industries of the conquered or dominated nations. After the cessation of British exports in spring 1940, the Continent (here: the Baltic, Mediterranean and western Europe) faced coal deficits of 36.4 million annual tons. Filling it was a matter of great urgency. On the one hand the Reich stood to gain a major adjunct to her war effort; if, however, no coal could be exported to the rest of Europe industry would remain at a standstill, populations freeze, and allies disappear. Coal planning for the Pax Germanica was characteristically flawed: it casually assumed that the Netherlands would continue to be self-sufficient and Belgium to be able to take over the Luxembourg market from the Ruhr as well as supply to France the 6.5 million annual tons Britain no longer delivered. In the Baltic and the Mediterranean areas, which lacked significant coal deposits, Ruhr coal was to share supply responsibilities with other German districts. But Italy remained a headache for the Ruhr. The syndicate was ordered to increase Italy's deliveries from a monthly average of 660,000 in May 1940 to 738,703 tons by April 1941. In Scandinavia, where Britain normally supplied 8.2 million tons of total annual imports of 18.0 million tons (and the Ruhr no more than 2.2 million tons), it was clear that the deficit could not be overcome still,

Ruhr coal exports to the area rose from an average of 187,000 monthly tons in 1939 to 382,000 in 1940 and to 460,000 in the first five months of 1941. These increases were necessary to maintain the barter trade for Swedish ore and Norwegian aluminium. As a result of this increased demand, shortages of coke and coal were beginning to hinder the increasingly critical steel production of western Europe by spring 1941.[35]

On 15 August 1941 Pleiger boasted to his patron, Göring, that 'in reality no armaments factory has had to reduce production for lack of coal'.[36] While this statement was true in a narrow sense, the RVK chief was well aware that the output declines of spring 1941 would soon change the situation for the worse. Within days of Pleiger's claim the rationing board, *Reichstelle Kohle*, ordered an across-the-board reduction of 20 per cent in all coal allocations. This measure was intended to force the closure of non-essential factories but did not improve the supply situation. By autumn, only the 'most important *(kriegswichtigsten)* raw materials factories such as explosives plants, artificial rubber works, synthetic petroleum refineries could be at all adequately supplied'. By November 1941 the Reichsbahn was down to a ten day stock-pile. By March and April of 1942, in spite of a mild winter, only the most critical factories *(Schwerpunktbetriebe)* were able to operate at full capacity.[37]

The failure to defeat Russia by winter 1941–2 threatened to worsen the situation. It meant that the Reich had to shift from a strategy of *Blitzkrieg* to one of total war. This required a huge increase in the output of armaments. To attain it, wasteful allocations had to be ended, design and manufacture simplified, idle factory capacity (especially in occupied Europe) put to use, and outputs of energy and raw material sharply increased. One of the most pressing tasks facing Speer was to solve the crisis in coal. This – a chief priority in the first six months in office – turned above all on the labour situation in the Ruhr.

But might it not have been possible to raise productivity by mechanization? With this goal in mind the Bergbau-Verein, the coal industry's 'think tank', had been reorganized and strengthened in early 1939. During the war it sponsored studies into all aspects of mine operations. They concluded that the most promising technology was still the cutter-scraper, a bulky and heavy piece of equipment used on a large scale in Great Britain and the United States but only to a limited extent in the Ruhr. Unfortunately, the Committee on Mining Methods reported in May 1941 that because of the softness of Ruhr seams the expense of introducing additional machines would be prohibitive. Further, machinery for automatic loading and conveyancing was still in the experimental stages.[38]

Productivity might also have been raised by shutting down inefficient mines and concentrating labour on good working points. The Bergbau-Verein concluded that by eliminating 38 shafts, output could be raised 10,000 tons a day – a theoretical increase of 2.0–2.5 per cent – but that this was impossible because of problems of grading, gas and electricity supply, etc. The Bergbau-

Verein refused to consider working only large veins on the grounds that it would be wasteful *(Raubbauwirtschaft)* to abandon small ones. Behind these technical objections was the industry's continued opposition to changing production methods. Thus Bergassessor Buskühl told the Bezirksgruppe:

> Under all circumstances all operations must be maintained. The suggestion to abandon small veins is worthy of some consideration assuming of course that tax provisions are first settled, but even here great caution is called for, and such measures should be regarded as a very last resort.[39]

But it was nearly impossible to work German miners any harder. This fact was recognized by everyone concerned with the coal problem. Pleiger described miners' morale vividly at the Zentrale Planung meeting of 15 July 1942. Production difficulties did not, he insisted, derive from ill-will, slacking, or any other form of resistance:

> The German miner has held out loyally *(brav und treu)* for two years – in spite of being the worst-paid in industry, with the longest hours (10 to 11 per day) . . . added to which is the [increasing serious] problem of air-raids.

Still, 'every miner worked two extra shifts *(Sonderschichten)* in 1941.' The productivity problem, as he explained it, was due to total physical exhaustion: 'Shop stewards have told me that even with the utmost effort *(beim besten Willen)* they can work no more.' And its cause was the lack of food: 'The loss of weight among miners is such that they are telling me, we don't want your money!' 'All they ask,' he added, 'is a pound of fat for each Sunday shift so that they can work twice as hard. . . . This is the mood in the West. . . . The miner is totally willing but at the end of his resources.' To pull through the miner needed more food but also 'relief in the form of the strongest and most healthy bodies from the mass of Russian prisoners-of-war.' Pleiger thought that it would then be possible 'to turn the good German miner into a supervisor or a work party chief *(Schachtmeister oder Vorhauer)* and he'll bring the Russians to the face'.[40] By the end of 1941 the industry was reaching similar conclusions with regard to the indispensability of Russian PoW labour. As put by Dr Martin Sogemeier, a long-time coal association official, 'when separated from their political commissars, the PoWs do pretty well . . . once they've been slapped into shape *(aufgepappelt)*'.[41]

The foreign labour conscription programme began early in 1942 when Bezirksgruppe Ruhr of the coal industry committed itself to raising outputs to 430,000 daily tons with the stipulation that, along with adequate provisioning, it would be supplied with 80,000 Russian PoWs. With this in mind, construction of new slave quarters started on a massive scale. On 21 March 1942 Speer appointed Gauleiter Fritz Sauckel of Thuringia to head the 'draft board'. As Generalbevollmächtigten für den Arbeitseinsatz (Plenipotentiary for Labour) he was vested with authority to override both DAF and the industry. In July the first campaign was set in motion, its targets based on Pleiger's estimate that the mines could 'digest' 20,000–25,000 slaves per month. Sauckel promised to deliver no less than 100,000 Russians in 180 days. In August the first large instalment reached the pits. Sauckel's programme, while never meeting its deadlines, would grow by leaps and bounds over the next twenty-four months. The number of Soviet PoW slaves increased from 18,832 in August to 33,738 in September, to 82,316 by mid-1943 and to a wartime high of 93,668 at the end of June 1944. The forcible recruitment of 'Workers-from-the-East' increased over the same period from 7632 to 31,331. As of June 1944 PoWs constituted nearly a quarter of the workforce, forced civilian labours from Poland and the Soviet Union a further 7 per cent, and 'other' foreigners an additional 6 per cent. This supplementary labour raised total mine employment (313,202 in December 1939) to 321,858 at the end of 1941, 363,654 in December 1942, and 400,297 in December 1943. In the final years of the war no more than 60 per cent of those at work underground were German.[42]

From the standpoint of the Reich war effort, the slave labour programme was by no means a failure. As early as October 1942 the management co-ordinator Bergassessor Hermann Winkhaus reported to Zentrale Planung the 'happy news' that outputs were increasing from 375,000 tons to 390,000 tons per day.[43] Thanks to the infusion of ever-greater numbers of slaves over the next year and a half, production levels remained stable. Little more than fear and discipline are responsible for this remarkable result.

The physical condition of the arrivals was appalling. According to Pleiger those brought from Stalino had been virtually stripped of their clothing by Romanian and Italian soldiers, 'lacked enough strength to throw a stone', were 'wasted' and would be of no economic value 'without a trip to a sanatorium'. (Such reports were unimportant to Speer, who sarcastically chided the RVK chief that it was 'none of your concern that the Führer deprived these people of their grain supply *(Getreidebasis)*'.) Some 40 per cent were too ill to be put to work and were dispatched elsewhere.[44] Those retained were little stronger. In October seventeen of them died at the Oberhausen mines of Gutehoffnungshütte from 'general weakness' *(Herzschwäche)*.[45] So many were perishing by December that the PoW section of the OKW directed they be buried not in coffins but butcher paper, adding that 'to spare the public unpleasant sights in case this should tear open in a storm on the way to interment, a single coffin [should] be kept handy for use until arrival at the grave site'. The directive concluded with pedantic grimness that, 'The corpse should be lifted out of the coffin at the time of burial, then interred properly, thus making it possible to put the properly disinfected coffin into service again.'[46] The mining official Oskar Gabel believed the condition of the Soviet PoWs to be so poor that they could not produce at more than a quarter of the German rate.[47]

The appalling living conditions of the mine slaves prevented any dramatic improvement in their health. They were normally housed 200 per wooden barrack (OKH *Pferdestallbaracken* 260/IX) without electricity, running water or surfaced floors. Toilet facilities consisted of trenches. Wool blankets, supposedly in short supply, were not provided. Predictably, procedures called for liberal spraying of the slave quarters with disinfectants. A compound consisted of four barracks surrounded by barbed wire. Rations were set at 'maintenance levels': 4400g of bread per week, 600g of meat, 300g of fat, 7000g of potatoes, 110g of sugar, and 25g of ersatz–tea.[48]

The strictest discipline was to be enforced and severe punishment applied. The operative Gestapo directive regarding the use of Soviet PoW labour, while emphasizing the need to avoid 'contamination with Bolshevik vices', called for the maintenance of near total separation between the two 'races'. Sexual relations were 'totally forbidden . . ., male offenders [to be] immediately put to death and female offenders sent to concentration camps'. Further, all 'unproductive categories' were to be at once 'referred elsewhere'. They included the sick, persons under fifteen and pregnant women. Finally, 'even the least sign of resistance is to be dealt with in ruthless fashion *(rücksichtlos)*, in the sense that weapons are to be used unsparingly. Fleeing Russians are to be shot at and killed.' Supervision of the foreign slaves by Gestapo agents being impossible, this responsibility was to be exercised by 'German supervisors, foremen, and workers who as members of the 'Factory Police' *(Werkschütz)* will wear armbands to identify themselves'.[49] To enforce such measures, the production chief at Concordia mine told the members of the council of trust:

> All of you, especially those who come into contact with the PoWs, are to be instructed on a continuous basis concerning your behaviour with regard to them. We must remain alert to prevent any sentimentality detracting from the authority of the German worker, for it can be dangerous if this happens. All persons are forbidden from giving the Russians [food] or doing him favours of any kind . . . Any breaches in these rules of conduct should be reported at once.[50]

Putting the mine slaves to work involved problems of both a technical and political nature. Procedures had to be devised for teaching the largely illiterate and completely untrained PoWs 'tool identification' and enough German to respond to commands. Instruction was for racial reasons to be kept to a bare minimum: 'It will in no way involve a labour training plan that leads in orderly fashion to the assumption of greater responsibilities. Professional education is to remain the exclusive privilege of Germans!'[51] After eight days of instruction and being 'slapped into shape' the slaves were introduced to the most menial and physically demanding of mine jobs. If within eight days, or subsequently, a Russian could not work to 50 per cent of the German level he was to be 'reassigned' to a labour camp.[52]

The influx of slaves placed considerable additional weight on the shoulders of the German miner. Initially one foreigner was to be attached to each German work party, but in many cases this was soon increased to four or five. To handle them the face worker *(Hauer)* was delegated life or death power over foreign slaves. It was he who decided on a weekly basis whether or not the 50 per cent standard had been met.[53] Contrary to the expectations of management and officialdom, this new responsibility was not necessarily welcome. In September 1942 – that is during the period when the first large instalment of foreign slaves was being put to work – German miners suffered an 'epidemic' of ulcers.[54]

Mistreatment often resulted from the fact that low PoW and East worker productivity cost the Hauer both money and effort. It was soon clear that a better approach to integrating the two groups into the work process had to be found. On 10 September 1942 Bergassessor Wilhelm Tengelmann suggested at a RWKS meeting that Soviet PoWs be allowed to form their own work columns. But a different approach was adopted. Noting that 'the inclusion of the Russians had dampened the enthusiasm of our boys, not least because of their effects on piecework rates', the Bezirksgruppe proposed that 'they be given a financial incentive to take foreigners into their work parties' and recommended that the foreigners' wages be set at 5–10 per cent below estimated productivity. In other words, 'when a Russian can produce at 60 per cent of the German rate, he should be given a share of 40–50 per cent'.[55] The wage table set the following equivalents:

Table 25 Wage table for Soviet PoWs (RM 000)

German worker	*Stalag worker*	*PoW share*
2–4	1.50	0.50
10–12	6.25	1.25
21–24	13.50	2.50
30–35	20.00	4.00
40–45	26.00	5.00
50–55	33.00	6.00
60–65	40.00	7.00
70–75	46.00	8.00

Source: Gutehoffnungshütte 400101482/0 'Lohntabelle für sowietische Kriegsgefangene', n.d.

This approach was a short-run success. According to Pleiger, the increased outputs of autumn 1942 were accomplished 'solely by dint of the harder work of the German miner in doing overtime and in training foreign labour'.[56] But instead of relief the miner received from Göring only empty words of praise:

> Although your workday is especially heavy, harder than that of any other job, you have toiled Sundays, and what's more, volunteered to do extra

> 'armaments shifts' *(Panzerschichten)*, donating your wages to the fabrication of weapons for the German armed forces. My thanks go in particular to those in [the Ruhr] who have fulfilled their duty unflinchingly and whose labour morale *(Schaffenseifer)* has never been found wanting.[57]

Over the long run, coal outputs could have been maintained only by infusing additional slave labour into the mines or reducing rates of attrition. The industry claimed credit for having been the first to appreciate the need for better treatment. An internal study of Gutehoffnungshütte concluded ponderously that

> The regulations governing the employment of foreign workers indicate an overall tendency to move gradually from an initially somewhat more severe concept of East Worker and PoW treatment to one emphasizing the provision of working conditions similar to those of Germans.[58]

But Labour Plenipotentiary Sauckel also deserves credit for advocating better treatment. On 15 July 1942 he warned coal administrators that 'If we do not succeed in satisfying the basic needs of foreign labourers for food and shelter it will be impossible to win them over in the struggle of the German people against the enemies of Europe.' A week later he pleaded to Zentrale Planung for a more humane approach, since

> no Russian, PoW or civilian, has become resistant to authority. This only happens when they are beaten. They have never experienced this in the USSR. When struck, they go mad. . . . When they get hit in Germany – I've heard it said a thousand times – they seek revenge.[59]

Treatment of the mine slaves did gradually improve enough to prevent any increases in rates of attrition. First, certain supervisory excesses were brought under a measure of control. These were numerous. The 'turf' above ground belonged to DAF and the Gestapo. Labour Front officials, frequently incompetent or corrupt, appointed similarly inclined camp bosses *(Lagerführer)* from the ranks of the slaves. Things were little better underground. German miners, acting as 'helpers' *(Wach- und Hilfsmannschaften)* of DAF and the Gestapo, often persisted in meting out brutal and arbitrary punishment. There was also an alarming increase in the suicide rate. As noted in an early 1943 circular of the Bezirksgruppe

> The Wehrmacht and civil authorities have complained that the treatment of PoWs leaves much to be desired. Beatings and other mistreatment continues. In the pits humane treatment of any sort is absent. It is obvious that no interest is shown for the fair handling of PoWs. How else can one explain the daily departures from the mines of bodies and of totally emaciated death-candidates *(Todeskandidaten)* . . .?[60]

On 26 August 1943, procedures were tightened up, it being directed that

> Punishment of PoWs can be ordered only by military officers. Since [it] normally results in the removal [of the offender] from production, all minor offences are to be brought first to the attention of management. Punishment is to be applied only after all attempts at constructive correction have been exhausted.

'No further chicanery', the directive concluded, 'will be tolerated'.[61]

Second, wages and living conditions also improved slightly. In September 1943 the Führer directed that to increase productivity Soviet PoWs should be allowed to carry pocket money of RM1 and to purchase limited amounts of sunflower seeds, majorka tobacco and soft drinks. Nor did he rule out for 'especially productive groups' the prospects of films, sports activities and radios. Beginning December 1943 'particularly productive miners' with three months' 'good time' could wear their 'East worker' badge on an armband instead of, as previously, over the left breast. In December wages for Soviet PoWs were raised to 80 per cent of German levels for 'equivalent work'. In the vital matter of food, however, little could be done. In September 1943 Director Kellermann of Gutehoffnungshütte, a firm which had provided supplementary ratios to PoWs, noted that any significant improvement in their poor diets would require the intervention of the political authorities.[62]

Given reasonable chances to survive the mine slaves proved willing to work hard. This by no means precluded the need for close supervision. According to a GHH report,

> Among the Russians . . . there is a high percentage of useful men, which is not to overlook the fact that they also include a certain number who damage the works whenever possible. Some of them, when left alone, do all kinds of mischief: tool boxes are broken into and tools hidden; some people walk off the job; packets are stolen from railroad wagons; food is taken and given to other foreign workers who then do not report for work . . . etc.[63]

Still, by April 1943 the productivity of Soviet PoWs had reached 80 per cent German levels, it had proved possible to employ them in work gangs under only loose German supervision, and retention rates (apart from 'natural' losses caused by death) were high. This contrasted with the continued high losses through flight of foreign civilians which mounted with the intensity of aerial bombardment. On 7 July 1943 it was ordered that subsequent drafts, the first for some 80,000 due in the mines by 1 September, were to be conducted at PoW camps.[64]

A second consideration also figured in this decision. With the Wehrmacht forced on the defensive it became more difficult to conscript. On 22 April 1943 a delegate of Sauckel's reported to Zentrale Planung that in the General Government

> labour draftees have been waging fierce resistance . . . They are registering but fail to appear to call-ups. Securing them is more or less a police matter . . . As is known, the situation in Poland is extremely grave. We've had to fight some real battles over this thing. Our people face serious dangers. In the last two or three weeks several of them have been shot including the director of the Warsaw labour office fourteen days ago at his desk, and yesterday still another official. So it goes at the moment. The conscriptions cannot be carried out, even with the utmost effort, without police reinforcements.[65]

The arrival of Polish East workers virtually ceased in mid-summer 1943. The supply of Russian PoWs, however, was abundant during most of the year, the number employed increasing from 43,131 in January to 77,935 in December. But by the end of February 1944 circumstances were such that, as one commentator put it, 'as a result of the general military situation, no more PoWs [were] to be had!' To aggravate the shortages, a March 1944 order from the OKW that all tuberculars be removed from the mines resulted in an immediate drop of 10 per cent in the number of Soviet PoWs employed. But shortages were already so severe by the end of 1943 that in spite of the unanimous opposition of the industry some 10,054 Italian military internees had to be sent to the pits. They proved, as feared, to be 'weak, malarial, susceptible to chills, and lazy'.[66] Additions to the labour force in spring 1944 consisted of PoWs reallocated from jobs elsewhere in the Reich.

In spite of sacrifice and suffering – much more of which was to come – the coal supply situation grew steadily worse over the months when the slave labour programme ran full tilt. While outputs remained fairly constant, current demand continued to rise, and on top of it came Speer's ambitious new steel campaign, the Iron Plan *(Eisenplan)*. The Iron Plan was the foundation for a planned increase in overall armaments outputs. It required an additional 500,000 tons of steel per month. In October 1942 the gap between the Reich's anticipated fuel needs and actual production was thrust before Zentrale Planung with remarkable suddenness. The presentation by Pleiger on the 23rd of that month of RVK's plans for the coal year April 1943–April 1944 amounted in Speer's view to a 'declaration of bankruptcy'. The RVK chief planned to make cutbacks in coal allocations of 20 per cent to the energy industry, of nearly 500,000 tons per month to the railroads, and of 340,000 tons per month to the foundry industry. The latter would have made it impossible to raise steel outputs above existing levels of 2.1 million tons per month, and this was *without* the Iron Plan. In a towering rage Speer tossed out the coal programme because 'less iron means fewer weapons, munitions, planes and tanks – and we are already consuming 80–90 per cent of our monthly munitions output. An [effective] 40 per cent cutback in allocation to steel is totally unacceptable!'[67] But what, apart from pumping more labour into the mines, could be done?

Reallocation was one possibility, and it was the main concern at no less than five meetings of Zentrale Planung in the last week of October and early November 1942. At them the remaining savings were 'squeezed' out of the coal economy. But whose ox was to be gored? Exports, where cutbacks had occurred earlier, appeared to be highly vulnerable but proved to be less so. State Secretary Landfried of the Ministry of Economics, the authority responsible for such matters, warned that this would cost the Reich its credibility. ('We promise everything and no longer deliver . . . and especially in coal we're far behind in our obligations') at a time when Germany was become increasingly dependent on the rest of Europe.

> Export [he emphasized] . . . equates with those things we depend on: a twelfth of our foodstuff supplies from Denmark as well as war-essential production from France, Greece, Norway, Croatia, Yugoslavia, Estonia, Spain, Portugal, Romania, Switzerland, Italy, and Sweden. We're not actually exporting but fuelling factories at work for us![68]

This was not a matter of choice: the Reich, he concluded, lacked the power to compel deliveries from abroad which, without sufficient coal exports, would surely come to an end. While Zentrale Planung agreed that Upper Silesia would take over 80,000 tons of the quota from the Ruhr, total exports were to decline only from 237,000 tons to 187,000 tons per month.

Domestic consumption was another use previously subject to cutbacks. In coal year 1942 some 5 million tons were diverted to industry, as was also done a year earlier. But Speer believed that, 'It is better to let people freeze a bit in their homes than allow arms production to go to pieces'. Acting on the assumption that German households were being better supplied with coal than British, he pressed hard for additional reductions. An investigation soon disclosed, however, that 'household allocation' in the Reich included small businesses while in Great Britain it did not. Per capita consumption of heating coal in homes was therefore actually already somewhat lower in Germany than in Britain (0.84 ton/person *v.* 0.87 ton/person). Savings of only 179,000 monthly tons were possible.[69]

The most significant savings were, surprisingly, made at the mines themselves. They came from the so-called 'self-consumption quota', the output that the vertically integrated firms reserved for their own use. Cutbacks were to occur on the basis of a complicated formula: 15 per cent from the 3.55 million tons subsumed under the 'self-consumption' quota (which approximated the 550,000 tons called for in the Iron Plan) followed by the retrocession to the tied-in mines of one-half the amounts achieved by savings in coke consumption. One purpose of this measure was to eliminate waste in the steel-making process, encourage the use of more scrap and high-grade ores, and so on. Savings of more than 10 per cent (450,000 tons) were believed possible. The other purpose behind it was political in nature: it was essential to give the impression to the Führer that Ruhr coal had been stripped of its last great privilege. As the Reich entered what was expected to be the decisive phase of the war Hitler called all existing institutional arrangements into question, including the right of industry to remain autonomous. As Speer threatened at the 3 November 1942 session of Zentrale Planung,

> we're on the verge of major decisions. The Fuhrer told me . . . a few days ago . . . in no uncertain way that [heavy industry] must meet its targets. At the same time, he added something very regrettable: industry had promised him that it could do the job on a 'self-administrative' basis. I have championed this argument, and it will be seriously undermined [if the targets are not reached].[70]

The spectre of expropriation was unmistakable. Its effect on production and supply was, however, moot.

There simply was no more 'give' in the coal economy. On 22 April 1943 Zentrale Planung discussed its problems exhaustively, concluding in effect that they were indeed hopeless. The coal plan for April 1943–April 1944 envisaged total Reich output (including lignite) of 312 million tons, significant increases over the 289 and 261 million tons *consumed* in the previous years. Total coal *produced* in the Reich in the same period had increased by 16 million tons. Some 10 million tons of this amount derived from work done on Sundays and holidays where no further gains were possible. Moreover, the total capacity of all Reich mines under 'optimum' conditions was rated at 290 million tons, and was predicated on increases of no less than 191,000 in the total employment of mine slaves. The official targets were no more realistic than earlier ones. How much coal really had to be produced to prevent the gradual breakdown of industrial production? Hans Kehrl, who soon would be named chief energy planner, estimated – and was not contradicted – that with outputs of less than 282 million tons and allocations less than 295 million tons 'the supply problem will be insoluble'. Coke was a particular weak point. The Iron Plan required some 68 million tons but with total mine output at 290 million tons only 58 million tons of coal could be coked. The fulfilment of the new steel programme's coal requirements, Kehrl concluded, would result in breakdowns throughout the industrial economy.[71]

This was prevented during coal year 1943 only by a combination of good luck, expedients and disruption elsewhere. The exceptionally mild winter of 1942–3 was a welcome reprieve. Still, by spring stocks were down by a half. In January and February allocations had to be reduced to all consumers except steel, artificial rubber, synthetic petroleum and armaments in order to maintain production in these critical industries. May and June brought shortages at cokeries and gas plants, and coking coal deliveries to the Reichsbahn also had to be reduced. In July the other German districts, above all Upper Silesia, received orders to deliver an additional 800,000 monthly tons to Ruhr customers. In September, the shortage of railway cars became more severe than that of coal, in part because of the additional demand resulting from the Silesian relief effort begun in July. This then had to be discontinued. At the same time the emergency caused by low water levels in south German hydroelectric dams made it necessary to start up inefficient coal-fired plants long out of operation. By December stocks of thermal coal had all but disappeared. In addition, the emergency shipments of huge amounts of small-sized Reichsbahn coals to the foundries for coking aggravated the weaknesses in the transport system, causing numerous stoppages. The gas works, the Hamburg wharves and many other important customers faced shutdowns by the end of the year. The 'loss on a large scale' of industrial output during winter 1943–4 was staved off thanks only to 'daily reallocations of coal'. In March 1944, temporary closures and reductions in operating levels climbed precipitously once again.[72] The United States Strategic Bombing Survey's (USSBS) summary report concluded that, 'The coal situation in [spring] 1944 provides the best indication that basic German industry had reached its practical limits in supporting a war economy.' This did not involve an increase in steel output which, contrary to Speer's hopes, failed in 1943 to rise above output levels of the previous year.[73]

The situation would have been still worse had not German miners been capable of extraordinary exertions. By the end of the year over 20 per cent of the German portion of the labour force was over fifty years old. In 1943 these men worked an average of 25.6 days per month, each of them forty-five minutes longer than normal. In June, weekly rations were cut by 100g. In addition to supervising the 87,000 foreigners at work underground, German miners also had to face increasingly intense air-raids. They were a minor problem until March 1943. But that month brought seven of them and April another four. In May came the famous RAF raid on the Mohne Dam. Worse was to follow. From March to July losses due directly to bombardment amounted to 215,000 tons, 166,170 tons, 242,840 tons, 813,278 tons, 563,948 tons and 515,327 tons respectively. But *indirect* losses of production were still more serious. Miners whose homes were destroyed, numbering 7288 in March alone, stayed away from work until they could find alternative accommodation for their families, and these were often far away from places of employment; the destruction of the tram system made commuting more and more difficult; and the same men who had toiled hard and long in the pits often found themselves obliged to do clearing and relocation work after hours. A rise in rates of absence and sickness was the consequence of such disruptions. By the end of 1943, losses of output due to air-raids exceeded those gained by the engagement of foreign labour. According to the unpublished contemporary account of the Ruhr coal industry during the war by Bergassessor Hans Spethmann, there was general agreement within the industry that no additional effort could be expected from the German miner. 'Extraordinary accomplishments', he states, 'occur in sport or in battle' but cannot be expected continuously over the long run. During the coming twelve months of 1945, he predicted 'the quantity and quality of the food supply would be decisive in production'.[74]

In early 1944 transportation replaced production as the immediate cause of the coal supply problem. While German output from April 1943 to April 1944 exceeded that of the previous year by 3.8 million tons, consumption shrank by 3.7 million tons, and stocks increased by 2.5 million tons. The pre-Normandy raids seriously aggravated the situation. Although by July the Reichsbahn had managed to repair most of the recent damage, the situation deteriorated rapidly soon thereafter. Coal wagons spotted in the Ruhr, according to the USSBS summary report,

> dropped from 20,200 daily in June and 18,200, in August to 14,500 daily in October, November, and December – insufficient for the normal requirements within the Ruhr itself. . . . Even more drastic was the decline in waterways traffic by 75 per cent in the final quarter [of the year].[75]

By November the inability to transport coal from the Ruhr was causing paralysis and breakdown throughout the industrial economy. The rails, power plants, gas works and chemical factories were down to an average of ten days' supply and work stoppages at many key production units had occurred. Munitions output was off 25–30 per cent and falling. On 11 November 1944 Speer 'wrote off' the Ruhr as irrecoverably lost, and therewith also the war itself: 'It is', he said, '. . . obvious that the loss of the Rhineland-Westphalia industrial area is unbearable for the German economy as a whole and for the successful prosecution of the war.'[76]

But the crisis in transportation relieved pressure on the mines at a time when they appear to have reached their technical limits. By the first half of 1944 plant as well as manpower was deteriorating rapidly. On 25 May 1944 Pleiger warned Zentrale Planung:

> The installations are no longer what they should be. [We are facing] increased losses and waste due to forced operations at higher capacities as well as inadequate deliveries of replacement parts, underground machinery, etc. This has led to major stoppages at many plants. We've had explosions and the like . . . and should expect greater difficulties in the future.[77]

Because by mid-1944 coal could not be moved from the pithead, outputs and mine employment dropped 40 per cent in the final year of the war. This slow-down made it possible to improve tunnelling and roofing as well as repair essential machinery.[78]

The 'breathing space' was of critical importance not only for the Ruhr but the German future. Even in its most punitive phases, Allied policy toward the defeated Reich recognized the necessity of restoring coal output in the Ruhr:

the economic recovery of Europe, as well as Germany, depended on it. Thanks to the preservation of plant, the power to withhold or deliver this critical commodity remained ultimately in German hands.

But the mine industry was incapable of staging a post-war comeback on its own, if for no other reason than financial exhaustion. Losses per ton of mined coal mounted from RM1.25/ton to RM8.49/ton by the end of 1944. Responsible for this result was a combination of controlled prices, which were held level for the duration of the war, and increased costs for wages (up 157 per cent) and 'social expenses' (up 172 per cent), both of which in large part stemmed from the foreign labour programme. Depreciations by contrast rose only 118 per cent and were quite insufficient. A British accountancy team sent to examine the mines in summer 1945 concluded that future mine operation would require massive official subsidies. The autonomy which it had sought so long to preserve *vis-à-vis* central authority was, for the Ruhr, the final casualty of the war.[79]

Notes

1 Bundesarchiv (BA) R3/1550 'Rede Reichsminister Speer auf der Rüstungstagung in Linz', 24 June 1944.

2 Wiener Library (WL), Pleiger Dok. 404, 'Eidesstattliche Erklärung Hermann Winkhaus', 14 June 1948; BA RIO VIII/2 'Sprechzettel für grundsätzliche Ausführungen; Westfälisches Wirtschaftsarchiv (WWA) F26/464 'Besprechung beim Reichskohlenkommissar', 17 December 1940; GHH 400101320/115 'Paul Walters Pläne', *Deutsche Allgemeine Zeitung*, 8 January 1941; 400101320/115 'Die Neuordnung der Kohlenwirtschaft. Umfassende Ziele und Pläne des Reichskohlenkommissars', *National-Zeitung, 9 January 1941;* 400101320/96; NIK 11,228 *'Erklärung Paul Pleiger', 31 July 1947.*

3 US National Archives (USNA), Spethmann IV/2, 15, 23; I, 56.

4 Matthias Riedel, *Eisen und Kohle für das Dritte Reich. Paul Pleigers Stellung in der NS-Wirtschaft* (Göttingen, 1973), 273 f.; BA Nachlass Spethmann V, 37 f.; GHH 400101330/42 'Sitzung des Ausschusses für Syndikatsfragen in der RVK', 19 August 1941; WL Paul Pleiger Dok. 403 'Eidesstattliche Erklärung Fr. Flick', 21 January 1948; NID-12876 'Interrogation of Paul Pleiger', 21 March 1946.

5 BA R7/590 Funk to Ley, 26 June 1939.

6 Westfälisches Wirtschaftsarchiv (WWA) F26/365 'Zur Nachwuchserwerbung, Bericht von Bergrat Ziekursch', 5 June 1942.

7 Gutehoffnungshütte (GHH) 400101305/9 'Statistische Angaben aus dem Ruhrkohlenbergbau. Zusammenfassende Darstellung seit Kriegsausbruch bis Juli 1944'.

8 BA Nachlass Spethmann III, 102 f.; WWA F26/3668 'Anlage zum Rundschreiben . . . Nr. 19 vom 27. Marz, 1940. G-N-B 300 XI, 9.3.40'.

9 USNA T83/45/3410993-3411746; T83/45/3411360 'Jungendarrestant Heinz-Günter Romeis; BA Nachlass Spethmann III, 17.

10 (BM) Bergbau Museum B13/1791 'Sozialpolitische Information Nr. 3/42. Frauen im Bergbau', BA R11/1144 'Was erwartet die Wirtschaft von der weiblichen Berufslenkung?' (n.d.)

11 GHH 400101320/96 Buskühl to Walter, 7 June 1940; WL Paul Pleiger Dok. 444 'Eidesstattliche Erklärung Hans Spethmann', 30 April 1948; BA Nachlass Spethmann IV, 61 f.; GHH 400101320/17 'Gremium', 13 March 1940; BM B12/1760 'Besprechung am 19.6.1940'.
12 USNA T83/42340813 Harpener to Bezirksgruppe, 31 July 1940.
13 WWA F26/393 'Vertrauensratssitzung', 15 July 1940; F26/393 'Vertrauensratssitzung', 29 May 1941; GHH 400101301/3 Staatspolizeilicheleitstelle Düsseldorf to GHH, 23 July 1940.
14 BA Nachlass Spethmann IV, 62; BM B13/1760 'Besprechung im Oberpräsidium in Münster', 19 June 1940.
15 ibid.; BA Nachlass Spethmann; GHH 400101330/27 Gabel to Sogemaier, 23 August 1940.
16 ibid., BA Nachlass Spethmann, 66; BM 12/1791 'Sozialpolitische Information Nr. 11/12/1942'; WWA F26/359 'Besprechung bei der Bezirksgruppe Essen', 8 August 1939.
17 GHH 400101301/3 'Förderung auf den Zechen', 26 June 1941.
18 USNA Spethmann, op. cit., IV, 1.
19 WWA F26/365 'Beiratssitzung der Bezirksgruppe Ruhr', 8 July 1941; BA R3/1726 '58. Besprechung der Zentralen Planung (Z.P.)', 25 March 1944.
20 GHH 400101301/3 Walter to Sogemaier, 10 July 1940.
21 BM B13/1760 'Besprechung (zu Ruk Nr. 748)', 4 September 1940; WWA F26/369 'Rundschreiben Nr. 10', 25 March 1941; BM B13/1760 'Besprechung im Landeshaus Münster (zu Ruk Nr. 748)', 4 September 1940; USNA Spethmann, op. cit., V, 13.
22 GHH 400101482/13 'Bericht über den Fremdarbeitereinsatz bei der Gutehoffnungshütte'.
23 WWA F26/393. 'Vertrauensratssitzung', 10 November 1941; BA R7/119 '52. Wochenbericht für den Bergbau', 21 November 1941.
24 GHH 400101301/3 Staatspolizeileitstelle Düsseldorf to GHH, 23 July 1940; WWA F 26/393 'Vertrauensratssitzung, 23 June 1941.
25 USNA T83/42/3408041 'Richtlinien über die Behandlung und den Arbeitseinsatz polnischen Zivilarbeiter . . .'
26 ibid.; USNA T83/42/3408116 'Der Höhere SS- und Polizeiführer bei den Oberpräsidenten von Westfalen', 22 July 1940.
27 WWA F26/393 'Vertrauensratssitzung', 29 May 1941.
28 BM B13/1760 'Besprechung im Landeshaus Münster (zu RUK Nr. 748)', 4 September 1940.
29 GHH 400101305/9 'Statistische Angaben aus dem Ruhrkohlenbergau. Zusammenfassende Darstellung seit Kriegsausbruch bis Juli 1944'.
30 BA Nachlass Spethmann V/2, 59.
31 ibid., IV 28.
32 Bergbau Verein, *Statistisches Heft. Produktions- und wirtschaftsstatistisches Angaben aus der Montanindustrie* (Essen, 1939); USNA Spethmann, op. cit., IV/2, 15.
33 Hoover Institution (HI), '6. Besprechung der Z.P.', 28 May 1942; GHH 400101320/96 'Aktennotiz', 16 December 1939.
34 HI, '10. Besprechung der Z.P.', 15 July 1942.
35 USNA Spethmann, op. cit., IV/2, *passim*.
36 BA RIO VIII/19 Pleiger to Göring, 15 August 1941.
37 WWA F26/365 'Aktennotiz, Bezirksgruppe', 24 November 1941; BA Nachlass Spethmann, V/2, 170.

38 GHH 400101330/33 'Bergbau Verein 2. Bericht über die Forschungs- und Entwicklungsarbeit' (Essen, 1941); BM B13/1790 'Berichte . . .', B13/1818, B15/423; BA/R7 Anl./63 Gabel to Gondemat, 28 December 1945; Ernst Buskühl 'Der Ruhrbergbau in der Leistungsprobe', *Der Vierjahresplan*, Jg.6/1942.
39 GHH 400101320/128 Kellermann to Welker, 13 October 1941; WWA F26/365 'Beiratssitzung der Bezirksgruppe Ruhr', 15 May 1942.
40 HI '10. Sitzung der Z.P.', 15 July 1942.
41 WWA F26/1365 'Beiratssitzung der Bezirksgruppe', 24 November 1941.
42 HI 'Besprechungen der Z.P.', no. 6, 28 May 1942, no. 10, 15 July 1942, no. 11, 22 July 1942; GHH 400101305/9 'Statistische Angaben aus dem Ruhrkohlenbergbau. Zusammenfassende Darstellung seit Kriegsausbruch bis Juli 1944'; GHH 400101320/18 'Sitzung des Beirats', 10 September 1942; BA Nachlass Spethmann VI, 89.
43 HI '17. Besprechung der Z.P.', 28 October 1942.
44 ibid.
45 GHH 400101301/3 'Sowjetrussische Kriegsgefangene', 21 October 1941.
46 GHH 400101330/17 'Merkblatt über den Einsatz sowjetrussischer Kriegsgefangener', 2 December 1942.
47 HI '17. Besprechung der Z.P.', 28 October 1942.
48 BM B13/1791 'Sozialpolitische Information Nr. 8/42', 1 August 1942; GHH 400101330/17 'Merkblatt über den Einsatz sowjetrussischer Kriegsgefangener', 2 December 1942.
49 GHH 4001482/14 'Gestapo. Merkblatt für die sicherheitspolizeiliche Behandlung der sowjetrussischen Arbeitskräfte . . .', 24 June 1942.
50 WWA F26/393 'Vertrauensratssitzung', 19 March 1942.
51 GHH 400101330/7 'Fördersteigerung durch Grosseinsatz von russischen Kriegsgefangener'.
52 WWA F26/370 'Richtlinien für den Einsatz russischer Kriegsgefangener', 17 September 1942.
53 GHH 400101330/7 'Fördersteigerung durch Grosseinsatz von russischen Kriegsgefangener', 22 July 1942.
54 GHH 400101320/18 'Sitzung des Beirats', 10 September 1942; 400101482/14 'Bezirksgruppe Steinkohlenbergbau Ruhr . . . 1943 Rundschreiben Nr. 43', 29 January 1943.
55 GHH 400101320/18 'Sitzung des Beirats', 10 September 1942; WWA F26/370 'Richtlinien für den Einsatz russischer Kriegsgefangener', 17 September 1942; F26/393 'Vertrauensratssitzung', 30 September 1942.
56 HI '17. Besprechung der Z.P.', 28 October 1942.
57 BA Nachlass Spethmann IV, 142.
58 GHH 4001482/13 'Bericht über den Fremdarbeitereinsatz bei der Gutehoffnungshütte', (n.d.).
59 HI 'Sitzungen der Z.P.', Nr. 10, 15 July 1942, Nr. 11 22 July 1942.
60 GHH 400101330/17 'Bezirksgruppe Steinkohlenbergbau Ruhr', 4 June 1943; 400101482/14 'Bezirksgruppe Steinkohlenbergbau Ruhr – 1943 Rundschreiben Nr. 43', 29 January 1943; 4001482/14 'Rundschreiben Nr. 170', 13 April 1943.
61 BM 1313/1791 'Sozialpolitische Information Nr. 10/43', 26 August 1943.
62 WWA F26/393 'Vertrauensratssitzung', 29 December 1942; GHH 4001026/10 'Sitzung des Unternehmerbeirats', 20 September 1943; 400101300/12 'Kriegsgefangene- und Ausländereinsatz', 24 September 1943; BA Nachlass Spethmann VIII, 716.

63 GHH 400101482/13 'Bericht über den Fremdarbeitereinsatz bei der Gutehoffnungshütte' (n.d.).
64 BA Nachlass Spethmann VIII, 69 f., 74.
65 HI '36. Besprechung der Z.P.', 22 April 1943.
66 BA Nachlass Spethmann VIII, 78, 83 f.
67 HI '16. Besprechung der Z.P.', 23 October 1942.
68 HI '16. Besprechung der Z.P.', 23 October 1942; HI 'Besprechungen' 17, 18, 19 (27 October, 28 October, 3 November 1942).
69 HI '18. Besprechung der Z.P.', 28 October 1942.
70 HI '23. Besprechung der Z.P.', 3 November 1942; '18. Besprechung der Z.P.', 28 October 1942.
71 HI '36. Besprechung der Z.P.', 22 April 1943.
72 BA Nachlass Spethmann VII, 178 f.
73 US Strategic Bombing Survey (USSBS), 'Summary Report,' op. cit., 96, 99–104.
74 BA Nachlass Spethmann IX, 74, 135–155; USSBS, 'Area Studies Division Report. The Effects of the Air Offensive Against German Cities', January 1947.
75 USSBS, Summary Report, op. cit., 99; BA Nachlass Spethmann IX, op. cit., 195–201.
76 BA R3/1528 'Speer. Denkschrift Ruhrgebiet', 11 November 1944.
77 HI '58. Besprechung der Z.P.', 25 May 1944.
78 B10S 'Technical report on the Ruhr coalfield (VI)' (London, 1946); BM B13/1790 'Vortrag über die Kohlenlage von Dr. Regul', 16 May 1944.
79 North German Coal Council, 'Interim report on the general economic and financial situation of the Ruhr mining industry', September, 1945.

7

WEST EUROPEAN HEAVY INDUSTRY IN THE NEW ORDER

In the period from the fall of France to VE Day the alliance of the Ruhr with its former cartel partners in western Europe was put to the test. Domination of the continent provided German coal and steel producers of the Ruhr with a unique opportunity to eliminate or take over foreign competition. By means of stock swaps which its victims made under duress the Reichswerke, Hermann Göring, became the largest conglomerate in the world during the few months from Anschluss to the invasion of Poland.[1] While a small minority of the Ruhr clamoured for a similarly aggressive policy, the majority decided in favour of a different, unspectacular one: to follow traditional aims and methods. This approach rested on a belief that wartime conditions were temporary and exceptional and would be followed by a peace in which 'business as usual' could be resumed. During the occupation the operators and foundrymen of the Ruhr tried to institutionalize the 'junior partnerships' which had developed over the previous fifteen years by reworking cartels along German lines, planning for the future, and establishing various kinds of communities of interest which would survive regardless of the war's outcome.

Business was not the sole carrier of German economic policy in New Order western Europe. It contended in this respect less with any single group, faction or bloc than with the chaos and confusion integral to the national socialist system, its nihilistic character. Hitler was fundamentally disinterested in economic policy in western Europe and this, while generally fortunate, opened the door to organized interests such as the Four Year Plan, party and SS for whom the purpose of conquest was simple plunder and the legitimate goal of occupation policy, politicide. They represented an ever-present threat to economic order and, if given free rein, might well have turned occupied western Europe into a kind of giant Poland.

But such a fate was not, at least for the present generation, clearly foreshadowed in Hitler's ruminations on policy. Other circumstances also combined to make it improbable. One was the existence in France and the Low

Countries of governments, or national representatives, pledged to economic collaboration. This often misunderstood policy amounted to an attempt to reduce the risks and rigours of occupation by supplying goods and services of value to the Reich's war effort. Another circumstance diminishing the likelihood of chaos was, paradoxically, German weakness in the face of Hitler's ambitions: the attainment of European hegemony by means of the *Drang nach Osten* (drive to the east) required an absence of conflict and a minimum of military commitments in the west. Those who stirred up resistance in the subject populations – radical Nazifiers for instance – represented a costly strategic luxury. The third circumstance was the growing demand in the Reich, felt as the scope of the war expanded, for supplemental sources of agricultural and industrial output. This called for a policy of 'rational exploitation', not the 'smash and grab' to which Nazi groups inclined. To harness the energies of industry in the occupied countries, the regime turned to German business. Technocrats, administrators and officials from industry staffed the numerous agencies responsible for raising industrial outputs in France and the Low Countries and guiding production into Reich armaments schedules. They wore two hats, as representatives of business and as agents of the regime.[2]

Producers and officials from the occupied countries supported, indeed promoted 'rational exploitation'. Its success was even more vital from the standpoint of their own national interests than it was to those of the Reich: so long as industry stood idle, losses would be enormous and, worse yet, productive resources, human labour above all, remain subject to seizure and removal. Opportunistic motives were of course at work in occupied Europe: many businessmen were only too eager to 'make a deal' with the conqueror. But even the shift in the tide of battle failed to bring about refusal to accept German orders or cause a breakage of economic links to the Reich. This would have been costly. But collaboration continued for other reasons as well. The producers of France and the Low Countries generally agreed on the efficacy of German organizational methods and expected that in the future world of economic giants co-operation with Reich producers would be essential.[3]

The Ruhr was in a position to meet the needs of its counterparts only about half way. When 'wearing hats' as agents of the regime, its representatitves were sometimes obliged to impose policies damaging to the industrial interests under their supervision. Worse still, business could not make policy at the top – in other words, influence Hitler's critical strategic decisions. Two consequences resulted from the low priority he assigned economic matters in western Europe. One was that although there were not initially severe shortages in the factors of production much of the manufacturing capacity of France and the Low Countries remained under-used. Depression-like conditions therefore obtained, which, aggravated by a catastrophic inflation, not only created high levels of unemployment, but reduced living standards precariously for those still at work. As feared, these conditions served as bait to the exponents of 'smash and grab'. The result was the forced labour drafts of 1943.

The second consequence of Hitlerian neglect was that by the time Albert Speer finally made his bid to put the industry of occupied western Europe to work systematically for the Reich, it was too late. By September 1943 neglect of the mines in Belgium, the Netherlands and northern France had set in motion a process of irreversible deterioration – drastic falls in productivity which could be only partially offset by adding to the total of man-hours worked – more severe even than the one occurring in the Reich. Lack of coal thus choked off any expansion of western European industrial production, writing *finis* to the story of Hitler's missed opportunity to gain an adjunct equal in economic potential to the industry of the Reich.[4]

In summer 1940 new political and administrative institutions were set up which would regulate the relationships between the Reich and western Europe for the remainder of the occupation. Hitler redrew the map in accordance with the aims of his strategy. The primary objective of the invasion of western Europe was to weaken France militarily and politically so as to prevent it from ever becoming a second front in a war against the USSR. In addition, France and the Low Countries were expected to serve as a staging ground for future operations against Britain. Territorial dismemberment was the result of the Franco-German armistice agreement. Only about a third of pre-war France remained unoccupied. It consisted of the southern portions of the country except for the ten *départements* closest to Italy (which the troops of that nation occupied) and the militarily more significant strip of territory, some fifty to sixty miles wide, which ran along the Atlantic coast from the Pyrenees north to German-occupied territory. A so-called line of demarcation cut off nearly all civilian contact between the occupied and unoccupied zones. A second line of demarcation restricted interchange between most of occupied France and the industrially critical areas of the north and east. Further, the two départements of Nord and Pas-de-Calais (which together raised some 60 per cent of French coal output) were attached to the administration of the Military Governor in Brussels rather than to his counterpart in Paris, hostages to a future peace treaty. Worse yet, the territories of the former Reichsland Elsass-Lothringen, which contained most of France's steel capacity as well as valuable ore beds, were reattached to Germany. They included the départements of Bas-Rhin and Moselle. Luxembourg was also incorporated into the Reich while Belgium (except for minor border 'rectifications') and the Netherlands were left outside its borders.[5]

Although these territorial arrangements remained largely in place for the entire period of German domination – the important exception being the German occupation of southern France in November 1942 – they were never intended to be permanent. Their temporary character was fully consistent with

Hitler's *Blitzkrieg* approach to governing which, while it did not necessarily make economic sense, was shrewd politically. By reserving the ultimate power of decision to himself he encouraged would-be *Machthaber* (wielders-of-power) to bid for his favour. Such contestants were also to be found among the conquered. Competition took place mainly between established groups pledged to co-operate so long as they remained in place and aspirants to power who through professions of political allegiance to the New Order hoped to introduce far-reaching, fascist-like changes in their societies. The long run favoured the 'conservatives'. Their assets included the existence of 'communities of interest' with the conqueror, the 'moral authority' conveyed by tradition, and dominant economic positions. The 'radical' alternative involved basing occupation rule on 'particularistic' fascist groups often in conflict with each other, whose ambitions sometimes collided with those of the Nazi Party, and whose leaders were generally unreliable, dishonest and unrealistic. In summer 1940 businessmen and civil servants in occupied western Europe set up the administrative machinery to attach their economies to the New Order. They adopted German methods of business organization, labour relations and raw materials rationing and created banking mechanisms with which to finance massive exports to the Reich.[6] The Reich should have welcomed these initiatives: it was short of personnel and increasingly in need of supplementary production.[7] Yet Berlin's acceptance of 'collaboration' was only qualified and it depended less on 'rational' policy-making than on the outcome of struggles for power.

The contest for west European heavy industry was of critical importance. The Ruhr won it, thus establishing its predominant influence in the occupied area. At the same time, the struggle left a legacy of administrative division that severely handicapped policy-making. It had both coal and steel dimensions. In steel the main contestants were Gauleiter Fritz Terboven of the Ruhr and his counterpart from Saar-Pfalz, Josef Bürckel. Otto Steinbrinck was Terboven's candidate for hegemon of west European foundries. A former U-boat captain, current SS Reserve General, and long-time associate of Friedrich Flick, Steinbrinck controlled with Terboven the largest shareholding in VS, the one held previously by Fritz Thyssen who had fled the Reich. Steinbrinck acted on behalf of the Ruhr. Bürckel's man was Hermann Röchling. This scion of a long line of Saar foundrymen was both rabid nationalist and technical genius, and therefore doubly threatening to the Ruhr. Although in early May 1940 Steinbrinck was named chief steel representative in the districts of Belgium, North France, and the district of Longwy, his territory did not include 'Meurthe-et-Moselle-Sud', the non-annexed section of eastern France which contained the bulk of the nation's foundry industry. In coal, the Saar was not a major force in policy-making. But in this field the Ruhr confronted the Göring interests. As the result of a bargain, the mines of Dutch Limburg and the Belgian Campine were placed under the administration of Bergassessor Bruch, a former employee of the Reichswerke. Various coal specialists on the staffs of the military government in Brussels and Paris, along with their regional subordinates, administered the rest.[8]

Outside of Röchling's 'sphere of influence' Steinbrinck and his deputies set up counterpart organizations to those in the Reich. In steel this was not difficult. The Belgian steel cartel, 'COSIBEL', was renamed 'SYBELAC' (Syndicat belge de l'Acier), with membership compulsory for all producers and the power to enforce German schemes for rationing raw materials and allocate orders from the Reich. The Comptoir Sidérurgique de France underwent a similar metamorphosis and emerged as 'CORSID' (Comité d'Organisation Sidérurgique de France). In both cases, pre-war officials remained in office. The coal cartels underwent more far-reaching changes. The pre-war federation of Belgian operators was centralized and became the Office Belge des Charbons. In north France the sometimes moribund producer associations formed 'COH', Comité des Houillières. A similar new syndicate was also organized for the mines of Dutch Limburg. The new cartels put the policy of collaboration on an institutional footing.[9]

This was not as easy to do in the territories annexed from France and Meurthe-et-Moselle-Sud, where a scramble for 'objects of industrial interest' took place between the Göring complex, the Röchling family and the Ruhr. The motives and strategies of the participants varied considerably. Still master-builder of the Reichswerke, Pleiger wanted desperately to acquire the 14.6 million additional tons of rated capacity necessary for his foundry to overtake VS as Germany's largest.[10] Röchling was keen on settling old scores, particularly with the de Wendel family, which in 1919 had taken over from its *saaroise* founder the beloved Karlshütte, Thionville. There was reason to believe that the Ruhr's historic grievances were equally strong since many firms had also lost steel holdings after the first World War. In early June 1940 the Minister of Economics, Walter Funk, took the precaution of warning them to contain *Annektationsgelüste* – 'annexation greed'.

Yet the only interest which could not restrain itself was one lacking prior involvement in the eastern French region. Friedrich Flick fervently desired to acquire Rombacher Huttenwerke/SA Acièries de Rombas owned by the Laurent group, a long-time Ruhr ally in the ISC. As regards Rombas/Rombach, Flick was again playing the maverick. Most other Ruhr steel interests suspected in fact that he was secretly allied with Göring, as in the earlier Petschek deal, so specious was the historical basis for his claim on the Laurent foundry.[11] Apart from Flick's, the Ruhr ambitions were quite modest. At the beginning of June, VS chairman of the Board, Ernst Poensgen, circularized the firms of the district in order to sound out their acquisition plans. The responses were not enthusiastic, the one from Hoesch even perfunctory. Two firms which had made acquisitions elsewhere, Krupp and Mannesmann, remained strangely silent. Director Kellermann of Gutehoffnungshütte actually objected to the request for the presentation of claims and drafted a memorandum enumerating them only after receiving assurances that the other big firms had already done so.[12] On 7 June 1940 Poensgen issued a directive which defined Ruhr policy for the remainder of the occupation on the basis of these responses. Its main points were as follows: transfer of mines and foundries would not take place until the restoration of peace unless other interests intervened: priority in access to *minette* should go to the firms of the area (Lorraine, Luxembourg and the Saar), only the surplus being guaranteed to the Ruhr; previous German owners should be given preference after peace in reacquiring former assets; and unexploited ore properties, unless returned to their owners, should be administered by a consortium of German steel producers. In an addendum to this document Poensgen added his 'personal plans' for Lorraine–Luxembourg after final military victory. They called for guaranteeing *minette* supplies to traditional consumers, strengthening the ore-coal trade with the Ruhr, 'rationalizing' production facilities, and integrating French producers with Ruhr firms when justified by cost criteria.[13] These plans were posited on the maintenance of traditional relationships with 'western markets' and industrial interests.

The power struggle over the steel districts of annexed France, and Luxembourg as well, was settled with a compromise in which the Ruhr, while holding the upper hand, still had to share power with the Göring and Röchling interests. There was to be no wholesale confiscation of property or machinery, and the redisposition of such assets would require the prior assent of the Franco-Belgian owners. Further, trustees were to be appointed for each foundry and administer the firms in their charge in a strictly businesslike manner, it being understood that the German overseers would receive preference in any post-war redistribution of assets. Similar arrangements were made with regard to the ore beds. This system of trusteeships worked to the advantage of both previous owners and the new masters: for the trustee the prospect of eventual acquisition offset the temptation to let plant run down, and when hopes for victory dimmed it was wise to restore properties in good condition.[14]

The trusteeship awards satisfied neither the Ruhr, the Saar, nor the Göring interests. Of the six Lorraine foundries, the Ruhr received mandates for three (Rombach/Rombas going to Flick), the Saar secured two (which included Karlshütte), and the Reichswerke one. In Luxembourg, one trusteeship was split between Ruhr and Saar, and a second went to VS. The third, over the dominant producer ARBED, was formally shared by the Ruhr and the Reichswerke. Röchling was extraordinarily bitter contending that, 'He who has fought receives nothing, but he who has never fought and therefore made money gets everything . . . Now that the battle in the west is over the helmet must be strapped on more tightly. This requires soldiers, not shopkeepers!'[15] For its part, the Reichswerke schemed incessantly for over a year to take over

ARBED which, if done in customary fashion, would have amounted to expropriation. But Pleiger encountered fierce resistance not only from the Ruhr but from Röchling and Gauleiter Gustav Simon of Trier as well. On 31 May 1941 General von Hanneken, acting on orders from the Chancellery in Berlin, ordered a truce in the interests of war production.[16]

The directors of the Ruhr mines pursued similar aims to Poensgen's, as indicated by the discussion over 'war aims' which took place in the aftermath of the campaign in western Europe. At issue was the shape of the future peace treaty. The minority represented by Director Sogemeier and the head of the mines section of the Economics Ministry, Gabel, held that the future would have an 'authoritarian cast' and provide opportunities 'to drop traditional methods and adopt production and consumption steering on a European scale'.[17] They favoured the organization of a continental producer syndicate (which Great Britain would be forced to join in a minority role), the creation of similar cost and price structures (which would have involved shut-downs on a large scale in Belgium and France), and the commitment of massive investments to German mines. The position that prevailed was less ambitious. The issue was a simple one, according to RWKS's Kellermann:

> Does the Führer really want another treaty of Versailles, in other words to write a book with countless clauses that enables men sitting around a green baize table to disrupt the economy? Or would he prefer to end this war with a short, precise document which while meeting our military demands will let industry solve economic problems?[18]

The demand for 'business as usual' could hardly be stated more baldly. Ernst Russel, the RWKS export chief, spelled this out in detail. He emphasized that 'while we must of course submit to the necessities of the war effort, traditional foreign marketing areas have to be served as before' and that pre-war cartel arrangements must be revived, including the coke and coal conventions with Great Britain. Russel also recommended treading lightly,

> it being unwise to require a compulsory syndicate for the English in a peace treaty because such a thing would have to be imposed, apart from which the heavy-handed application of political pressure violates the policy of promoting economic co-operation. The English [he added] should take minimum steps towards organizing themselves to work with us, but this, once done, will allow their government to recommend reaching an understanding with the continental group.[19]

Such a 'hands-off' policy was also to apply in principle to the coal districts of occupied western Europe. As Bergassessor Lübsen wrote to Sogemaier on 14 August 1940:

> Our goals concern only export. How Holland, Belgium, and France dispose of domestic markets does not interest us. Of course we have interests in these countries, but we can handle them with general provisions in a peace treaty. It would also be a good idea to create conditions in these lands similar to our own, not to mention analogous cost and price structures. . . . This will take a gradual, natural development growing out of increased economic interrelationships.[20]

The events of the occupation would reveal the wisdom of this course: left to themselves, the businessmen of occupied western Europe would work out their own accommodations to the economic realities of the New Order and, having done so, find them acceptable.

The 'war aims' proposals of Ruhr coal and steel echo a general policy line which, while only one ingredient in the national socialist brew, was important. It emerged from the summer 1940 discussions of the so-called New Order planning staff headed by State Secretary Gustav Schlotterer of the Ministry of Economics. The participants included, in addition to various officials, representatives of key export interests: Dr Ilgner of IG Farben, Drs Kimmich and Abs of the Deutsche Bank, Dr Pildner of the Dresdner Bank, Paul Reusch of Gutehoffnungshütte and Dr Blessing of the Reichsbank. These figures consulted privately with key businessmen in the occupied countries, among them the Belgians Alexandre Galopin (governor of the Société Générale de Belgique), Baron Paul de Launoit (head of the Banque de Bruxelles/Confinindus/Brufina complex) and A.E. Janssen (director of the national bank) and the Dutchmen, Drs Hirschfeld (secretary general of the Ministry of Economics), Woltershom (Rotterdam Bank) and Fentener van Vlissingen (diverse interests). Each of them along with the German members of the Schlotterer committee, would be very prominent in the economic affairs of Hitler's Europe.

As 'concrete results' of the discussions Schlotterer reported agreement on a number of points: first, 'The necessity of a Europe-wide market area, and thereby the liberation of inner-European commerce from duties, non-tariff barriers, and currency differentials'; second, 'the recognition of the sovereignty of small states'; third, 'the conclusion of international agreements on the private rather than official level'; and fourth, 'the maintenance of trade and financial relationships with the outside world'. Another matter was of special interest. According to Schlotterer's account,

> The Belgian industrialist Baron de Launoit introduced for discussion the fact that the economic area Ruhr–South Holland–Belgium–Lorraine–Luxembourg–north France is, as regards coal and iron, a natural economic region whose political division impairs technical progress and damages the interests of the working population. Coal and steel industrialists should break through these borders and co-operate in economic matters.

This idea was taken up in subsequent discussions, as were a number of others. Proposals included the setting up of unified systems of transportation, the 'rationalization of industry' on a European scale, the creation of multinational European corporations, and above all the organization of a European customs union *(Wirtschaftsunion)* on an essentially private basis in which members would hold shares in 'the manner of a pool'. What was meant by this was that the cartel principle should apply as a principle of organization; each member would have a quota to be brought, sold, traded, increased or diminished as required by changing circumstances. This, in Schlotterer's words, would amount to,

> An economic *Paneuropa* (Greater Europe) that would not involve a merger of states but a union of national economies on the basis of treaties between nations, run by similar economic associations and organizations, and only supervised by public authorities with powers limited to the issuance of general directives and expressly forbidden to intervene in operations.[21]

The vision of the New Order planning staff never disappeared in the years from 1940 to 1944. It kept flickering amidst the tempests of occupation and war, thanks to men like the French Minister of Industrial Production, Jean Bichelonne, for whom the occupation provided an opportunity to solve long-term economic problems with the aid of German methods. As he put it in a speech of 21 September 1942, 'The Great Depression which began in the United States in 1929 has given pause to both businessmen and economists. . . . The doctrinaire solutions have failed.' Bichelonne added that while in France small business interests and 'liberals' in the economy had largely frustrated the increasingly more ambitious legislative attempts to encourage state-regulated cartelization (the laws of 1884, 1935 and 1938) these influences had been eclipsed:

> Now Germany, with its Reichsstellen, Fachgruppen, and Wirtschaftsgruppen, with its Ministry of Economics and above all through its unquestionable successes attained by means of such institutions – so Germany, I say, has provided us with the model of economic leadership, methodically organized with a view to practical accomplishment.[22]

The experience of many French, Dutch, Belgian and Luxembourgeoise businessmen reinforced such sentiments. Many of them found it possible to 'make deals' in New Order Europe. The creation of industrial ententes between German interests and their partners in France and the Low Countries is an important if seldom discussed feature of the war years. Such agreements took place in many fields. French examples include the creation of a Franco-German (IG Farben) dyestuffs monopoly for domestic markets, a three-nation cartel (including Italy) for rationalizing the automobile industry which, among other achievements was responsible for the Porsche-designed Renault '4 cv', the formation of a synthetic fibre consortium with German producers and the organization of joint ventures in aluminium smelting. Similar arrangements were quite common in coal, steel and related fields.[23]

Motives ranging from the purely defensive to the highly adventurous were behind the conclusion of such deals. The alliance that grew up around ARBED serves as an example of the former. In mid-August 1940, Karl Goetz of the Dresdner Bank, who was acting as an agent of Göring and clothed with a mandate to promote share exchanges weighted to favour Reich interests *(Kapitalverflechtung)*, arrived in Brussels to entreat, threaten and possibly force the two Belgian holding companies which controlled ARBED to part with their equity in the Luxembourg steel enterprise. One of these interests was the Banque de Bruxelles headed by the ambitious Baron Paul de Launoit, the other the Société Générale de Belgique, the *primus inter pares* of Belgian finance. Although Goetz at times went into carpet-biting fits of rage, threatening expropriation after victory, his mission ended in failure because, as he was reminded by the Société Générale's representative, 'we are playing a threesome that includes your neighbour, the Deutsche Bank'.[24] The close relationship between the Deutsche Bank and the Société Générale antedated the war.[25] This was the responsibility of Hermann J. Abs who, since 1937 had orchestrated the Deutsche Bank's orderly takeover of Société Générale positions in south-eastern and eastern Europe – a 'natural consequence' of increasing German political power in the area. The ARBED deal of summer 1940 strengthened their ties. In order to protect its position, the Société Générale sold the Deutsche Bank one half of its ARBED stock, which put Abs on the board of directors of the Luxembourg steel firms but still left the Belgians with the largest packet of shareholdings. An addendum to this understanding stipulated that in the event of an 'unfavourable' outcome of the war the DB would retrocede its ARBED interests to the Société Générale. Thanks to Abs's agreement to 'prevent significant amounts of ARBED shares from finding their way into undesirable hands', it was possible to frustrate repeated attempts of the Dresdner-led Göring combine to acquire shares over open markets. ARBED remained effectively in the hands of a trustee who 'managed it as if it were any other German firm'.[26] The business connections that ran to and from the Ruhr over Köln and Aachen to Luxembourg, Belgium and France remained intact.

But new ones formed as well, for instance, with the Netherlands around the figure of Dr Frederick H. Fentener van Vlissingen. Fentener van Vlissingen was the unofficial leader of one of the powerful but diverse interest groups dominating the highly complicated world of Dutch industry, trade and finance, the one that developed around the coal carrying traffic between Rotterdam and the Ruhr. His father founded and jointly owned with RWKS the main Dutch wholesaler, Steenkolen Handelsvereeniging, which normally handled about 10 per cent of total Ruhr solid combustible sales. In 1929 and 1933 Fentener van Vlissingen engineered agreements to stop the Limburg mines from underbidding the Ruhr on the Dutch market. He next organized the only large Dutch steel mill (Koninklijke Hoogovens, Ijmuiden) and through a series of complicated financial transactions, arranged an exchange of shares between it and the Ruhr firm, Phönix AG. When it later became a part of VS, Fentener van Vlissingen controlled between 10 and 12 per cent of Germany's largest steel producer. In this field, as in coal, he had become *the* indispensable business intermediary between the Reich and the Netherlands.

After 1933 he built upward and outward, aided by his diverse personal connections. A former tutor to Princess Juliana, he, and his wife, became close personal friends of Queen Wilhelmina. One of his daughters married a son of German Foreign Minister Ribbentrop. In 1935 Fentener van Vlissingen was elected president of the International Chamber of Commerce on the strength of his ability 'to bridge the gap' between the economic differences of democracies and dictatorships.[27] Reich officialdom was extraordinarily solicitous of his interests. When he proposed a 'huge deal' involving Ruhr coal exports, which in the view of the German Ministry of Economics 'would have enriched him inordinately', the ambassador in the Hague sprang to his defence on the grounds 'that we need him very much indeed for our proposed Dutch–German association and do not want to risk angering him until the thing is running perfectly'.[28]

Fentener van Vlissingen was the logical man to head the Dutch section of the 'German–Dutch Society', organized on 21 January 1937 by Ribbentrop in order to 'deepen and broaden economic relations between the two countries'. The association also brought together certain Dutchmen who later participated in the tractations of the New Order planning staff. In August 1940 Fentener van Vlissingen was a major force behind the organization of the General Committee for Economic Collaboration, a spearhead organization of Dutch big businessmen and senior officials whose first principle was 'you *can* do business with Hitler'.

The rise in Fentener van Vlissingen's business fortunes paralleled those in political realms. In the 1930s he was elected to supervisory boards in nearly every important branch of Dutch industry save oil, soap and electrical machinery but including overseas trading companies, a railway equipment manufacturer, a sugar refinery, an aircraft manufacturer, dry dock and shipbuilding operations. But his most important connection, especially during the occupation, was as chief representative of Dutch interests on the huge rayon combine, Vereinigte Glanzstoff-Algemeene Kunstzijde Unie (AKU). The German half of this enterprise, VG of Wuppertal, was the largest producer of fibres in the Reich. AKU was the fourth largest enterprise of any kind in the Netherlands, and had often provided economic advisers to the Dutch government. The relationship between the Dutch and German halves was made deliberately complicated in order to obscure where ultimate control of the company rested. This was necessary lest world war impeded the global operations of the firm. AKU held 90 per cent of VG's common stock, which in turn held 30 per cent of AKU. But those who voted the forty outstanding preference shares controlled the company. These were held equally by Germans and 'persons from the Netherlands', among whom was a representative of the de Bary bank in Amsterdam, an affiliate of the Deutsche Bank. In fact, Fentener van Vlissingen and the German representative, Abs of the Deutsche Bank, decided policy matters privately.[29] Thanks to the confusion concerning the national identity of VG/AKU it was never necessary for the firm to 'choose sides'. It successfully played the chameleon. This ambiguous behaviour, according to a report of the US military police department in The Hague, even involved channelling AKU/VG war profits over Zürich into US and British war industries. By the end of the war Fentener van Vlissingen's personal wealth had become so great that he founded his own bank, Vlaer en Kol, Utrecht. As if to complete the circle, the trust department of the new institution managed the huge Dutch holdings of Werner Carp, the largest shareholder in Gutehoffnungshütte and heir to one of the great Ruhr fortunes.[30]

Idealism could also blend with opportunism in the creation of 'communities of interest'. According to Baron Kurt von Schroeder, the Baron de Launoit was 'a veritable Eurovisionary', his mind fertile with ideas for Belgo-German co-operation in the fields of chemicals, electric power, construction, and heavy industry. De Launoit's main steel holding, Ougrée-Marihaye, entered a convention with the Otto Wolff firm to set up a 50:50 holding company to pool his own interests and those of the Société Générale in ARBED, a number of other steel firms, as well as in the Campine mines, for which the Belgian side would receive compensation in the form of Ruhr mining shares. On 2 February 1941, de Launoit organized a 'secret and private bureau within [one of his two holding companies] "Brufina" ', to study possible fields of collaboration with the Dresdner Bank. He discussed these with Dresdner Board Member Rasche as late as March 1943, one must assume out of a belief that his schemes would outlive German defeat.'[31]

'Communities of interest' could also grow out of sheer political necessity. Take the one which developed around a certain purchase of confiscated Jewish property by Dutch and Saar investors. It resulted from an attempt initiated by Bichelonne in early 1942 to regain control over the foundries of 'Meurthe-et-Moselle-Sud'. This could not be done, he feared, unless some means could be found to provide operating subsidies for the firms, whose deficits were too large for the French state to make good. With the help of something called TREDIFINA, Ernst Röchling – the allegedly francophile custodian of the family's interests in Paris – found the solution. TREDIFINA was a holding company originally set up by the government of the Netherlands in 1921 (and which included participation of several 'blue ribbon' figures from German finance and industry) to provide credits for Dutch exports to the Reich. In early 1941, however, its assets were blocked. To secure a decision of the Reich Ministry of Economics to release them, the managing director of TREDIFINA, one Kreuter, agreed to enter a partnership with Ernst Röchling. It involved organizing Société de Crédits et d'Investissements (SCI). The new finance enterprise soon bought up the 'Aryanized' holdings of the department store Galeries Lafayette as well as bauxite mines near Toulon, a railway equipment manufacturer and a considerable amount of valuable real estate in central Paris. With the 80 million francs of its capital remaining unspent, SCI provided a loan with which the French state 'bailed out' the foundries of Meurthe-et-Moselle-Sud. They were then restored to their French owners who, of course, continued to work under German contract. These shenanigans left an unpleasant taste, although from the standpoint of overall Dutch, but especially French, economic interests they represented a lesser evil.[32]

The harsh realities of a system in which fundamental decisions depended on the whims of a Hitler and the battles of rapacious and short-sighted interest groups made a mockery of the visions of technocrats and ambitious businessmen. Until September 1943, the pleas to Berlin of Bichelonne that France was ready to accept a far larger volume of German orders, of the Galopin Committee in Brussels, that with modest food imports industrial outputs could be sharply raised, or of the Dutch national bank president that continued economic tampering by German Nazis interfered with the smooth functioning of an economy already at the disposal of the occupying power – these things went largely unheeded. The extended hand of collaboration received only a limp-wristed shake. This might not have been the case if after conquest Hitler had vested a single authority with the amplitude of powers necessary to enforce a consistent line of economic policy in western Europe. Instead responsibility remained divided and the area as a whole failed to receive priority treatment at the top levels of policy-making.

Once order had been restored and a few political scores settled, the industry of western Europe served as a catch-basin for demand spillover from the Reich. (The then current German term for subcontracting abroad, *Auftragsverlagerung*, meaning literally order-*dis*placement, suggests the light in which this activity was viewed.) To be sure, order books thickened at a fairly steady rate as the scope of the war widened and shortages of both war-critical and consumption goods increased. In Belgium, France and the Netherlands a wide range of production installations were put under long-term German contract over the first eighteen months of the war. In Belgium as elsewhere they varied in size and product from the artisanal wicker-ware weavers of the Campine (who wove standard-issue shell baskets for the Wehrmacht) and the garment-makers of Binche (who put the entire single industry of their town at the disposal of the Luftwaffe), to growing family-sized enterprises like the furniture manufacturer de Coene of Courtrai (who built fully furnished barracks for German troop units), to branches of foreign multinationals such as Ford of Antwerp, Fibranne-Fabelta of Solvay-AKU/VG (which placed their operations at the disposal of German contractors) to the giant foundries of Liège and Charleroi dominated by the holding companies (which supplied the usual profiles), and to the Fabrique Nationale, owned by the Société Générale (which simply changed invoices after May 1940 when making deliveries of its famous infantry weapons).[33]

Still, ample industrial capacities remained unused all over occupied western Europe until well into 1942. In March of that year Hermann Röchling noted in a letter to Hitler, 'The steel industry of Lorraine and Luxembourg is not being exploited at even 30 per cent of capacity, that of Meurthe-et-Moselle and Longwy at not even 20 per cent, and that of Belgium-North France at only 30 per cent.'[34] Röchling's initiative fell on fertile ground: in early summer he was empowered to take every means necessary to double steel outputs. Thus began a campaign of brow-beating. In disregard of the comfortable working relationships arrived at by Steinbrinck, Röchling ordered the foundries of western Europe to accept orders at his dictation regardless of financial consequences. He offered the steel producers of western Europe subjugation and economic ruin.[35] Yet even his drastic methods could hardly have resulted in more than a temporary increase in steel outputs: to secure the coke necessary for raising steel production would have required a crippling reduction in deliveries to the rest of industry not to mention intolerable cutbacks in allocations for domestic consumption.

The coal problem focused on France. While the coal import-export traffic of Belgium and the Netherlands was roughly even, the French normally faced a deficit of 15.5 million annual tons. Of this amount, 7.5 million tons was normally imported from the UK, 1.5 million tons from Poland and some 6.9 million tons (including 55 per cent of total coking coal requirements) from the Reich. The British blockade prevented the exportation of 3 million annual tons of Dutch bunker coal and this traffic might have been diverted to France. Outputs also could have been increased by 3 million tons in Dutch Limburg and the Belgian Campine without new investments. Assuming savings in French coal consumption of 5 per cent, it would have been at least theoretically possible to maintain industrial outputs in France and the Low Countries at 1936–8 levels. With extreme care, superb organization, and unqualified technical co-operation the coal deficit in western Europe *could* have been overcome.[36]

There was no shortage of good intentions at the outset. The main task facing the coal delegate of the Brussels Military Administration was to pave the way for 'international co-operation after the war', which involved 'helping the mines at all times in remaining healthy and productive, assuring an adequate return, and rooting out problems, [since] this was the best way to maintain production'.[37] Such an approach was warmly welcomed. According to an account typical of summer 1940, the German official responsible for liaison with the north French district noted that

> Herr Duchemin, the chief of mines, offered [us] his unqualified support, facilitated visits [to the local firms], and in general was extremely helpful and informative. The various mine directors . . . were nearly all ready to show us around and fill us in on their operations. [With one exception] the managers were extremely obliging and not in the least bit resentful. The mission could be accomplished quickly.[38]

Mine production in Belgium, north France and the Netherlands was restored in remarkably short order, reaching average 1936–8 levels in each place by September 1940. Thereafter the situation began to deteriorate, first in Belgium, then in the Netherlands, and finally in north France. The underlying problem, especially in Belgium and north France, was the food shortage. As with fuel, Berlin merely assumed that occupied western Europe would be agriculturally self-sufficient. Planning was all but absent. Although pre-war France could feed itself and the Netherlands was an important exporter of dairy products, Belgium (and north France) depended on imports for slightly more than one-half of total consumption requirements. Under the rules governing trade in the New Order it was impossible to offset this deficit with imports from either the Reich or neighbouring France and the Netherlands. Although the population would survive by planting every available square metre of terrain, the first winter of occupation brought severe food shortages and the threat of famine. In December potato rations became all but unobtainable in Belgium. Ominously, groups of miners' wives appeared in front of city halls throughout Wallonia, waving potato sacks in silent protest. Serious strikes broke out in Liège in mid-January, involving some 2800 to 3500 miners. Spreading throughout the southern district they ran intermittently through the spring and culminated with a work stoppage by 10,000 miners on 17 May. The same month another 17,672 walked off the job in the Campine. Disturbances soon spread across the border to north France, continuing through June. The military administration eventually managed to suppress the strikes with ultimata and promises of something to eat. Those who returned to work were fed by men of the Wehrmacht from a railway canteen *(Hilfszug Bayern)*, which could be shunted from siding to siding as necessary. In addition, local German military authorities set up numerous works' kitchens at the mines to assure that underground workers received their full ration allotments. But these were mere stop-gap measures. Without a commitment from the top, little could be done to solve the food problem, protect miners' health or maintain production in the long run.[39]

The creation of RVK under Pleiger in March 1941 might have provided an opportunity to take the situation in hand. It was not, however, until August that a 'Western Coal Committee' was set up under Oskar Gabel, the senior Reich mine official. But Gabel accomplished little. He failed to gain the release of Belgian and French miners who remained as PoWs in the Reich. While recognizing 'that the diet of miners in Belgium and north France is wholly inadequate', he did nothing to correct the situation since 'the Reich cannot make any food available'. In March 1942 Gabel finally directed that miner rations in western Europe be raised to the standard of German 'heaviest workers'. But here, as well, impediments of an ideological character continued to hinder effective policy-making. Gabel stipulated that miners should be issued increased rations only after working a seven-day week of eight and three-quarter hours a day and also that the food allotments should specifically not include supplements of fish, sugar, tobacco, etc. which would bring parity with miners in the Reich. The additional food required would be found by further reducing civilian rations in the occupied countries. As of December 1943 official rations for 'heaviest workers' in the Netherlands, actually somewhat higher than those in the other western districts, were only 88.9 per cent of German levels for bread, 90.9 per cent for fat, and 76.4 per cent for meat.[40]

In November 1942 an authority called BEKO-West (Beauftragte des Reichs für die Kohle in den besetzten und angegliederten Gebieten – der Leiter der Gruppe West) was set up under Steinbrinck to impose unified control over the coal districts of France and the Low Countries. The appointment provided the Ruhr with compensation for an administrative *coup d'état* in June 1942 which had resulted in the takeover by Hermann Röchling of responsibilities for administering the entire steel industry of western Europe, including those previously exercised by Steinbrinck.

Steinbrinck proved to be well qualified to win a deeper commitment from the mine operators, from whom great sacrifices were to be required. He also had the necessary personal prestige to tighten control over allocation by reducing quotas of domestic coal for civilian and Wehrmacht consumption. Here Steinbrinck enjoyed a measure of success, managing to increase Belgian coal allocations to France by an annual rate of 245,000 tons in spite of output declines of 3 million annual tons in the year following his appointment. He also deserves credit for having checked the rapid deterioration of mine supplies. Still, he made no progress in solving the most critical problem, labour; the undernourishment resulting in sickness, 'slacking' and absenteeism that made it necessary to increase labour inputs to maintain outputs, which in turn accelerated the physical and financial exhaustion of the mines.[41]

The fact that the fall in productivity was much greater than in the Ruhr stems from a fundamental difference in attitudes between German miners and those in the occupied countries. The latter simply refused to suffer more hardship than necessary for survival. This had an immediate bearing on outputs. Pleiger pointed out to Zentrale Planung on 21 August 1942 that while in the Reich it was possible to make up losses by laying on Sunday shifts,

> [This] actually brings . . . declines in the occupied countries. In Belgium I [then] get only 30 to 35 per cent of normal yield and on the following Monday 60 per cent instead of 100. Belgians do not want to work holidays and I cannot compel them to do so. I have no German supervisors there – only Belgians.[42]

The continued failure to provide adequate rations was the chief cause of the steady decline in miner productivity. The official increases ordered by the Gabel committee were a poor guide to nutritional reality. Especially in north France and Belgium allocation steadily approached breakdown as inflation raged, leaving the populace with no choice but either raise its own foodstuffs or engage in dealings on the so-called *marché clandestin* (black market). To cope with this situation most employers in strategic industries such as coal set up (with the tacit encouragement of the occupation authorities) on-site food dispensaries supplied from the black market. To eat one had at least to appear for work. The military administration in Brussels estimated that employer 'food paternalism' added 36 per cent to wage and salary costs. But even this was not enough. Most miners had families to feed and therefore either took home a portion of the food intended to keep them productive *(Mundraub)* or stayed off the job in order to work in home gardens or trade stolen coal on the black market. The latter caused extraordinarily high levels of miner absenteeism. In north France this increased from 10.96 per hundred in 1942 to between 14 and 16 the following year. In the Netherlands, absenteeism increased steadily from a pre-occupation rate of 9.8 per hundred shifts to an alarming 22.7 in early 1944. Those in Belgium rose even faster to higher levels.[43]

It was difficult to use foreign labour to offset such losses: the Reich had prior claim, doubts surrounded the supervisory abilities of non-German miners, resistance was feared, and – consistent with usual national socialist approaches – treatment of the foreigners would have to be substantially worse in the occupied countries than in the Reich itself. As Pleiger described the results, 'among the Russians [in the Campine] a kind of epidemic has taken hold. There have been cases of self-mutilation and outbursts of hysterical screaming. No one goes willingly into the pits.' For these reasons foreign mine employment did not rise above 10 per cent of the total until autumn 1943.[44]

By adding thirteen hours to the working week and increasing the size of the native labour force by about a quarter it was possible to maintain coal outputs in north France, the Netherlands, and the Belgian Campine at approximately 1941 levels during 1942 and 1943 (Table 26). But such methods did not succeed in the long-worked, labour-intensive, and inefficient mines of the southern basin, where outputs dropped at rates of about 15 per cent per year. As a result, by autumn 1943 Belgium as a whole was able to raise coal at only about 40 per cent of pre-war rates.

Table 26 Coal outputs in western Europe, 1938–1943 ('000 tons)

	Belgium	*France*	*The Netherlands*
1938	29,580	46,502	13,537
1940	25,608	39,286	—
1941	26,604	41,740	—
1942	24,084	41,866	12,329
1943	23,748	40,536	12,497

Sources: Alan S. Milward, *The New Order and the French Economy* (Oxford, 1970), 183f.; Fernand Baudhuin, *L'economie Belge sous l'occupation allemande* (Brussels, 1945), 396; Rijksinstitut voor Oorlogsdocumentatie (RO) Beko-West-Verbindungsstelle Holland, *Jahresbericht 1943*.

The political situation also slipped out of control. 'In the measure that belief in ultimate German victory waned', according to the somewhat delicate wording of an administrative history written by the chief of the coal branch of the Brussels military government, ' . . . supervisory personnel became concerned lest their activity be viewed by the Allies as providing aid to the enemy.'[45] In a November 1942 meeting of Zentrale Planung Pleiger cited sabotage as a cause of output decreases in the occupied territories.[46] Soon there would be outright rebellion. On Thursday 29 May 1943 a serious strike broke out at the Limburg mines in protest at a Wehrmacht order for the recall of former PoWs. Six hundred miners were immediately arrested. The following day the secret police *(Sicherheitsdienst)* SD announced that unless work was resumed 160 hostages would be shot. By Sunday some three-quarters of the strikers were back at work, too late, however, for the seven 'ring-leaders' already sentenced. They were executed the following morning. The mine directors at first refused to provide the police with lists of the strikers but eventually submitted them when ordered to do so by the Dutch Secretary General for Finance, Dr Hirschfeld. One board member of the Staatsmijnen, Groothoff, was placed under indefinite arrest as a warning to the others to take prompt pre-emptive measures to forestall future strikes.

In October still more severe strikes broke out, this time around Lille, in protest against Sunday wages, inadequate food supplies and general exhaustion. Some 38,600 miners stopped work and refused an order of the prefect to return to the pits. By means of police 'dragnets' *(Grossaktionen)* in various miner settlements 620 recalcitrants were arrested, 43 tried, and 14 sent off to 'labour camps' even though the German authorities were unable to discover the leaders of the strike or even determine that it had had political causes. But the protests continued for five days, affected 46 out of 114 mines, and brought about 40 per cent decreases in output.[47] October and November brought sporadic disorders to Belgium, including a sit-down strike in Liège lasting over thirty days. It was broken by sealing an entire shift underground for twenty-eight hours. Opposition also took passive forms. Three thousand supposedly sick miners, for instance, left the mines permanently in late summer and early autumn of 1943. By winter the general resistance to work had resulted in irreversible output declines which, accelerated by shortages of critical supplies such as steel and pit-props, and later by the stepped-up pace of the bombing raids in preparation for the Normandy landing, reduced coal output in Belgium and north France by 60 per cent.[48]

This fall in coal production nullified Speer's attempt to raise industrial outputs in western Europe. But its prospects were dismal from the outset because industrial coal reserves had fallen to precariously low levels as a result of the 'crash programme' in steel launched by Röchling a year earlier. In order to increase coke and coking coal deliveries to Lorraine (which could not prevent a doubling of Ruhr exports to the area in 1943) the Saar foundryman found it necessary to short-change other consumers. In Belgium, allocations for all non-steel uses dropped more than 40 per cent in the six months following the introduction of the Röchling programme. In France, deliveries to industry, 442,000 monthly tons in 1941, dropped to 380,000 in 1942, and 307,000 for the first months of 1943. The share of industry in total French coal consumption, itself a fairly steady 65 per cent of pre-war levels, actually fell from 36 per cent to 32 per cent.[49]

The decline in productivity along with the costs of black market provisioning had a catastrophic impact on mine finances. In the Netherlands profits per ton of Fl 0.9 and Fl 0.44 in 1940 and 1941 turned into losses of Fl 1.29 and Fl 1.6 in 1942 and 1943. In north France a similar trend developed. In Belgium, matters were much worse. There the mines roughly broke even over the first eighteen months of the occupation, but at the beginning of 1943 net losses per ton rose to BF10.36 in spite of a 'temporary' subsidy from the government to offset some 42.38 per cent of the gross amount. By the end of the year, the tonnage deficit had increased to BF39.34 in spite of tripled subsidies. Over 1943 total monthly mine losses increased from BF65 to BF114 million. In 1944, for which no figures are available, they were surely still more frightening. According to the report of the investigating German accountancy firm, after 1942 amortizations were also virtually eliminated. By the end of the occupation, the financial reserves of the Belgian mines were wiped out and plant nearly wrecked by overuse.[50]

But such blemishes on the record of German administrator-businessmen did not prevent French, Belgian and Dutch producers from springing to the defence of their Reich colleagues during the trials of industrialists organized by the Allies after the war. Steinbrinck, a defendant in the 'Flick Case', arrived at Nürnberg with a bulging briefcase of *Persilscheine* (clean bills of health). The testimonials from Belgium included one from the former head of SYBELAC, the 'beefed-up' steel cartel, who commended Steinbrinck for 'correct behaviour', noting that he had done everything in his power to aid Belgian workers. A letter from Count Lippens, an influential statesman, praised the defendant's 'understanding' of Belgian concerns and emphasized his 'lack of enthusiasm' in discharging his wartime mission. A note from a director of John Cockerill SA praised Steinbrinck's 'respect for the patriotic attitudes of Belgian industrialists', and numerous others expressed gratitude for his 'comprehension of the Belgian temperament'. Charges against Steinbrinck of 'economic spoliation in the occupied territories' were dropped.[51] Flick also came to trial well-prepared. At Rombach, where he had been trustee, Flick made heavy investments, in hopes of retaining possession after the war. Jacques Laurent, the French owner of the steel firm, described the German production manager as having

> behaved towards the directors and employees with moderation and a genuine grasp of the exceptional circumstances. He made every effort to help the engineers repatriate their furniture. During the expulsions of August and November 1940 he was responsible for laudable attempts to prevent the departure of numerous Lorrainers, especially workers and clerical staff. I personally witnessed his courageous stand in this matter *vis-à-vis* the Nazi authorities.[52]

Even Hermann Röchling, tried at a special tribunal set up in Rastatt, escaped severe censure. An affadavit of Humbert de Wendel, whose family interests Röchling was pledged to destroy, described this political fanatic as an essentially rational if misguided figure. De Wendel considered

> the defendant a pan-Germanist of the old school, who gave total support to Hitler because he saw in him a man capable of achieving the 'Deutschland über Alles!' But [Röchling] did not swallow all the stupidity of the Nazi Party. . . . He was a man of the Reichswehr [sic] but not the Gestapo.[53]

According to de Wendel, Röchling opposed Gauleiter Bürckel's expulsion of French personnel, frustrated Gestapo plans to place operatives in factories, and intervened on numerous occasions with the police on behalf of French employees. While it is difficult to verify these interventions, Röchling did make financial provisions to enable the French employers to maintain operations at company headquarters in Paris. By all accounts, the Röchling-appointed German administrators responsible for supervising production at individual French firms were excellent. The German administrator of the Neuves-Maison foundry claimed to be on the best of terms with its director general, M. Taffenal, and factory manager, M. Thédral. Thédral, he claimed,

> was a frequent and regular guest who came on a friendly basis. . . . My French visitors were often astonished to see in my apartment the well-known picture of the allied armies entering flag-bedecked Strasbourg after Armistice Day. Of course, I never removed it. At the end of my activities [he continues] . . . M. Thédral offered me his company car, a big Renault, in order to reach home, adding that I had done so much for the factory that the loss of the car would be a small thing.[54]

Conflicts of interest, management breakdowns and different national loyalties did not ruin the tradition of co-operation developing in west European heavy industry since 1926. The events of the war strengthened it. The Ruhr behaved reasonably. German organizational methods spread and familiarity with them increased. The web of *Interessengemeinschaften* thickened. The common threat which all producers faced from the Nazi agents of chaos forced them to coalesce into a conspiracy against the vicissitudes of politics. Under the motto 'Better the worst industrialist than the best Gauleiter!' producers tried wherever possible to solve business and political problems among themselves. The war also witnessed long-range planning attempts which gave expression to a common vision of the future. It featured a Europe run as a single economic unit by its captains of industry.

Notes

1 US National Archives OMGUS, Control Office for Germany and Austria 58–2/2 39.00 'German Industrial Complexes. The Hermann Göring Complex'.
2 John Gillingham, *Belgian Business in the Nazi New Order* (Ghent, 1977), 37 f.
3 ibid., 65 f., 163 f.; David Barnouw and Ruurd Stellinga, 'Ondernehmers in Bezet Nederland: De Organisatie-Woltershom', *Cahiers voor de Politieke en Sociale Wetenschapen*, 1(4) May 1978, 3–99.
4 John Gillingham, 'Die Europäsierung des Ruhrgebietes: Von Hitler bis zum Schuman-Plan', in K. Düwell and W. Köllman (eds) *Rheinlandwestfalen im Industrie zeitalter*. (Bd. 3: Vom Ende der Weimarer Republik bis zum Land Nordrhein-Westbalen.) (Wuppertal, 1984) 179–89.
5 Alan S. Milward, *The New Order and the French Economy* Oxford, 1970), 51 f.
6 Gillingham, *Belgian Business*, *passim*.
7 Robert Paxton, *Vichy France: old guard and new order, 1940–1944* (New York, 1972), 51 f., 2346; Werner Warmbrunn, *The Dutch under Occupation, 1940–1945* (Stanford, 1963), *passim*.
8 US National Archives (USNA) T501107/675 f. '11. Teil. II Abschnitt, 1. Bergbau und Kohlenwirtschaft', NI 2023 'Röchling Affadavit'; NI 275 Poensgen to Flick, 27 June 1940.
9 Gillingham, *Belgian Business*, 72, 127 f; Etienne Dejonghe 'Penurie charbonnière et répartition en France (1940–1944)', *Revue de la Deuxieme Guerre Mondiale*, 26 April 1976, 21 f.
10 Nïrnberg Industrialists (NI) 322 'Objet: usines nationales Hermann Goering. Participation a l'industrie sidérurgique', 29 May 1941; Weiner Library (WL) Dok. Pl. Nr. 115 'Vorschlag Pleiger zum Aufbau der Hermann Göring Werke', 9 November 1941; NI 3023 'Erklärung Hermann Röchling', 18 December 1946.
11 Bundesarchiv (BA) R13I/621 'Besprechung im Kleinen Kreis'; NI 3517 Flick to RWM, 7 October 1940; NI 3463 'Herrn Flick zur Rücksprache', 13 July 1943; NI 5395 'Notiz für Herrn Flick', 26 July 1941; NI 31 'Biography of Dr Flick'.
12 WL Pl. Dok. 127 Fritz von Bruck, Dir. Hoesch to Paul Korner, 2 August 1940; Gutehoffnungshütte (GHH) 400101306/27 Kellermann to Lübsen, 11 February 1941; 400101306/27 'Beteiligung GHH bei der Verteilung der Eisenindustrie Lothringen-Luxemburgs (n.d.)'; 400101306/27 'Besprechung mit Poensgen', 26 August 1940.

13 BA R2/30287 'Eisenhüttenwerke in Lothringen und in Luxemburg'; GHH 401101306/27 'Wg EsI, Rundschreiben Tgb. Nr. 11788 R/Mu', 26 July 1940; Rijksinstituut voor Oorlogsdokumentatie (RO), HR13 'Circulaire Tgb. Nr. 11788 R/Mu22', 6 August 1940.
14 GHH 400101306/27 'RWM II EM 3–31132/41 III,' 21 February 1941.
15 Rijksinstituut voor Oorlogsdocumentatie (RO), HR 79 Röchling to Hanneken, 1 February 1941; HR 78 Röchling to Körner, 24 January 1941; GHH 400101306/27 Röchling to Reichert, 6 August 1940.
16 BA R7/839 RWM III, Wog 17927/40, 23 September 1940; R2/30287 'Eisenhüttenwerke in Lothringen und in Luxemburg' (n.d.); R2/30287 fol 1. 'Bericht vom 11. Februar 1944, ARBED'; R7/840 fol. 1 'Verordnung zum Schutz der Wirtschaft in Luxemburg', 30 January 1941; NI 966 Bormann to Lammers, 6 June 1941; NI 343 Simon to Lammers, 6 June 1941; NI 344 Simon to Körner, 15 May 1941; USNA OMGUS 58–1/2 'File note Kurzmeier', 16 November 1941; 'File note Abs', 3 April 1941; Schröder to Abs, 29 April 1941; 'File note Abs to Kurzmeier', 21 September 1943.
17 GHH 400101320/98 'Sogemaier. Zur künftigen Gestaltung der europäischen Kohlenwirtschaft', June 1940; BA R7II/615 'Referat II Bg/5, 8 August 1940 "Vorbereitung der Friedensverhandlungen und des wirtschaftlichen Aufbaus im deutschen Machtbereich" '; R7II/615 Bezirksgruppe Ruhr to RWM Funk, 7 September 1940.
18 GHH 400101320/98 Lübsen to Huber, 27 May 1940.
19 Westfälisches Wirtschaftsarchiv, Dortmund (WWA) F26/464 (Denkschrift Russel, n.d.); F26/464 'Erwägungen zu einer europäischen Kohlenordnung nach dem Kriege', 22 July 1940 (by Russel); GHH 400101320/98 Janus and Russel to Funk *re* 'Deutsch-englisches Kohlenverständnis nach dem Krieg'.
20 GHH 400101320/98 Lübsen to Sogemaier, 14 August 1940; BA R7 II 652a 'Denkschrift zur Neuordnung der europäischen Steinkohlenwirtschaft, August 1940; BA Nachlass Spethmann, vol. V, p. 28 f.
21 NI 11375 'Deposition of Gustav Schlotterer (RWM) concerning his career, the economic New Order for Europe, and IG Farben's position in the German economy', 20 September 1947.
22 Auswärtiges Amt Ha Pol IIa Frankreich, Wirtschaft 6–1/7976 f. 'Vortrag von Generalsekretär Bichelonne. "Die Grundzüge der Wirtschaftsführung in Frankreich" '; Ha Pol II Frankreich, Wirtschaft 6/a 7976 f. 'Vorträge der Tagung Deutscher Industrie- und Handelskammern und französische Chambres de Commerce vom 18. bis 21. September in Paris'; Ha Pol IIa Frankreich. Wirtschaft 6/1 370308 f.; Michel to Göring, 'Verstärkung des deutschen wirtschaftlichen Einflusses in Frankreich'; BA R24/745 Karl-Robert Ringel, 'Die organisatorische Grundlagen der französischen Wirtschaftspolitik (n.d.)'.
23 NI–119 'Note für den Vorsitzenden . . . bei der deutschen Waffenstillstande Delegation', 3 June 1942; USNA T120/757/349434 'Über die Zusammenarbeit der Automobilindustrien Deutschlands, Italiens und Frankreichs'; T120/757/349447 f. 'Deutsch-französische Industrieverflechtung', 18 July 1942; T120/757/349455 'Bildung eines deutsch-französischen Wirtschaft-Büros'.
24 John Gillingham, 'The politics of business in the economic *Grossraum*: the example of Belgium', *Studia Historiae Oeconomicae*, 14, 1979 (Poznan, 1980), 32.
25 ibid., 32–4.
26 USNA OMGUS, *Investigation of the Deutsche Bank (1947)*, Exhibits 181, 209, 298, 203, 387.

27 USNA OMGUS, Economics Branch 56–1/2 'The Vereinigte Stahlwerke complex'; 56–2 'Final report on the investigation of AKU', August 1946.
28 AA Ha Pol. II a Frankreich Industrie 3/1 Deutsche Gesandtschaft to Benzler, 22 February 1937; Emil Hilfferich, *1933–1945 Tatsachen. Ein Beitrag zur Wahrheitsfindung* (Jever, 1969), 274.
29 USNA OMGUS 56–1/2 'Extracts from the final report on the investigation of AKU', 1 August 1946; OMGUS, 'Interrogation of Kurt Frh. von Schroeder', 2 November 1945 *Deutsche Bank, Final Report*, exhibit 248; OMGUS, *Deutsche Bank, Final Report*, exhibits 413, 414, 418.
30 USNA OMGUS 56/1/2 Legal Division, Folder AKU Edward H. Degener USMPO/ Haag, 'Dr Fentener van Vlissingen'.
31 John Gillingham, 'The Baron de Launoit: a case study in the "politics of production" of Belgian industry during Nazi occupation' (Parts I and II), *Revue Belge d'Histoire Contemporaine* 6 (1–2), 1974, 1–60; NI 6106 'S.D. Tractations Brufina-Dresdner Bank. Doc. Rasche'; CIOS Target No 4/57 'Rocket propellant production in Bruxelles'.
32 USNA OMGUS 58–2/2 'Dr Kreuter', 4 March 1947; 58–2/2 'Report on Alexander Kreuter. OMGUS Financial Investigation Section'; RO TGD 1261 'Vernehmung Eugène Roy', 3 March 1947; TGD 1229 'Niederländische Militärmission beim internationalen Kontrollrat in Deutschland'; TGD 1224 'Statement by Dr Kreuter', 4 March 1947; TGD 1226 'Erklärung Kreuter, 13 April 1948; Martin, op. cit., 205 f.
33 Belgian Military Tribunal, 'Zake Roex Eerste Limburgsche Reit en Teenvlechterij', 'Affaire Fibranne-Fabelta-Requisitoire', in 'Zake de Coene-Requisitoire', Tailleurs de Binche, Requisitoire; Gillingham, *Belgian Business*, *passim*; Gillingham, 'The Baron de Launoit', *passim*.
34 RO TG 206 Röchling to Hitler, 19 March 1942.
35 RO TG 215 'Affadavit Greiner'.
36 GHH 400101206/26 'Bericht Knepper', August 1940; Fernand Baudhuin, *Histoire économique de Belgique 1914–1939*, II, 10; 400101306/20 'Der nordfranzösische Steinkohlenbergbau', 25 May 1940.
37 USNA T501/107/690 11. Teil. II Abschnitt, 1. 'Bergbau und Kohlenwirtschaft'.
38 GHH 400202306/26 'Bericht Ritter, GBAG, July 1940'; 4001011306/26 'Aktenbericht Haeck, 23 June 1940'.
39 USNA T50/102/473 f. 'Tätigkeitsbericht der Militärverwaltung Nr. 5', 7 July 1940; T501/103/99 TB10, October 1940; T501/103 375 TB11, November 1940; T501/103/650 TB12, December 1940; T501/104/166 TB15, March 1941; T501/104/ 314 f. TB16, April 1941; T501/104/1012 'Jahresbericht der Militärverwaltung für das erste Einsatzjahr'.
40 RO 'RWMII Bg, 3281/42', 14 March 1942; 'Sitzung des Westkohlenausschusses', 6 August 1941; 'Sitzung des Westkohlenausschusses', 9 December 1941; RO 'Beko West. Verbindungsstelle Holland, Jahresbericht 1943'.
41 USNA T501/101/683 f. '11. Teil II Bergbau und Kohlenwirtschaft'.
42 Hoover Institute (HI) '13. Sitzung der Z.P.,' 21 August 1942.
43 USNA T501/107/977 f. '11. Teil. Wirtschaftslenkung und Wirtschaftskontrolle'; Gillingham, 'The Baron de Launoit', 49; Milward, op. cit., 207; RO 'Beko-West, Verbindungsstelle Holland. Jahresbericht 1943'.
44 HI '13. Sitzung der Z.P.', 21 August 1942; GHH 400101305/9 'Statistische Angaben aus dem Ruhrkohlenbergbau', op. cit.
45 USNA T501/107/692 11. Teil. II Abschnitt, 1 'Bergbau und Kohlenwirtschaft'.
46 HI '23 Sitzung der Z.P.' 3 November 1942.

47 HI 15,091 'Bergarbeiterstreik in Holland', 8 May 1943; NI 2659 'OFK Tgb. Nr. 18/1143 Bergarbeiterstreik', 28 October 1943.
48 USNA T501/105/844 'TB26, Oktober–Dezember 1943'; T501/106/964 'TB28, April 1944'.
49 Gillingham, *Belgian Business*, Dejonghe, op. cit., 46.
50 USNA T501/107/771 f. 'Bergbau und Kohlenwirtschaft'; Dejonghe, op. cit., 51; RO 'Beko-West Verbindungsstelle Holland. Jahresbericht 1943'.
51 WL Steinbrinck Doks. 3, 3a, 6, 7, 8, 13, 16, 17, 23, 36, 383.
52 RO TGD714 'Attestation de Jaques Laurent', 25 July 1946.
53 RO TGD64 'Déclaration de M. Humbert de Wendel (LSFF673)'.
54 RO TGD588 'Déclaration Friedrich Amende', 28 March 1948.

CONCLUSION

The history of Ruhr coal from 1933 to 1945 unfolded within a context of economic regulation whose central feature was 'industrial self-administration'. This system was not specifically national socialist in inspiration but rather grafted on to traditional German practices of 'organized capitalism', which during the 1930s were admired by many businessmen and economic policy-makers in Europe. 'Industrial self-administration' allowed business to run its own affairs on the condition that it implement regime policy. Rewards were to be proportional to service in the national cause.

Two types of accommodation to this system were possible, partnership or partial integration. Further research will be required to determine how they worked out case by case and branch by branch. Among factors playing a role were structural considerations such as size, organization, market orientation, methods of financing and labour problems. The importance of management philosophy and political predilection must also not be underrated.

Ruhr coal adapted quite differently from IG Farben, the 'model' Nazi corporation, to the Third Reich, and the two may well stand at opposite ends of the spectrum. The distinctions between them are fundamental. To fulfil his extravagant ambitions the Fuhrer needed more than co-operation from German industry, namely *commitment*. This quality was strikingly evident at IG Farben, whose managers designed and administered the Four Year Plan. By the beginning of the war, its synthetics factories produced no less than half the petroleum consumed in the Reich. Without its extraordinary achievements, Hitler would have been unable to field a modern air force. Thanks to them, the chemical firm expanded from an oversized trust to an awesome megacorporation between 1933 and 1945.

Ruhr coal may be the 'worst case' example of industry–regime relationships during the Nazi years. The mines' difficulties, already in evidence during the *Gleichschaltung* process, became increasingly severe from 1936 to 1939 because the industry refused either to expand subsurface operations or otherwise play a prominent role in energy planning. Inadequate preparations led to acute fuel shortages before and during the war and therefore also to the deterioration of labour and plant, bitter disputes over allocation, the imposition of a coal commissar, and slow-downs in armaments production. The formation of a regime-sponsored consortium, Reichsvereinigung Kohle, and the creation of savings in distribution came too late to make inroads into the coal problem. The use of slave labour, which exhausted the mines, kept output fairly steady but failed to meet rising coal demand. The unwillingness of coal management to grasp the initiative in the manner of an IG Farben – its lack of a comparable sense of commitment – reduced Germany's ability to wage the Second World War. In respect to their potential contribution to the success of Hitler's enterprise, the operators came up short.

They also compare unfavourably with miners. Hitler was less concerned with the souls of those who worked underground than with their bodies. These he exploited mercilessly. Both managers and policy-makers agreed that miners deserved high commendation for their willingness to sacrifice. The success of national socialist labour policy is hard to explain. It was in some respects little more than a gloss on traditional industry paternalism. Still, Hitler did eliminate unemployment and increase opportunities for promotion. The Gestapo was never far away. Appeals to patriotism had at least some effect. These things did not eliminate class hostility or make life pleasant. They did, however, prevent German miners from impeding production. Comparisons with Belgium, north France and the Netherlands are worthwhile. In the occupied countries miner refusal to make sacrifices brought sharp falls in output which hobbled whole sections of the industrial economy.

The incomplete integration of the Ruhr mining industry into the national socialist political system can be attributed partly (as regime administrators often complained) to a lack of managerial dynamism – to the Malthusianism so prevalent in European industry during the 1930s. This was in most respects a barren decade for the mines. There were no significant technological developments. Growth was unimpressive. The industry remained a captive of strategies dating from the late 1920s. Even in cases where it tried to benefit from the new opportunities opened by Hitler's *Autarkiepolitik*, failure was the rule. One cannot overlook a distinct closed-mindedness. Industry spokesmen reacted with neuralgic hypersensitivity to *all* advice or criticism from 'mine-foreign' *(Bergfremde)* persons. Management gave the regime little credit for sponsoring policies of direct benefit to the mines, such as those from 1933 to 1936 in trade, labour and organization. To technocrats such as Speer mobilizing the Ruhr coal industry must have seemed like moving a graveyard.

The partial integration of the collieries into the political system had another cause as well. The Bergassessoren were anti-parliamentary and pro-authoritarian but not Nazified. They were, of course, ready to co-operate with Hitler. They supported the regime in general matters of social and economic policy, even on occasion soliciting the support of party offices. A refusal to support the war effort would have been unthinkable. Yet the Ruhr never identified itself with Hitler's aims or methods. It did not employ slave labour by choice. It made no major deals which depended on German victories. It did not pin its fate to military or party contracts. The mines preferred traditional ways of doing business to anything the regime could offer as an alternative. Above all else the coal industry wanted stability, including in foreign policy. In this sphere its interests collided head on with those of the regime.

The history of the Ruhr belongs to western Europe as a whole, not merely the Reich. This is partly the result of geology, partly also of a tradition dating from between the wars. Its milestones are the International Steel Cartel of 1926, the coal and steel agreements of the 1930s and, subsequently, the German administration of western Europe during the Second World War. Over this period as a whole there developed business partnerships, parallel sets of institutions, shared business methodologies, similar political outlooks, even a 'community of fate' *(Schicksalsgemeinschaft)* – thanks to which, the Ruhr survived.

After 1945 its fate depended on decisions made in Washington by men committed to ridding Germany of the 'evils of cartelism' as well as the industrialists and financiers believed responsible for having 'brought Hitler to power'. How, precisely, European recovery was to take place once the mines and foundries had been shut down (or while they were being reorganized administratively) was a problem the US occupation authorities were never able to resolve. And there was a further diplomatic one: how could Ruhr industry be revived without threatening Germany's neighbours and recent victims, France above all? These questions became even more pressing as Cold War battlefronts hardened and the creation of a strong capitalist West German state became a matter of highest priority. US policy towards the Ruhr none the less remained beset with contradictions – encouragement to produce on the one hand, threats to expropriate on the other. France – which had invested massively in the renovation of her own heavy industry – remained adamantly opposed to economic revival in the Ruhr. Policy had run into an impasse.[1]

The industrialists found the way out. In spite of the upheavals of the post-war years managerial continuity remained intact. The most prominent figure in the Ruhr Steel Trusteeship, which ran the industry on behalf of the British occupation authorities, was Heinrich Dinkelbach, who before the war had served on the board of Vereinigte Stahlwerke. His counterpart in coal, Heinrich Kost, was equally prominent in the years from 1933 to 1945. These men could count on support from well-placed foreign allies. Aloyse Meyer, successor to Mayrisch as head of both ARBED and the ISC was reinstated as chairman of the Luxembourg steel trust after a brief period of arrest. He frequently intervened with the Allies to promote the restoration of Ruhr industry. Frederick H. Fentener van Vlissingen did no less in this respect. The director of a Dutch royal commission to prosecute wartime economic collaborators, he did not hesitate to make use of his automatic *entrée* with the occupation authorities. André François-Poncet was named economic adviser to the French military government in Mainz.[2]

The first evidence that industrialists might be seeking private solutions to the Ruhr problem came with the disclosure of the so-called 'Pferdmenges mission' named after the Köln banker close to Konrad Adenauer. In the first week of November 1947 Pferdmenges approached the Comité des Forges through the de Wendel family and Aloyse Meyer. He had a truly astonishing offer: to cede a 50 per cent share of the Ruhr iron and steel industry to French interests. The Köln banker acted on instructions from an informal industry directorate consisting of Dr Hermann Reusch of GHH, Dr Hermann Wenzel of VS, Dr Karl Jarres of Kloëkner, Johannes Semler (formerly the German director of the Bizonal Economic Administration) and Bergassessor Heinrich Kost. Although the French begged off entering detailed negotiations, allegedly from fear of being branded collaborators, they did agree in principle on the necessity of arriving at some form of 'Franco-German settlement' *(politische Lösung)*.[3]

The steps taken between November 1948 and January 1949 to restore Ruhr industry to German control encouraged the French to take the initiative. On 15 January 1949 the American Consel General in Bremen reported that

> Rumours abound [concerning] the activities of such officials as the French Ambassador François-Poncet, who is reported to have had recent discussions with Dr Hermann Reusch, Managing Director of GHH and a leading spokesman for the iron and steel industry. Reusch is . . . reported to have been in Paris recently to discuss with French officials the organization of Ruhr industry.

By summer, there were numerous reports of European steel men 'taking tea together'.[4]

Within a few months the experts in the French Plan, directed by Jean Monnet, began to draft a blueprint for a new coal and steel authority which, in the end, provided a way around the diplomatic problems faced by the Allies. Although in all likelihood the greatest statesman of his generation, Monnet has not yet found a biographer. His motives in proposing a European supranational heavy industry organization remain obscure. There can be no doubt, however, about the 'nature of the beast' itself. Although described as 'liberal' in order to appease the American public, Monnet's proposals sounded very much like a call for a government-sanctioned supercartel. The responsibilities of the new organization were to include those exercised earlier by the international syndicates along with some new ones: investment planning, co-ordination of sales, standardization of product, compensation for changes in market share, rationalization and joint exportation. A new High Authority was to serve as the executive branch but existing national producer associations would provide statistical input, formulate and propose policy, and enforce the High Authority's directives. Monnet's proposals brought institutions and practices into the sphere of public policy which up to then had been conducted only semi-officially or privately.[5]

They also provided the nub of the Schuman Plan, the French offer of 9 May 1950 to enter a coal–steel pool with West Germany on the basis of equality which served as a blueprint for the European Coal and Steel Community (ECSC), founded in April 1951. This event also brought an end to Allied control of the Ruhr, the restoration of private ownership and the perpetuation of western European heavy industry traditions. The ECSC ushered in the present era of European economic integration on the Continent. The men who managed Ruhr coal, and steel, have left a living legacy. The nature and significance of their work deserve further examination.

Notes

1 US National Archives (USNA) State Department 862.551/1–145 'Die Entflechtung und Neuordnung der eisenschaffenden Industrie. Treuhandverwaltung . . . (150pp.)', April 1948; Henry Wallich, 'Economic orientations for postwar Germany: critical choices on the road to currency convertability', *Zeitschrift für die gesamte Staatswissenschaft*, Bd. 137/3, September 1981, 405; 'Economic reconstruction in Europe: the reintegration of western Germany: a symposium'. (Zgs-Reconstruction-Symposium); James S. Martin, *All Honorable Men* (Boston, 1950), *passim*.

2 Martin, op. cit., 40–1, 49, 279; USNA OMGUS 56–1/2 Legal Division, Folder AKU. Edward Degener USMPO/Haag, 'Dr Fentener van Vlissingen'.

3 USNA State Department 862.6511/12–2447 Altaffer to Secretary of State, 24 December 1947; 862.6511/3–2548 'Further information regarding alleged offer to French Industry . . .', 25 March 1948.

4 F. Roy Willis, 'Schuman Breaks the Deadlock', in F. Roy Willis (ed.) *European Integration* (New York, 1975), 19–38.

5 William Diebold, *The Schuman Plan: A Study in Economic Cooperation* (New York, 1959); Dietmar Petzina, 'The origins of the European coal and steel community: economic forces and political interests', in ZgS-'Reconstruction Symposium', 450–468.

SELECTED BIBLIOGRAPHY

Abelshauser, Werner 'Problem des Wiederaufbaus der westdeutschen Wirtschaft 1945–1953', in H.A. Winkler (ed.) *Politische Weichenstellungen in Nachkriegsdeutschland* (Göttingen, n.d.).

— *Wirtschaft in Westdeutschland 1945–1948* (Stuttgart, 1975).

Adamthwaite, Anthony *France and the Coming of Second World War* (London, 1980).

Arndt, H.W. *The Economic Lessons of the 1930s* (London, 1963).

Ausschuss zur Untersuchung der Erzeugung und Absatzbedingungen der deutschen Wirtschaft (Enquête Ausschuss) *Die deutsche Kohlenwirtschaft* (Berlin, 1929).

Bagel-Bohlan, Anje *Hitlers industrielle Kriegsvorbereitungen 1936–1939* (Koblenz, 1974).

Bahnhoff, H. 'Stand und Entwicklungsmöglichkeiten in der Zechenkraftwirtschaft des Ruhrbergbaus', *Glückauf*, 28 December 1933.

Barkai, Avram 'Die Wirtschaftsauffassung der NSDAP', *Aus Politik und Zeitgeschichte*, Heft 9/1975.

Barnouw, David and Stellinga, Ruurd 'Ondernehmers in Bezet Nederland: De Organisatie-Woltershom', *Cahiers voor de Politieke en Sociale Wetenschappen*, 1 (4), May 1978.

Baudhuin, Fernand *L'Economie belge sous l'Occupation, 1940–1944* (Brussels, 1945).

— *Histoire économique de Belgique, 1914–1939* vols I, II (Brussels, 1946).

— *La Belgique et la Hollande: Les Finances de 1939 à 1945* (Paris, 1950).

— 'Die Kleinstaaten und der gemeinsamen Markt' *Europa: Besinnung und Hoffnung* (Zurich and Stuttgart, 1957).

— *Histoire économique de Belgique, 1945–1956* (Brussels, 1958).

— *Belgique 1900–1960. Explication économique de notre temps* (Brussels, 1961).

Baumont, Maurice *La grosse industrie allemande et le charbon* (Paris, 1928).

Becker, Peter W. 'The Basis of the German War Economy under Albert Speer, 1942–1944', (Stanford, 1971).

Becker, Willy 'Die deutsche Mineralölwirtschaft' (diss., Berlin, 1936).

Beckerath, Herbert von *Grossindustrie und Gesellschaftsordnung* (Tübingen, 1954).

Benzolverband, *Vierzig Jahre Benzolverband 1893–1938* (Bochum, 1939).

Bergbau, Verein *Der Ruhrbergbau im Wechsel der Zeiten* (Essen, 1933).

— *Statistisches Heft. Produktions- und wirtschaftsstatistische Angaben aus der Montanindustrie* (Essen, 1939).

Bettelheim, Charles *L'economie allemande sous le nazisme* (Paris, 1946).

Bilanz des Zweiten Weltkrieges. Erkenntnisse und Verpflichtungen für die Zukünft (Oldenburg, 1953).

BIOS 'Technical report on the Ruhr coalfield', vol. 1 (London, 1947).

— 'Report on the petroleum and synthetic oil industry of Germany', (London, 1947).

Birkenfeld, Wolfgang *Der synthetische Treibstoff, 1933–1945: Ein Beitrag zur nationalsozialistischen Wirtschafts- und Rüstungspolitik* (Göttingen and Berlin, 1964).
Bonnell, Allen T. *German Control Over International Economic Relations* (Urbana, 1940).
Borkin, Joseph *The Crime and Punishment of IG Farben* (New York, 1978).
Bower, Tom, *Blind Eye to Murder. Britain, America amd the Purging of Nazi Germany – A Pledge Betrayed* (London, 1981).
Bracher, K.D., Sauer, W. and Schulz, G. *Die nationalsozialistische Machtergreifung* (Schriften des Instituts für politische Wissenschaft, Bd. 14) (2nd, enlarged edn, Köln and Opladen, 1962).
Brady, Robert A. *The Rationalization Movement in German Industry: a study in the evolution of economic planning* (Berkeley, 1933).
— *The Spirit and Structure of Fascism* (London, 1937).
Brandt, Karl *Germany's Agricultural and Food Policies in World War II, vol. I, II* (Stanford, 1953).
— *The Management of Agriculture and Food in the German-occupied and Other Areas of Fortress Europe* (Stanford, 1953).
Braunthal, Gerhard *The Federation of German Industry in Politics* (Ithaca, 1965).
Bruch, Arnold 'Die Neuordnung der deutschen Kohlenwirtschaft seit 1938' (diss. Köln, 1936).
Bry, Gerhard *Wages in Germany 1871–1945* (Princeton, 1960).
Buck, Horst-Günter 'Die Entwicklung des Ruhrbergbaus seit der Weltwirtschaftskrise', (diss., Köln, 1950).
Bühring, Otto *Wesen und Aufgaben der industriellen Wirtschaftsgruppen als fachliche Spitzengliederung der Industrie im Rahmen der Organisation der gewerblichen Wirtschaft* (Berlin, 1940).
Bullock, Alan *Hitler: A Study in Tyranny* (New York, 1962).
Buxton, Neil K. 'Coal mining' in Aldcroft, D. and Buxton, N. (eds.) *British Industry Between the Wars* (London, 1979).
Carroll, Berenice A. *Design for Total War: Arms and Economics in the Third Reich* (Studies in European History XVII, The Hague, 1958).
Castellan, Georges 'Bilan social du IIIe Reich', *Revue d'histoire moderne et contemporaine* vol. xxv, July–September, 1968.
Clay, Lucius D. *Decision in Germany* (New York, 1950).
Czichon, Eberhard *Wer verhalf Hitler zur Macht?* (Köln, 1967).
Dallin, Alexander *German Rule in Russia* (London, 1957).
Davis, Joseph S. *The World Between the Wars, 1919–1939: An Economist's View* (Baltimore, 1975).
Degrelle, Léon *La Cohue de 1940* (Lausanne, 1945).
Dejonghe, Etienne 'Le Nord et le Pas-de-Calais pendant la première année d'Occupation (juin 1940–juin 1941)', *Revue du Nord*, vol. LI, Nos. 2, 3, October–December, 1969.
— 'La reprise économique dans le Nord et le Pas-de-Calais', *Revue d'Histoire de la Deuxième Guerre Mondiale* 77, 20th year, July 1970.
— 'Un mouvement séparatiste dans le Nord et le Pas-de-Calais sous l'occupation', *Revue d'histoire moderne et contemporaine*, vol. XVII, January–March 1970.
— 'Les problèmes sociaux dans les entreprises houillères du Nord et du Pas-de-Calais durant la seconde guerre mondiale', *ID.*, (vol. XVIII, January–March, 1971).
Deutsches Institut für Konjunkturforschung *Die deutsche Wirtschaft zwei Jahren nach dem Zusammenbruch. Tatsachen und Probleme* (Berlin, 1947).

Deutsches Institut für Wirtschaftsforschung *Die Deutsche Industrie im Kriege, 1939–1945* (Berlin, 1954).
Dlugoborski, Waclaw (ed.) *Zweiter Weltkrieg und sozialer Wandel. Achsenmächte und besetzte Länder* (Göttingen, 1981).
Doering, Dörte 'Deutsche Aussenwirtschaftspolitik 1933–5', (diss., FU/Berlin, 1969).
Domeratzky, Louis *The International Cartel Movement* (Washington, 1928).
Edwards, Corwin *et al.*, *A Cartel Policy for the United Nations* (New York, 1945).
Ehrmann, Henry W. *Organized Business in France* (Princeton, 1957).
Eichholtz, Dietrich *Geschichte der deutschen Kriegswirtschaft 1939–1945* Bd. I (1939–1941), (Berlin, 1969).
Einzig, Paul *Hitler's New Order in Europe* (London, 1941).
Emmendorfer, E. 'Die geschäftlichen Beziehungen der deutschen Eisen-, und Stahlindustrie zur eisenschaffenden Industrie besetzter Gebiete 1939–1945' (Köln, 1955).
Erbe, René *Die nationalsozialistische Wirtschaftspolitik im Lichte der modernen Theorie* (Zürich, 1959).
Esenwein-Rothe, Ingeborg *Die Wirtschaftsverbände von 1933 bis 1945* (Schriften des Vereins für Sozialpolitik. Gesellschaft für Wirtschafts- und Sozialwissenschaften. Neue Folge, Bd. 37) (Berlin, 1965).
Facius, Friedrich *Wirtschaft und Staat: Die Entwicklung der staatlichen Wirtschaftsverwaltung in Deutschland von 17. Jahrhundert bis 1945.* (Schriften des Bundesarchivs Bd. 6) (Boppard, 1959).
Federau, Franz *Der zweite Weltkrieg und seine Finanzierung in Deutschland* (Tübingen, 1962).
Feldman, Gerald *Army, Industry, and Labor, 1914–1918* (Princeton, 1966).
— 'Big Business and the Kapp Putsch', *Central European History* (vol. VI, No. 2, June 1971).
— 'Arbeitskonflikte im Ruhrbergbau', *Vierteljahrshefte für Zeitgeschichte* Heft 2/1980.
Fischer, Wolfram *Die Wirtschaftspolitik Deutschlands 1918–1945* (Lüneburg, n.d.).
Ford, Franklin L. 'Three Observers in Berlin: Rumbold, Dodd, and François-Poncet', in Gordon Craig and Felix Gilbert (eds.) *The Diplomats*, 1919–1939 (vol. II) (Princeton, 1953).
Forstmeier F. and Volkmann, H.-E. (eds.), *Wirtschaft und Rüstung am Vorabend des Zweiten Weltkrieges* (Düsseldorf, 1975).
— *Kriegswirtschaft und Rüstung 1939–1945* (Düsseldorf, 1977).
Fritz, Martin *German Steel and Swedish Iron Ore 1939–1945* (Göteborg, 1974).
Gebhardt, Gerhard *Ruhrbergbau. Geschichte, Aufbau, Verflechtung seiner gesellschaftlichen Organisationen* (Essen, 1957).
Geer, Johann Sebastian *Der Markt der geschlossenen Nachfrage*. Eine morphologische Studie über die Eisenkontingentierung in Deutschland 1937–1945. (Nürnberger Abhandlungen zu den Wirtschafts- und Sozialwissenschaften, Heft 14) (Berlin, 1961).
Gillingham, John 'The Baron de Launoit: a case study in the "Politics of Production" of Belgian industry during Nazi Occupation', (Parts I and II) *Revue Belge d'Histoire Contemporaine* V, 1974, 1–59.
— 'Die Rolle der Privatwirtschaft im Dritten Reich', *Zeitgeschichte* (1974).
— *Belgian Business in the Nazi New Order* (Ghent, 1977).
— 'Die Ruhrbergleute und Hitlers Krieg', in Hans Mommsen (ed.) *Glück auf Kamaraden!* (Düsseldorf, 1979).
— 'The politics of business in the economic *Grossraum*: the example of Belgium', *Studia Historiae Oeconomicae* No. 14 (Poznan, 1980).

— 'Ruhr coal miners and Hitler's war', *Journal of Social History* V/15/4, 1982.
— 'Die Europäsievung des Ruhrgebietes: Von Hitler bis zum Schuman-Plan' in Kurt Düwell and Wolfgang Köllman (eds) *Rheinland-Westfalen im Industriezeitalter* (Bd. 3: Vom Ende der Weimarer Republik bis zum Land Nondrhein-Westfalen) (Wuppertal, 1984).
— 'How Belgium Survived: The Food Supply Problems of an Occupied Nation' in B. Martin and A. S. Milward (eds) *Agriculture and Food in the Second World War* (Hannover, 1985).
Gruchmann, Lothar *Nationalsozialistische Grossraumordnung. Die Konstruktion einer 'deutschen Monroe-Doktrin'*, (Schriftenreihe der Vierteljahrshefte für Zeitgeschichte, No. 4) (Stuttgart, 1962).
Hallgarten, G.W.F. *Hitler, Reichswehr und Industrie* (Frankfurt, 1955).
Heiber, Helmut (ed.) *Hitler's Table Talk, 1941–1944* (London, 1953).
— *Hitlers Lagebesprechungen* (Stuttgart, 1962).
Henschel, Volker 'Wirtschafts- und sozialhistorische Brüche und Kontinuitäten zwischen Weimarer Republik und Dritten Reich', *Zeitschrift für Unternehmensgeschichte* 28. Jg. Heft 1/1983.
Herbig, Ernst and Jüngst, Ernst (eds) *Bergwirtschaftliches Handbuch* (Berlin, 1931).
Herbst, Ludolf 'Die Krise des nationalsozialistischen Regimes am Vorabend des Zweiten Weltkrieges und die forcierte Aufrüstung', *Vierteljahrshefte für Zeitgeschichte*, 26 Jg./No. 3 1978.
Herrmann, Walther 'Die Wiederaufbau der Selbstverwaltung der deutschen Wirtschaft nach 1945', *Zeitschrift für Unternehmensgeschichte*, 23 Jg. Heft 2/1978.
Hexner, Ervin *The International Steel Cartel* (Chapel Hill, 1943).
Heyl, John D. 'Hitler's economic thought: a reappraisal', *Central European History* (vol. VI No. 1, March, 1973).
Hinrichsbauer, August *Schwerindustrie und Politik* (Essen, 1948).
Hitler, Adolf *Mein Kampf* (19th impression, New York, 1941).
Hoffmann, Stanley 'The effects of World War II on French society and politics', *French Historical Studies* (vol. II, spring 1961).
Homze, Edward L. *Foreign Labor in Nazi Germany* (Princeton, 1967).
Hughes, Thomas Parke 'Technological Momentum in History: Hydrogenation in Germany, 1898–1933,' *Past and Present* (No. 44, August, 1969).
Hüttenberger, Peter *Die Gauleiter, Studie zum Wandel des Machtgefüges in der* NSDAP. (Schriftenreihe der Vierteljahrshefte für Zeitgeschichte) (Stuttgart, 1969).
International Labour Office *The World Coal Mining Industry*: vol. 1 *Economic Conditions* (Geneva, 1938).
Institut für Konjunkturforschung (ed.) 'Die Wettbewerbslage der Steinkohle', *Vierteljahrshefte zur Konjunkturforschung* (Sonderheft 34) (Berlin, 1933).
Institut für Zeitgeschichte *Das dritte Reich und Europa* (München, 1957).
International Labour Office *The World Coal Mining Industry* (vol. I: *Economic Conditions*) (Geneva, 1938).
— *The World Coal Mining Industry* (vol. II: *Social Conditions*) (Geneva, 1938).
Jacobsen, Hans-Adolf (ed.) *Dokumente zum Westfeldzug* (Göttingen, 1960).
Jacquemyns, G. *La Société belge sous l'occupation allemande, 1940–1944*, vols I–IV (Brussels, 1950).
— 'Réactions des travailleurs belges sous l'Occupation', *Revue d'histoire de la deuxième guerre mondiale*, 31, July 1958.
Jaeckel, Eberhard *Frankreich in Hitlers Europa* (Stuttgart, 1966).
Jaeger, Hans 'Business history in Germany: a survey of recent developments', *Business History Review*, No. 1 Spring 1974.

Jäger, Jörg-Johannes *Die wirtschaftliche Abhängigkeit des Dritten Reiches vom Ausland dargestellt am Beispiel der Stahlindustrie* (Berlin, 1969).
— 'Sweden's Iron-Ore Exports to Germany, 1937–1944', *Scandinavian Economic History Review*, v. XV., Nos. 1–2 (1967).
Janssen, Gregor *Das Ministerium Speer: Deutschlands Rüstung im Kriege* (Berlin, 1968).
Karlbom, Rolf 'Sweden's iron-ore exports to Germany, 1933–1944', *Scandinavian Economic History Review*, v. XIII, No. 1. (1965).
Karpa, Fritz 'Die Gründe der Krise 1931/32 und ihre Überwindung' (diss., Königsberg, 1934).
Kartelle in der Wirklichkeit, Festschrift für Max Metzner (Köln, 1963).
Kehrl, Hans *Krisenmanager im Dritten Reich*. (Düsseldorf, 1973).
Kiersch, Günther *Internationale Eisen- und Stahlkartelle* (Essen, 1954).
Kindleberger, Charles *The World in Depression* (Berkeley, 1973).
Kittler, Werner *Der internationale elektrische Energieverkehr in Europa* (München and Berlin, 1933).
Klein, Burton H. *Germany's Economic Preparations for War* (Cambridge, 1959).
Kocka, Jürgen '1945: Neubeginn oder Restauration?' in Carola Stern *et al.*, *Wendepunkte deutscher Geschichte 1848–1945* (Frankfurt, 1979).
Kuisel, Richard *Capitalism and the State in Modern France* (New Haven, 1981).
Kwiet, Konrad *Reichskommissariat Nederlande: Versuch und Scheitern nationalsozialistischer Neuordnung* (Schriftenreihe der Vierteljahrshefte für Zeitgeschichte, No. 17 (Stuttgart, 1969).
Lacqueur, Walter (ed.) *Fascism: A Reader's Guide* (Berkeley, 1976).
Länderrat des Amerikanischen Besatzungsgebiets *Statistisches Handbuch von Deutschland* (München, 1948).
Lange, E.G. *Steinkohle. Wandlungen in der internationalen Kohlenwirtschaft* (Leipzig, 1936).
Levy, Hermann *Industrial Germany: a study of its monopoly organizations and their control by the state* (New York, 1935, 1966).
Liefmann, Robert *Cartels, Concerns and Trusts* (New York, 1932).
Lochner, Louis *Tycoons and Tyrant: German industry from Hitler to Adenauer* (Chicago, 1954).
Ludwig, Karl-Heinz *Technik und Ingenieure im Dritten Reich* (Düsseldorf, 1974).
Martin, James S. *All Honorable Men* (Boston, 1950).
Mason, Edward *Controlling World Trade* (New York, 1946).
Mason, Tim *Arbeiterklasse und Volksgemeinschaft* (Opladen, 1975).
— 'Labor in the Third Reich', *Past and Present* (No. 33, April. 1966).
— 'The primacy of politics – politics and economics in national socialist Germany' in S.J. Woolf (ed.), *The Nature of Fascism* (London, 1968).
— 'Some origins of the Second World War', *Past and Present* (No. 29, December 1964).
Meinck, Gerhard *Hitler und die deutsche Aufrüstung* (Wiesbaden, 1959).
Milward, Alan S. 'Could Sweden have stopped the Second World War?' *Scandinavian Economic History Review*, v. XV, Nos. 1, 2 (1967).
— *The German Economy at War* (London, 1965).
— *The New Order and the French Economy* (Oxford, 1970).
— *Der Zweite Weltkrieg* (München, 1977).
Ministry of Economic Warfare. 'The minerals industries', *Economic Survey of Germany* (London, 1944).
— 'The Oil Industry', *Economic Survey of German Industry* (London, 1946).
— 'Foreign Trade', *Economic Survey of Germany* (London, 1945).

— 'Fuel, power, and public utility services', *Economic Survey of Germany* (London, 1945).
Mommsen, Hans 'Sozialpolitik im Ruhrbergbau' in D. Petzina *et al.* (eds) *Industrielles System und politische Entwicklung in der Weimarer Republik* (Düsseldorf, 1974).
— 'Die Bergarbeiter an der Ruhr, 1918–1933', in Hans Mommsen (ed.) *Arbeiterbewegung und Nationale Frage* (Göttingen, 1979).
Monnet, Jean *Memoirs* (London, 1978).
Muthesius, Volkmar *Ruhrkohle: 1893–1943* (Essen, 1943).
Nauwelaerts, Gérard *Petroleum: Macht der Erde* (Tilburg, 1931).
Neumann, Franz *Behemoth* (New York, 1943).
Nocken, Ulrich 'Interindustrial conflicts and alliances in the Weimar Republic: experiments in social corporatism' (diss., UC, Berkeley, 1974).
North German Coal Council 'Interim report on the general financial situation of the Ruhr mining industry', September report (Essen, 1945).
Oberste Kriegsführung der Wehrmacht, Wehrmachtsführerungsstab *Kriegstagebuch 1940–1944*, vols I–III (Frankfurt, 1961–5).
Ollsson, Sven-Olof *German Coal and Swedish Fuel, 1939–1945* (Göteborg, 1975).
Orlow, Dietrich *The Nazis in the Balkans: a study of totalitarian politics* (Pittsburgh, 1968).
Overy, R.J. 'Transportation and rearmament in the Third Reich', *Historical Journal*, XVI (1973).
— 'Cars, Roads, and Economic Recovery in Germany, 1933–1938', *The Economic History Review* 1975, 3.
— 'The German Pre-war Aircraft Production Plans', *English Historical Review* 90/1975.
Parker, William N. 'Fuel supply and industrial strength: a study of the conditions governing the output and distribution of Ruhr coal in the late 1920s', (diss., Harvard, 1950).
— 'Entrepreneurship, industrial organization and economic growth: a German example', *Journal of Economic History*, 1954, 380–400.
Parker, William and Pounds, Norman J.G. *Coal and Steel in Western Europe: the influence of resources and techniques on production* (London, 1957).
Paxton, Robert *Vichy France: old guard and new order 1940–1944* (New York, 1972).
Peterson, Edward N. *Hjalmar Schacht: for and against* (Boston, 1954). *The Limits on Hitler's Power* (Princeton, 1971).
Petzina, Dietmar 'Hitler und die deutsche Industrie. Ein kommentierter Literatur- und Forschungsbericht', *Geschichte in Wissenschaft und Unterricht* (6 August 1966).
— *Autarkiepolitik im Dritten Reich* (Stuttgart, 1968).
— 'Die Mobilisierung deutscher Arbeitskräfte vor und während des Zweiten Weltkrieges', *Vierteljahrshefte für Zeitgeschichte* (18 Jg., 1970).
— 'Probleme der weltwirtschaftlichen Entwicklung in der Zwischenkriegszeit', *Forschungen zur Sozial- und Wirtschaftsgeschichte* (Bd. 23) (New York and Stuttgart, 1981).
— 'Gesellschaft in der Bundesrepublik Deutschland – Aspekte sozialen Wandels seit dem Zweiten Weltkrieg', in Horst Ueberhorst (ed.) *Geschichte der Leibesübungen* Bd 3/2 (Berlin, 1982).
Pfahlmann, Hans *Fremdarbeiter in der deutschen Kriegswirtschaft* (Darmstadt, 1968).
Picker, Henry *Hitlers Tischgespräche im Führerhauptquartier 1941–1942* (Stuttgart, 1955).

Plum, Günter 'Die Arbeiterbewegung während der nationalsozialistischen Herrschaft', in Jürgen Reulecke (ed.) *Arbeiterbewegung am Rhein und Ruhr* (Wuppertal, 1974).
Pollard, Sidney *The Development of the British Economy* (London, 1962).
Pounds, Norman J.G. *The Ruhr: a study in historical and economic geography* (New York, 1965).
Regul, Rudolf *Die Wettbewerbslage der Steinkohle* (Sonderheft 34 der Vierteljahrshefte zur Konjunkturforschung) (Berlin, 1933).
— *Energiequellen der Welt* (Schriften des Instituts für Konjunkturforschung. Sonderheft 44) (Berlin, 1937).
Reichert, J.W. 'Ein Rückblick auf das zehnjährige Bestehen der internationalen Stahlverbände', *Stahl und Eisen*, Heft 48, 1936.
Riedel, M. *Eisen und Kohle für das Dritte Reich. Paul Pleigers Stellung in der NS-Wirtschaft* (Göttingen, 1973).
Riedel, Matthias 'Die Eisenerzversorgung der deutschen Hüttenindustrie zu Beginn des Zweiten Weltkrieges', *Vierteljahresschrift für Sozial- und Wirtschaftsgeschichte* Bd. X 58, Heft 41, 1971.
Rox, Thérèse *Mineralölwirtschaft und Minieralölpolitik in Deutschland unter besonderer Berücksichtigung des Erdöls* (München, 1937).
Rudzio, Wolfgang 'Die ausgebliebene Sozialisierung am Rhein und Ruhr . . .' *Archiv für Sozialgeschichte* Bd., 1978.
Sauvy, Alfred, *Histoire économique de France entre les deux guerres* (Vols I–IV) (Paris, 1965–75).
Scharf, Claus and Schröder H.-J. *Politische und Ökonomische Stabilisierung Westdeutschlands 1945–1950*. Fünf Beiträge zur Deutschlandpolitik der westlichen Allierten (Wiesbaden, 1977).
Scheer, W. and Gröbner, W. *Die Entwicklung der Steinkohlenveredelung in den letzen 20 Jahren* (Essen, 1941).
Schmalenbach, Eugen, *et al.*, *Gutachten über die gegenwärtige Lage des Rheinischenwestfälischen Steinkohlenbergbaus* (Berlin, 1928).
Schoenbaum, David *Hitler's Social Revolution* (New York, 1966).
Schröder, H.-J. 'Deutsch-französische Wirtschaftsbeziehungen 1936–1939', *Beihefte der Francia* Bd., 10, (Paris, 1982).
Schumann, Hans-Gerd *Nationalsozialismus und Arbeiterbewegung* (Hannover/ Frankfurt, 1968).
Schunder, Friedrich 'Die wirtschaftliche Entwicklung des Ruhrbergbaus seit der Mitte des 19 Jahrhunderts', in K.E. Born (ed.) *Moderne deutsche Wirtschaftsgeschichte*, (Köln and Berlin, 1960).
Schweitzer, Arthur *Big Business in the Third Reich* (Bloomington, 1964).
— 'Business Power under the Nazi Regime', *Zeitschrift für Nationalökonomie*, Bd. XX, Heft 3–4 (Wien, 1960).
Schwenger, Rudolf *Die betriebliche Sozialpolitik im Bergbau* (Schriften des Vereins für Sozialpolitik 186/I) (München/Leipzig, 1932).
Schwerin von Krosigk, Lutz *Es geschah in Deutschland. Menschenbilder unseres Jahrhunderts*. (Tübingen and Stuttgart, 1951).
Seebold, Gustav-Hermann *Ein Stahlkonzern im Dritten Reich. Der Bochumer Verein 1927–1945*. (Wuppertal, 1981).
Seubert, Rolf *Berufserziehung und Nationalsozialismus. Das berufspädagogische Erbe und seine Betreuer* (Weinheim, 1977).
Sölter, Arno, *Das Grossraumkartell. Ein Instrument der industrieller Marktordnung im neuen Europa*. (Dresden, 1943).

Sörgel, Werner *Metallindustrie und Nationalsozialismus* (Frankfurt, 1965).
— 'Die Neuordnung des industriellen Organisationswesens, 1933–1935', in H.J. Varain (ed.) *Industrieverbände in Deutschland* (Köln, 1973).
Speer, Albert *Inside the Third Reich* (New York, 1969).
Spencer, Elaine Glovka 'Business bureaucrats and social control in the Ruhr, 1896 to 1914', in H.-U. Wehler (ed.) *Sozialgeschichte Heute: Festschrift für Hans Rosenberg zum 70. Geburtstag* (Göttingen, 1974).
Stegmann, Dirk 'Zum Verhältnis von Grossindustrie und Nationalsozialismus 1930–1933', *Archiv für Sozialgeschichte*, XIII, Bd., 1973.
— 'Kapitalismus und Faschismus in Deutschland 1924–1934', *Gesellschaft. Beiträge zur Marxistischen Theorie VI* (Frankfurt, 1976).
— 'Antequierte Personalisierung oder sozialökonomische Faschismus-Analyse?' *Archiv für Sozialgeschichte*, XVII Bd., 1977.
Stockder, A.H. *Regulating an Industry* (New York, 1932).
Stocking, George W. *Cartels in Action: Case Studies in International Business Diplomacy* (New York, 1946).
Svennilson, Ingvar *Growth and Stagnation in the European Economy* (Geneva, 1954).
Taylor, Graham D. 'The Rise and Fall of Antitrust in Occupied Germany, 1945–48', *Prologue*, spring 1979, v. II, No. 1.
Tenfelde, Klaus 'Mining festivals in the nineteenth century', *Journal of Contemporary History*, 13 (2), April 1978.
— 'Bergarbeiterkultur in Deutschland', *Geschichte und Gesellschaft* 5. Jg/Heft 1, 1979.
Tengelmann, W. *Die Steinkohle in der Elektrowirtschaft* (Herne, 1936).
Teppe, Karl 'Zur Sozialpolitik des Dritten Reich dargestellt am Beispiel der Sozialversicherung', *Archiv für Sozialgeschichte*, 17, 1977.
Thomas, Georg *Geschichte der deutschen Wehr- und Rüstungswirtschaft 1918–1943/5* (Schriften des Bundesarchivs/14) (Boppard, 1966).
Trials of War Criminals before the Nürnberg Tribunal under Control Council Law No. 10 (vol. 2 'The Milch case', vol. 6 'The Flick case', vols. 7–8 'The IG Farben case', vol. 9 'The Krupp case', vol. 13–14 'The Ministries' case') (Washington, 1952).
Tschirbs, Rudolf 'Der Ruhrbergmann zwischen Privilegierung und Statusverlust: Lohnpolitik von der Inflation bis zur Rationalisierung (1919 bis 1927)', in Gerald Feldmann (ed.) *Die deutsche Inflation. Eine Zwischenbilanz* (Berlin and New York, 1982).
Turner, Henry 'The *Ruhrlade*, secret cabinet of heavy industry in the Weimar Republic', *Central European History* v. III, no. 3, September 1970.
— *Faschismus und Kapitalismus in Deutschland* (Göttingen, 1972).
— 'Hitlers Einstellung zu Wirtschaft und Gesellschaft vor 1933', *Geschichte und Gesellschaft* Jg. 2, Heft 1, 1976.
Uhlig, Heinrich *Die Warenhäuser im Dritten Reich* (Köln, 1950).
Ulshofer, Otfried *Einflussnahme auf wirtschaftliche Unternehmungen in den besetzten nord-, west-, und südosteuropäischen Ländern während des zweiten Weltkrieges* (Tübingen, 1958).
Umbreit, Hans *Der Militärbefehlshaber in Frankreich 1940–1944* (Boppard, 1958).
US Federal Trade Commission *Report (of the FTC) on International Steel Cartels* (Washington, 1948).
United States Strategic Bombing Survey *The Coking Industry in Germany* (Washington, January, 1945).

— Overall Effects Division *The Effects of Strategic Bombing on the German War Economy* (Washington, October 1945).
— 'Area studies division report: the effects of the air offensive against German cities' (Washington, 1947).
Unverferth, Gabrielle 'Die Verbandspolitische und ökonomische Entwicklung des Ruhrbergbaus von der Machtergreifung bis zum Vierjahresplan', (MA thesis, Ruhruniversität Bochum, 1975).
Wagenfuhr, Rolf *Die deutsche Industrie*. Gesamtergebnisse der amtlichen Produktionsstatistik (Berlin, 1939).
Wagner, Elisabeth (ed.) *Der Generalquartiermeister*. Briefe und Tagebücheraufzeichnungen des Generalquartiermeisters des Heeres, General der Artillerie Eduard Wagner. (München and Wien, 1963).
Wagner, Wilfried 'Die deutsche Besatzungspolitik in Belgien während des zweiten Weltkrieges', (Frankfurt, 1968).
Wallich, Henry 'Economic orientations for postwar Europe: critical choices on the road to currency convertability', *Zeitschrift für die gesamte Staatswissenschaft*, Bd., 137/3, September 1981.
Warmbrunn, Werner *The Dutch under Occupation 1940–1945* (Stanford, 1963).
Wedekind, Erich 'Die Rationalisierung im Bergbau und ihre ökonomischen und sozialen Auswirkungen', (diss, Köln, 1930).
Der Weg zum industriellen Spitzenverband (no author), (Darmstadt, 1966).
Weisbrodt, Berndt *Schwerindustrie in der Weimarer Republik: Interessenpolitik zwischen Stabilisierung und Krise* (Wuppertal, 1978).
Welter, Erich *Der Weg der deutschen Industrie* (Frankfurt, 1943).
— *Falsch und Richtig Planen*. Eine kritische Studie über die deutsche Wirtschaftslenkung im Zweiten Weltkrieg. (Veröffentlichungen des Forschungsinstituts für Wirtschaftspolitik an der Universität Mainz, Bd. 1) (Heidelberg, 1954).
Wendt, Bernd-Jürgen *Economic Appeasement: Handel und Finanz in der britischen Deutschlandpolitik* (Düsseldorf, 1971).
Wiester, Erich *Ausbau der deutschen Treibwirtschaft* (Dortmund, 1935).
Willis, F. Roy *The French in Germany* (Stanford, 1962).
Winkler, Heinrich A. (ed.) *Organisierter Kapitalismus* (Kritische Studien zur Geschichtswissenschaft, Bd. 9) (Göttingen, 1974).
Wolsing, Theo *Untersuchungen zur Berufsbildung im Dritten Reich* (Schriftenreihe zur Geschichte und Politischen Bildung, Bd. 24) (Kastellaun, 1977).
Youngson, A.J. *The British Economy, 1920–1957* (Cambridge, Mass., 1960).

INDEX